A Nest of Singing Birds

100 years of the New Zealand School Journal

1966 *** SCHOOL JOURNAL

A Nest of Singing Birds

100 years of the New Zealand School Journal

Learning Media
Te Pou Taki Kōrero

This publication was produced in partnership with

MINISTRY OF EDUCATION
Te Tāhuhu o te Mātauranga

With generous support from

bluestar
BLUE STAR PRINT - NEW ZEALAND

Printing by Format
Binding by Printlink

Also supported by

Wakefields DIGITAL
Pre-press services

Spicers Paper
Printed on Media Satin Matt artpaper

Published 2007 by Learning Media Limited,
Box 3293, Wellington, New Zealand.
www.learningmedia.co.nz

This book has been published with the support of *School Journal* writers past and present who have generously given permission for their work to be included.

The photographs on pages 13, 14, 18, 38 (top left), 50, 55, 101, and 123 are published courtesy of the Alexander Turnbull Library, Wellington. Their reference numbers are p. 13 Woodcocks School, 1913, F-148159-1/2; p. 14 William Pember Reeves, F-018264-1/1; p. 18 Clarence Edward Beeby and Beatrice Beeby, F 031264-1/2; p. 38 Frank Sargeson, F-65722-1/2; p. 50 James Keir Baxter, 1/2-003020-F; p. 55 Louis Albert Johnson, F-19115-1/4; p. 101 Staff Sgt Russell Clark, EP 18/4 Obits-Dead-Ca-Cn; p. 123 John Pascoe, PA Coll-6075-04.

The photograph on page 20 was first published in the *Arts Year Book*, no. 7, 1951.
The photographs on pages 40 and 46 were first published in *Landfall*, no. 53, March 1960.

Edited by Margaret Cahill
Designed by Penelope Newman

Dewey number 052.083

Soft cover edition
ISBN 978 0 7903 2627 6
Item number 32627

Front cover illustration by Jill McDonald, original cover illustration for *School Journal*, Part 2 Number 2, 1966
Back cover and endpaper illustrations by Jill McDonald

Contents

Foreword

A Nest of Singing Birds is a gorgeous honouring of the centenary of the *School Journal*. It reminds me of James K. Baxter's child's view of school: "a hot jungle, full of life, colour and noise, smell, violence, joy and grief, where alligators and birds of paradise swap yarns daily". [1]

At ten, I read my older brother's 1941 Part 3 *School Journals*, glutting myself on the remarkable selection of poems by Davies, E. B. Browning, Scott, Swinburne, Thackeray, Belloc, Cowper, Longfellow, Mary Lamb, Drayton, Dekker, and Clare and extracts and adaptations from Cervantes, Shakespeare, Addison, Austen, Swift, Dickens, Reade, Marryatt, Defoe, Leigh Hunt, Zola, Twain, Hawthorne, Borrow …

Eurocentric the *Journal* may have been, dubious on Māori matters but, unlocking a gateway beyond Waharoa, it helped me understand something of myself and others through story which, in Margaret Mahy's great words, "confers structure upon us". I have those *Journals* still, strung in their ink- and tear-blotted folder.

After leaving the bush, I developed much of my teaching around the *School Journal*, became its editor, encouraged students in its use, and wrote for it. While I havered and dithered over the risks, it was Tolstoy's "How Much Land Does a Man Need?", which I first read in the *School Journal*, that clinched my decision to accept the vow of poverty and become a full-time writer for children.

Gregory O'Brien's text is moving, stimulating, provocatively arguable. Should the *Journal's* didacticism increase or lessen? What is its pedagogic justification? Should teachers control it? Should this national treasure be given to private enterprise? Should it be an instrument of cultural nationalism? Like it or not, the *School Journal* has always been a vehicle for propaganda, for social engineering, yet the doctrinaire and politically correct have been unable to repress its bursting vitality.

The *Journal* of my childhood had few illustrations; my imagination was nourished by having to provide them. Today's *Journal* is image-loaded, befitting an age in which the picture dominates the word, the wrapping supersedes the contents. In the less verbal and more illustrative nature of today's *Journal*, I see a move from the Apollonian to the Dionysian, but then I'm a grumpy old joker who knows that literacy is the master tool and that good illustration is its own justification rather than a futile competitor with television or video games. I comfort myself with the thought that what the child takes from the *Journal*, as from our teaching, is not always what we intend, and I remember Dr Beeby's wise words: "In a school book a small child from a barren home may make his first contact with literature and the arts". [2]

A Nest of Singing Birds – squawking, cheeping, jabbering, alone or in occasional sweet harmony – is a centennial Hooray! for the *School Journal* that – like the child itself – is anarchic, vigorous, and fertile as the New Zealand bush.

Jack Lasenby

Wellington
January 2007

Clare Bowes, illustration for *School Journal*, Part 1 Number 2, 1965

Introduction: Revisiting the School Journal

There are many histories that could be written of the New Zealand *School Journal*. *A Nest of Singing Birds* is a visual and verbal unfolding of one such history. The *Journal*, particularly since the mid-twentieth century, has played an integral part in the growth of the local imagination and of the artistic consciousness of the country. While acknowledging the editors and administrators – not to mention the children – this book focuses on the artists and writers who have been central to the *Journal*, a great many of whom also played a major part in the development of New Zealand arts and literature beyond the pages of the *School Journal*.

Working on this book, and the National Library Gallery exhibition that accompanies it, involved going through over two thousand back issues of the *Journal* spanning 1907–2006, to seek out contributions that encapsulated or were suggestive of crucial points in the development of the publication. The stories of Maurice Duggan and Witi Ihimaera tell us a lot about how the *Journal* was positioned during the 1950s and 1970s respectively; the artworks of Russell Clark, Jill McDonald, and Dick Frizzell speak of the period in which they were created, as do the poems of William Pember Reeves and James K. Baxter. The layout and page design of the *Journal* also tell the story of the publication, directly and indirectly, from the achingly conformist mastheads of the early years, by way of the idealistic, refined designs of Russell Clark and E. Mervyn Taylor, to the unfettered graphics of Vanya Lowry from the 1970s – and onwards towards the computer-generated designs of the present.

Juliet Peter, cover artwork, *School Journal*, Part 4, Autumn 1957

Over a century of dizzying change, there is one central aspect of the *Journal* that has not altered – its preoccupation with literacy, with encouraging children to read. Excellent writing, good artwork, and high production standards have long been considered a crucial part in achieving this. For a great number of New Zealanders, the *School Journal* was the beginning of a lifetime of reading. Relatively early in its history, it came to occupy a central place in classrooms and homes. Art historian Athol McCredie writes:

> *For generations of New Zealanders the stories and appearance of the* School Journal *have been an element of their cultural consciousness – remembered as evocatively as the smell of stale school milk, the feel of chalk and finger paint, and the steamy atmosphere of a classroom of wet bodies on a rainy day.* [1]

Scott Kennedy, cover illustration, Penelope Newman, design, *School Journal*, Part 4 Number 1, 2006

The artwork and writing reproduced here hint at a few of the reasons why the *Journal* has become such a reference point and object of affection for so many New Zealanders. This book is also a portrait of a children's publication that unintentionally became, as Dick Frizzell suggests, an "unauthorised history" of New Zealand art and, as Margaret Mahy says, cheerily, "one of New Zealand's leading literary magazines". It is not an attempt to explain the machinations of what has always been a complex and mutable organisation. A linguist, educationalist, or sociologist would row a very different course across the very great lake that is School Publications/Learning Media. Specialists in non-fiction would propose other histories, and I hope they do. Books could be written about the relationship between the *Journal* and national identity, biculturalism, and multiculturalism as well as between the *Journal* and the Department/Ministry of Education. The changing ways in which the publication has been used within and outside the classroom (and its relationship to the curriculum) are other topics only touched upon here. A vast archive of School Publications materials – much of it still uncatalogued – is housed at the National Archives in Wellington, awaiting future scholars and writers.

The life of an institution such as School Publications is seldom without conflict and occasional controversy. Over the century of its existence, the *Journal* has been a topic of much debate and some contention. The relationship between such a lively and varied publication and the government was, for a start, never going to be straightforward. Illustrator Peter Campbell has described the School Publications Branch, where he worked during the late 1950s, as:

> *at once a crown jewel for the Department of Education and a recalcitrant child. It was not always an harmonious place. There were minor scandals and ructions, but if that was the price for a steady stream of teaching material which was excellent, home grown and home-orientated, it was thought to be well worth paying.* [2]

Acknowledging that pitfalls and hurdles, controversies and arguments are integral to the history of such a healthy, diverse publication, *A Nest of Singing Birds: 100 years of the New Zealand School Journal* is a celebration of all of it. It is an acknowledgment of a publication that has served an exemplary function in the life of the country – a kind of sustainable farming of the New Zealand heart, mind, and soul.

School Journal illustrator Clare Bowes as a young girl:
"In 1948 or 49, an editor from the *Education* magazine visited my school, Belmont Primary, and two of us were chosen to have our photos taken reading the *School Journal*. I believe they were published in an issue of *Education* in that year."

While the *School Journal* sprang to life with surprising gusto in 1907, it lost much of its character and identity during World War One, when the overriding concerns of empire and nationhood effectively squashed the fledgling publication. The 1920s and 30s passed without much ostensible drama on the *Journal's* pages, its prime purpose being, or so it appears, to save youngsters from the related evils of bad grammar and juvenile delinquency. Until the 1940s, illustrations were few and contributors' names were unstated (unless you happened to be a long-dead inhabitant of the English literary canon).

From that decade onwards, however, the history of the *Journal* takes on a very different character. It reflects a concerted effort to understand and express what it means to be a New Zealander. It is not only a story of good management and strategic planning but of happenstance as well. Particularly since the 1940s, there have been many instances when, by good fortune or editorial vision, remarkable contributions have surfaced in the *Journal* –

Bernard Dobbie, illustration for Aesop's fable "Wolf and Dog", *School Journal*, Part 2 Number 3, 1991

among them Brian Sutton-Smith's "Our Street" series, Janet Frame's stories, Margaret Mahy's first poems, and the two stories, "Teddy and the Witches" and "The Procession", that launched her writing career in 1961. At these points in time, the *Journal*, wittingly or not, found itself riding the crest of a creative and imaginative wave that swept New Zealand on the back of an emerging nationalistic and modernist art and literature.

As well as attending to the work of regular contributors, such as Russell Clark, E. Mervyn Taylor, Juliet Peter, and Roy Cowan, this book records some of the remarkable occasional submissions – among them Louise Henderson's drawings, which accompanied Celia Manson's "Children in New York" in October 1947. There are many other notable cameo appearances on these pages from the likes of Frank Sargeson, Colin McCahon, Robin White, Ralph Hotere, cartoonist Murray Ball and, in Summer 1955, Edmund Hillary, who contributed an account of the ascent of Mount Everest. I imagine a *School Journal* editor at his or her desk, sizing up these marvellous verbal and visual offerings in much the same way as Professor Kirk lovingly beholds his giant squid at Island Bay, in *School Journal,* Part 4, 1956.

Louise Henderson, cover artwork, *School Journal*, Part 3, October 1947

Richard Barwick, illustration for J. A. F. Garrick's "Giant Squids and Sperm Whales", *School Journal*, Part 4, Summer 1956

Yvonne Bendall, cover artwork, *School Journal*, Part 1, May–June 1955

Geoffrey Notman, cover artwork, *School Journal*, Part 2 Number 2, 1995

Trawling the great lake of *School Journals*, there were many revelations and surprises. In April 1951, an entire Part 1 *Journal* was devoted to "Earthworms". Among its contents were an elegant cover drawing of woven-together worms, a set of instructions on how to make your own wormery, and a useful cross-section explaining its inner workings. After some weeks of going through *School Journal* archives, I was struck by the unusually high percentage of stories by or about Māori that featured kaimoana (see Witi Ihimaera's "The Pupu Pool", page 75) and, even more prevalently, eels. Did this reflect the zealous commissioning of stories by a succession of editors who all happened to be fishers and/or eel-catchers? Looking for a European equivalent to the eels, the only species that figured anywhere nearly as prominently in Pākehā articles and stories was, or so it seemed, the hedgehog (with cats, dogs, and elephants running along behind). Future scholarship will, no doubt, be pending on this matter.

In one of the first stories ever published in the *School Journal*, "The Lighthouse" (Number 2, 1907), a boy called Willie, who has long dreamed of visiting the lighthouse near his home, is finally granted his wish. The keeper takes him to the top of the tower and shows him a lamp, around which are arranged pieces of three-sided glass:

"'What are these for?" asked the boy, pointing to the pieces of glass round the lamp.

"The glass makes the light seem very much brighter from a distance," answered the keeper.

"See how small the lamp is! Yet a sailor can see the light thirty miles away."

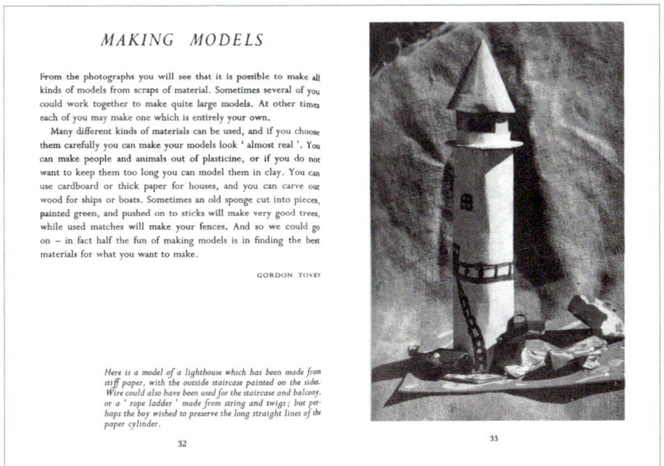

MAKING MODELS

From the photographs you will see that it is possible to make all kinds of models from scraps of material. Sometimes several of you could work together to make quite large models. At other times each of you may make one which is entirely your own.

Many different kinds of materials can be used, and if you choose them carefully you can make your models look ' almost real '. You can make people and animals out of plasticine, or if you do not want to keep them too long you can model them in clay. You can use cardboard or thick paper for houses, and you can carve out wood for ships or boats. Sometimes an old sponge cut into pieces, painted green, and pushed on to sticks will make very good trees, while used matches will make your fences. And so we could go on – in fact half the fun of making models is in finding the best materials for what you want to make.

GORDON TOVEY

Here is a model of a lighthouse which has been made from stiff paper, with the outside staircase painted on the sides. Wire could also have been used for the staircase and balcony, or a ' rope ladder ' made from string and twigs; but perhaps the boy wished to preserve the long straight lines of the paper cylinder.

32

33

Article by Gordon Tovey, with illustrations (see left) by John Drawbridge and photography by Olaf John, *School Journal*, Part 3, Winter 1954

Conrad Frieboe, cover illustration for *Looking at New Zealand*, *School Journal*, Part 3, May 1948

The image of the lighthouse reappears in James K. Baxter's satirical play *The Bureaucrat* (1967), which was inspired by his time as an editor at School Publications. The main character recounts a story about an uncle who kept a kerosene lamp burning in the window of his cottage overlooking the sea so that fishermen could take their bearings from it: "There was no lighthouse on that coast. But they could steer by the light of a kerosene lamp in somebody's window."

Speaking on behalf of educationalists in general, Baxter's character then declares: "We've gone one better. We're the ones who install lighthouses." [3]

The editors of the *Journal* might indeed be thought of as the lighthouse keepers, responsible for the publication's upkeep and for "lighting the lamp". But – and this is where Frame, Mahy, and company enter the picture – it is the writers and artists who put in place the pieces of glass, the prisms through which the light is amplified and reaches the world.

The *School Journal* has, indeed, functioned as a beacon over the one hundred years of its life so far. And the message it has been broadcasting has made generations of young New Zealanders aware of a coastline – and a country – that was, and still is, changing shape. To our good fortune, this is a coast on which the fair winds of the imagination and human spirit continue to blow.

Gregory O'Brien
Wellington
January 2007

Both Ends of the Telescope:

Looking at the School Journal 1907–2007

Juliet Peter, detail of cover artwork, *School Journal*, Part 4, Winter 1956

Looking back to the *School Journal's* beginnings in 1907 is like gazing down through the skyward end of a telescope, peering back to that distant point in time when a group of educationalists decided the children of the Dominion would do well to have their own form of literary edification. From there, the *Journal's* history comprises both a number of exceptional individual achievements, by writers, artists, editors, and teachers, and a concerted group effort to realise a range of shared objectives that reflect, as editor P. R. Earle has written, "consciously or unconsciously – both continuities and currents of change in the community". [1] As needs and aspirations have changed over the century, not only has the *Journal* encapsulated those shifts, but it has also inadvertently influenced them. While the *School Journal's* chief function was, from the outset, to teach children to read, it would be naïve not to discern in it an attempt to shape the sensibilities of the country.

Returning to the other end of the telescope and imagining the view, from the vantage point of 1907, looking forward in time, it is hard to think what the founders of the *Journal* would make of the publication in its present form. We can only guess at their degree of incomprehension when confronted with a not untypical 1997 *School Journal* that included a short story about girl surfers, an interview with a vegetarian, an article about growing dreadlocks (including some useful Rasta hair-care tips), and a feature about computer viruses. Needless to say, the *Journal's* founders might be pleasantly surprised that their periodical had not only survived but that it had thrived and, a number of times during its hundred-year history, been upheld as a leading publication of its kind. In an essay in the *Arts Year Book*, Number 7, 1951, J. C. Beaglehole pronounced the *Journal* second to none in the world and made a point of commending its stated mission "to provide 'reading material' for children who inherit New Zealand as well as western civilization". The publication, he elaborated, had come to serve the fundamental purpose of making children feel:

> *that life in New Zealand can be a worthwhile and interesting experience, that New Zealand has a tradition and contemporary ways of living of its own; that New Zealanders are doing fascinating and important things here and now, that can best be written about and drawn by New Zealanders.* [2]

Life was rather quiet in 1907. There were no wars in the world. Local disasters were minor ones: there was a grass fire on the Port Hills in Christchurch in February, and in May a woman was killed in a tram accident in Brooklyn, Wellington. It was headline news that herrings were stranded in Picton in September by a high tide ... In 1907, New Zealand was proclaimed a Dominion – an event that in itself makes this year an important one in our history.

"Fifty Years Ago: The Life of New Zealand in 1907" by John Pascoe,
School Journal, Part 4, Summer 1957

While these are familiar sentiments in 2007, sixty years ago they were not.

In its initial form, the *School Journal* resembled a traditional English reader, and much of the content was culled from imported literary sources. It also offered some good colonial instruction in tree-chopping and civilised living. In the minds of its founders, the *Journal* was a tonic and a subtle enforcer of colonial values. Looking at it from a slightly different angle, current *Journal* editor Tricia Glensor considers the early issues were designed "not so much to change the world as to enshrine and preserve the values of a world that was soon to disappear forever". [3]

The *School Journal* was not without precedent. A government-produced anthology of writings by local authors, *The New Zealand Reader*, had been produced in the 1890s, the brainchild of "that remarkable Minister of Education", [4] as Brent Southgate has called him, William Pember Reeves. A historian and poet of some standing, Pember Reeves prescribed for the New Land an intellectual, creative life imported from Mother England, coexistent with a passionate awareness of New Zealand nature and history. He believed the colony needed to start producing its own literature instead of having to slavishly rely on imported material.

NEW ZEALAND.—EDUCATION DEPARTMENT.

The School Journal.

PART III.—FOR CLASSES V AND VI.

At least one copy of each Part should be filed in the school as a School Record.

VOL. XII.—No. 6.] WELLINGTON. [JULY, 1918.

School-gardens at Whangarei.

THE PASSING OF THE FOREST.

All glory cannot vanish from the hills—
Their strength remains, their stature of command,
Their flush of colour when calm evening stills
Day's clamour, and the sea-breeze cools the land.
Refreshed when rain-clouds swell a thousand rills,
Ancient of days in green old age they stand
In grandeur that can never know decay,
Though from their flanks men strip the woods away.

NEW ZEALAND.—EDUCATION DEPARTMENT.

The School Journal.

PART III.—FOR CLASSES V AND VI.

At least one copy of each Part should be filed in the school as a School Record.

VOL. XI.—No. 7.] WELLINGTON. [AUGUST, 1917.

ENGLAND.

Glory of thought and glory of deed,
Glory of Hampden and Runnymede,
Glory of ships that sought far goals,
Glory of swords and glory of souls,
Glory of songs mounting as birds,
Glory immortal of magical words,
Glory of Milton, glory of Nelson,
Tragical glory of Gordon and Scott,
Glory of Shelley, glory of Sidney,
Glory transcendent that perishes not—
Here is the story, here be the glory—England!
Shatter her beauteous breast ye may;
The spirit of England none can slay!
Dash the bomb on the dome of St. Paul's—
Deem ye the fame of the Admiral falls?
Pry the stone from the chancel-floor—
Dream ye that Shakespeare shall live no more!
Where is the giant shot that kills
Wordsworth walking the old green hills?
Trample the red rose on the ground—
Keats is beauty while earth spins round!
Bind her, grind her, burn her with fire,
Cast her ashes into the sea—
She shall escape, she shall aspire,
She shall arise to make men free;
She shall arise in a sacred scorn,
Lighting the lives that are yet unborn;
Spirit supernal, Splendour eternal—
England!

—Helen Gray Cone.

William Pember Reeves
Photograph courtesy of the Alexander Turnbull Library

A writer as well as a politician, William Pember Reeves (1857–1932) was Minister for Education, Justice, and Labour in the Liberal Government during the 1890s. He was subsequently appointed New Zealand's Agent-General in London. While he never returned to New Zealand, two years after his departure in 1896, he published *The Long White Cloud: Ao Tea Roa*, which remained a standard history of the country for over half a century. His poems and articles continued to appear in the *School Journal* long after his death.

"In 1908, its first full year of publication," writes P. R. Earle, "105 of the 132 prose items in the three parts were on 'social studies' subjects – history, geography and civics, as they were then called." [5] Notable also during the first year of publication was a series of "Maoriland Fairy Tales" (with titles like "Jack, the Fairy, and the Moa") and, in a Part 1 *Journal*, "What a Maori Thought of Captain Cook".

Pember Reeves hovers above the early history of the *Journal* like a godfather figure. On its front cover, *School Journal*, Part 3, July 1907 featured the opening stanzas of his "The Passing of the Forest", a poem that was reprinted often during the following two decades. In its 1907 incarnation, the poem was followed by an exhortation to the young of the Dominion that they become guardians of Pember Reeves' beloved forest. Subsequent issues of the *Journal* continued to promulgate this kind of environmental awareness while, in the same breath, promoting Pember Reeves' poetic prowess.

With the outbreak of World War One, the pastoral, bucolic tradition made way for a deluge of anthems and marching songs. Alongside all this tub-thumping nationalism (of which militarism was presented as an essential component), articles extolling the virtues of flora and fauna continued to trickle through. However, in this new context, even these articles were coloured with patriotic fervour – as if the forests of Northland were somehow contributing to the war effort.

NEW ZEALAND.—EDUCATION DEPARTMENT.

The School Journal.

PART III. — FOR CLASSES V AND VI.

At least one copy of each Part should be filed in the school as a School Record

VOL. I.—No. 3.] WELLINGTON. [JULY, 1907.

THE PASSING OF THE FOREST.

Gone is the forest world, its wealth of life,
Its jostling, crowding, thrusting, struggling race,
Creeper with creeper, bush with bush at strife,
Warring and wrestling for a breathing-space:
Below, a realm with tangled rankness rife;
Aloft, tree columns, shafts of stateliest grace.
Gone is the forest nation. None might stay;
Giant and dwarf alike have passed away.

Gone are the forest birds, arboreal things,
Eaters of honey, honey-sweet of song,
The tui, and the bell-bird—he who sings
That brief, rich music we would fain prolong;
Gone the wood-pigeon's sudden whirr of wings;
The daring robin, all unused to wrong.
Wild, harmless, hamadryad* creatures, they
Lived with their trees, and died, and passed away.

* Wood-nymph.

NEW ZEALAND—EDUCATION DEPARTMENT.

The School Journal.

PART III. — FOR CLASSES V AND VI.

At least one copy of each Part should be filed in the school as a School Record.

VOL. II.—No. 1.] WELLINGTON. [FEBRUARY, 1908.

THE MAKING OF NEW ZEALAND.

God girt her about with the surges
And winds of the masterless deep,
Whose tumult uprouses and urges
Quick billows to sparkle and leap;
He filled from the life of their motion
Her nostrils with breath of the sea,
And gave her afar in the ocean
A citadel free.

Her never the fever-mist shrouding,
Nor drought of the desert may blight,
Nor pall of dun smoke overclouding
Vast cities of clamorous night,
But the voice of abundance of waters,
Cold rivers that stay not or sleep,
Greets children, the sons and the daughters
Of light and the deep.

The winds of the sea and high heaven
Speed pure to her, kissed by the foam;
The steeds of her ocean undriven,
Unbitted and riderless roam,
And clear from her lamp newly lighted,
Shall stream o'er the billows upcurled
A light as of wrongs at length righted,
Of hope to the world.

—WILLIAM PEMBER REEVES,
High Commissioner for New Zealand.

Typically, for a *School Journal* during the war years, the Part 1 issue for June 1915 offered a quaint tale about a French girl who brewed coffee daily for the front-line soldiers. As well as the lyrics to "God Save the King", an account of the life of Joan of France and, on the back cover, "My Native Land" in the key of E, the issue included a fable that began: "A shining river-fairy looked up and down her stream and smiled. 'It is beautiful,' she said." While the conflict in Europe dominated the *Journal*, there was still room for a little, measured, escapist fantasy – as the cover of the subsequent Part 1 *Journal* also makes plain (see below).

ARBOR DAY NUMBER.

NEW ZEALAND.—EDUCATION DEPARTMENT.

The School Journal.

PART I.—FOR CLASSES I AND II.

At least one copy of each Part should be filed in the school as a School Record.

Vol. IX.—No. 6.] WELLINGTON. [July, 1915.

THE NEW FAIRYLAND.

"What can we do?"

Compared with more recent issues, the early *Journals* were slim and not particularly well designed, with few illustrations. Children were expected to file the year's issues in a specially made cover, and they usually took them home each night to learn their spelling words, a passage of verse, or a passage set for the next day's dictation. At the end of the year, the *Journals* became their own property.

A Guide to the School Journal (1994).

In the *Penguin History of New Zealand* (2003), Michael King underlined the powerful influence the *School Journal* had been on the developing sense of New Zealand identity. The legend of Kupe as popularised in a 1916 *Journal* became, according to King, "a founding myth every bit as majestic as the stories that Pākehā settlers carried with them from Europe". This account of the discovery of New Zealand also incorporated, he continued, "a series of adventures around the New Zealand coast involving moa, greenstone and a fight with a giant octopus".

E. Mervyn Taylor, cover illustration, *School Journal*, Part 4, August 1947

King also ascribed to the publication (and to the writings of a handful of earlier writers including William Pember Reeves) a key role in promoting the erroneous belief that Aotearoa had been the traditional Māori name for New Zealand. "After decades of repetition, Māori themselves came to believe that this was so. And, because shared mythology is ultimately more pervasive and more powerful than history, it became so." [6]

A far more lamentable lapse in the veracity of the early *Journal* was a 1916 account of the Moriori people in which, the *Penguin History* relates, they are described as a people of inferior culture. "No one knows whence they came, nor why they came … They were ocean waifs occupying three canoes that had been carried away by a storm from some island to the westward … They had a habit of looking sideways out of the corners of their eyes, and were an indolent and chilly folk [who] afterwards settled the Chatham Isles. In their new home they were peace-loving, timorous and lazy …" King noted that just about every statement in the *Journal* account was demonstrably wrong, yet "for hundreds of thousands of New Zealand children, the version of Moriori history carried in the *School Journal* and other publications which drew from that source, reinforced over 60-odd years by primary school teachers, was the one that lodged in the national imagination". [7]

An official acknowledgment of – and apology for – this misinformation and its negative effects is to be integrated into the Waitangi Tribunal settlement of the Moriori claim.

168 THE SCHOOL JOURNAL. [PART II.

INDEX TO PART II, VOLUME II, 1908.

By Authority: JOHN MACKAY, Government Printer, Wellington.
[38,050/10/08—11341

A glance at a Part 2 *Journal* index from 1908 gives a sense of the mixture of local and imported content offered in the early *Journals*.

AN EMPIRE DAY MESSAGE.

TO THE BOYS AND GIRLS OF THE BRITISH EMPIRE, FROM THE EARL OF MEATH.

WATCHWORDS: RESPONSIBILITY, DUTY, SYMPATHY, SELF-SACRIFICE.

BOYS AND GIRLS OF THE BRITISH EMPIRE,—

May you realize more and more fully as you grow older your great indebtedness to the British Empire — a majestic community of free nations, freely governing themselves, owing its being to vast sacrifice, enterprise, and valour on the part of your fathers and predecessors, bound together by one King, one Flag, and one Navy, comprising more than a fifth part of the human race, and occupying more than a fifth part of the earth's surface—a federation the like of which the world has never known before!

May you bear in mind that, of the allied peoples of this Empire, each one looks to the others for practical sympathy, protection, and co-operation; and that not only the State to which you belong, but also the Empire itself, looks to you to be ready in time of need, to think, to labour, and to bear hardships in its behalf! May you excel in the practice of Faith, Courage, Duty, Self-discipline, Fair-dealing, Even Justice, Good Citizenship, Loyalty, Patriotism, and Sympathy, and thus by your own individual action aid in elevating the British character, strengthening the British Empire, and consolidating the British Race!

At the outset of the Gallipoli campaign in 1915, the *Journal* was reporting events in a manner not dissimilar to that of the popular press, loudly praising the heroism of the Australasian soldiers who, in the words of Sir Ian Hamilton, gloriously "upheld the finest traditions of our race during this struggle still in progress". On Empire Day, June 1917, the Part 3 *Journal* carried a message to the "boys and girls of the British Empire" (see above). While the Armistice marked the end of the war in Europe, articles glorifying the conflict continued to appear in the *Journal* until well into the 1930s.

Amidst the New Zealand content published between the wars, the *Journal* regularly included material relating to Māori culture, largely because, as Diana Beaglehole has pointed out, this was:

> *a period when considerable interest was being shown in "The Maori", especially by creative artists and those associated with the Polynesian Society ... the prevailing assumption that Maoris were a dying race gave a certain impetus to collecting and recording information related to them.* [8]

For the most part, the 1920s and 30s passed inauspiciously, with a significant percentage of *Journal* content lifted straight from English publications. Not a lot remained of either the *Journal's* original flair or its lively sense of the local. While William Pember Reeves still appeared as a contributor, his influence was on the wane. It was not until 1939 and the establishment of the School Publications Branch that the *Journal* would enter a new, dynamic phase.

Whatever the limitations of its viewpoint, however, the *School Journal* certainly had a positive influence during its first quarter century. It was often the only reading material available for adults, particularly those living in outlying areas, as well as for children. In a country where people were frequently moving around, it standardised the resources available in schools and was distributed free to each child until the late 1940s, at which point it was decided that copies be given to schools rather than individuals, enabling teachers to access class-sets from previous years.

While the Depression went more or less unmentioned in the *Journal*, the 1931 Napier earthquake elicited a message – more a God-like pronouncement – from the Director of Education, imploring the youngsters of the nation to give up their sweets and cinema money to aid the afflicted.

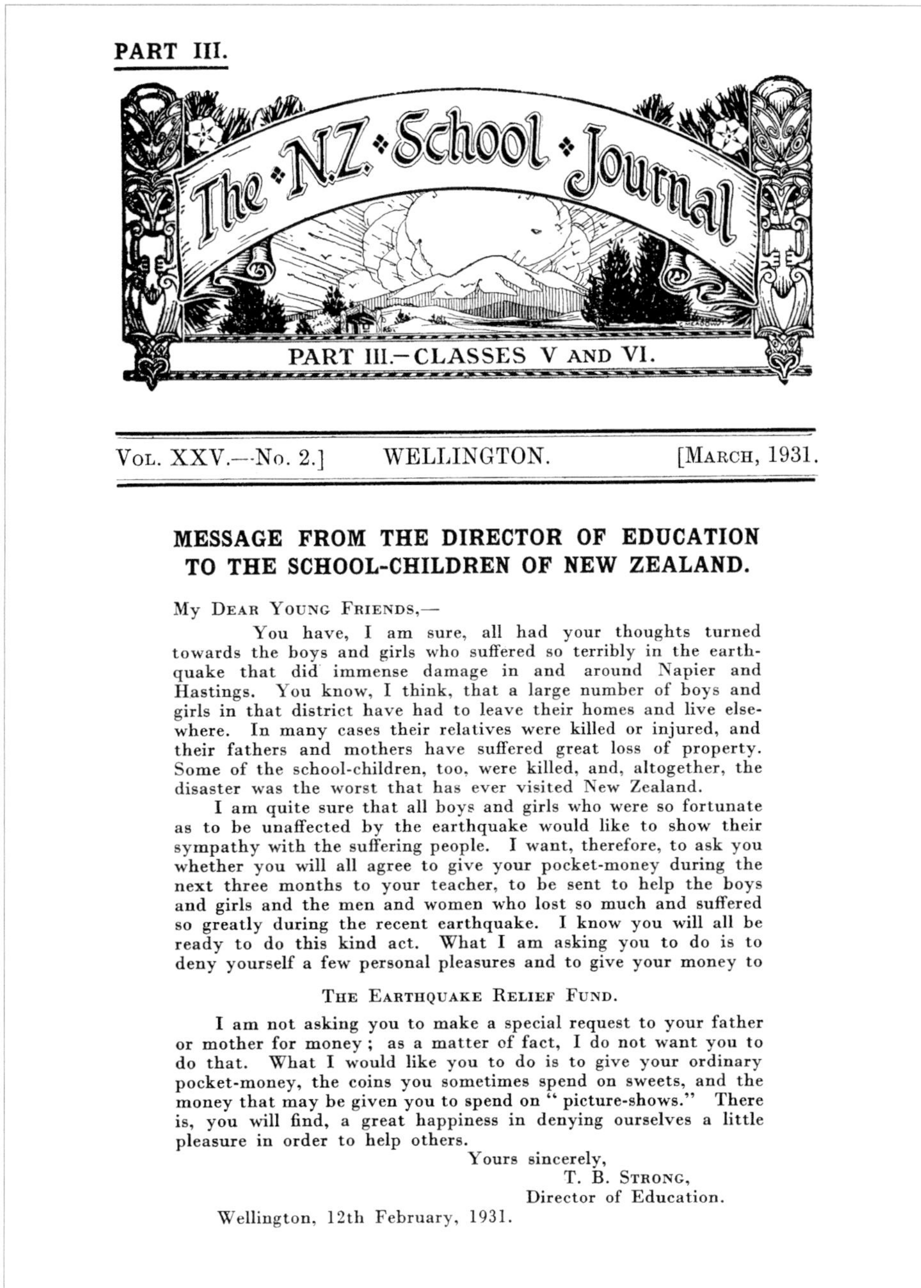

PART III.

The N.Z. School Journal

PART III.—CLASSES V AND VI.

VOL. XXV.—NO. 2.] WELLINGTON. [MARCH, 1931.

MESSAGE FROM THE DIRECTOR OF EDUCATION TO THE SCHOOL-CHILDREN OF NEW ZEALAND.

MY DEAR YOUNG FRIENDS,—

You have, I am sure, all had your thoughts turned towards the boys and girls who suffered so terribly in the earthquake that did immense damage in and around Napier and Hastings. You know, I think, that a large number of boys and girls in that district have had to leave their homes and live elsewhere. In many cases their relatives were killed or injured, and their fathers and mothers have suffered great loss of property. Some of the school-children, too, were killed, and, altogether, the disaster was the worst that has ever visited New Zealand.

I am quite sure that all boys and girls who were so fortunate as to be unaffected by the earthquake would like to show their sympathy with the suffering people. I want, therefore, to ask you whether you will all agree to give your pocket-money during the next three months to your teacher, to be sent to help the boys and girls and the men and women who lost so much and suffered so greatly during the recent earthquake. I know you will all be ready to do this kind act. What I am asking you to do is to deny yourself a few personal pleasures and to give your money to

THE EARTHQUAKE RELIEF FUND.

I am not asking you to make a special request to your father or mother for money; as a matter of fact, I do not want you to do that. What I would like you to do is to give your ordinary pocket-money, the coins you sometimes spend on sweets, and the money that may be given you to spend on "picture-shows." There is, you will find, a great happiness in denying ourselves a little pleasure in order to help others.

Yours sincerely,
T. B. STRONG,
Director of Education.

Wellington, 12th February, 1931.

Clarence Edward Beeby (1902–98)
Detail from photograph, courtesy
of the Alexander Turnbull Library

After studying law, Clarence Beeby decided to commit himself to primary teaching out of a sense of moral purpose that would eventually lead him into the Education Department. A hugely influential figure, Beeby became Director of Education and oversaw the beginnings of the School Publications Branch, which was founded in 1939 within the Education Department. In 1992, P. R. Earle recalled:

> *Beeby gave impetus to a new movement for broadening education, and particularly giving it a more local, national focus. So the publications component of the Department was expanded into a branch, the School Publications Branch, to produce textbooks, syllabuses, handbooks, bulletins for primary and post-primary schools and later a magazine for schools called* Education. [9]

The objective was to make New Zealand appear to its future citizens "more important and worthwhile than anything else". Beeby pronounced:

> *We could no longer be content with the educational theories and practices of the Old World, however warmly we felt about them, not with the textbooks we imported from it, not indeed with the pale copies of them we ourselves produced.* [10]

Juliet Peter, illustration,
School Journal,
Part 4, Spring 1956

The year 1937 marked the beginning of a period of major change in education circles. A national conference for teachers and educationalists two years after the election of M. J. Savage's Labour Government gave a new impetus to bolster New Zealand content in the *Journal* and also to make it less dominated by dogged, practically minded articles and stories. The *Journal* would henceforth strive to engage the curiosity and imaginations of children as well as aiming to connect with their daily lives. With the appointment of Beeby as Director of Education in 1940, the *School Journal* was effectively reborn.

During his twenty years in that position, Beeby oversaw a remarkable period in the history of School Publications and in education generally. Responsible for a programme of wide-ranging reforms, he created the Physical Education and Arts and Crafts branches through which, as Roger Hardie writes:

> *"the bright-eyed and bushy tailed" newly graduated teachers were employed in an itinerant capacity to inject revisionary practices into schools in their specialist subjects, while progressively influencing the whole curriculum to become increasingly concerned with flexible, responsive and creative education.* [11]

The relationship between the *School Journal* and the Arts and Crafts Branch would prove useful in years to come, with many of the art teachers involved contributing to the publication. Importantly, School Publications did not exist in isolation. It was part of a changing, dynamic educational scene, just as it was becoming part of a lively literary and art scene.

As well as bolstering creativity in its readers, the *School Journal* had to continue to meet specific requirements in the areas of maths and social studies. The approach to these, under Beeby, was ground-breaking. In the case of mathematics, examples were drawn from the children's experience of home and country. As P. R. Earle writes:

> *The new ideas in education came in on a wave of nationalism that started before the second world war. It was strengthened by the fact that New Zealand had celebrated its centenary (Pakeha New Zealand, that is) and had an independent division in that war.* [12]

George Woods, illustration for "Don Quixote and the Lions", *School Journal*, Part 3, February 1943

In the years up to and during World War Two, the *School Journal* had featured many of the classic writers of Western literature, among them Shakespeare, Cervantes, Jane Austen, Jonathan Swift, and Mark Twain. There were numerous outdoor adventure stories and, puzzlingly, an extraordinary number of animal stories with titles like "Two Thousand Million Pigeons", "Frisk, the Picnic Dog", and "A Fishy Story". In the tradition of the English Boy's Own Reader, *Journal* stories and articles from 1944 bore titles such as "Harris in Hampton Court Maze", "The Inventor of the All-Hearing Ear", "Quentin Durward Is Befriended", "Eight Lions Get Loose", "How Does a Horse Gallop" and, most memorably of all, "Boring under the Southern Alps". Like the prose, the poetry chosen for publication between 1939 and 1945, given events elsewhere in the world, was pointedly lighthearted. Typically, a Part 3 *Journal* from 1939 included the poems "I Will Make You Brooches", "The Names Come Ringing down the Way", "Master Rabbit", and "Miss Thompson Buys Fish".

BOY SCOUTS SPRAY WITH WATER AND SANDBAG AN INCENDIARY BOMB.

Russell Clark, illustration for *School Journal*, Part 3, March 1942

Since the present war began, more than 60,000 Boy Scouts in England have earned the National Service Badge for constant war service. They have worthily upheld the Scout promise to "help other people at all times".

One of the very few items published that engaged directly with World War Two was "Boy Scouts Help to Defend Britain", in the Part 3 *Journal*, March 1942. The tone of this piece, based on a Boy Scouts' Association of London booklet, was close to the nationalistic rant of the First World War *Journals*. Such writing was, however, the exception rather than the rule during the war period. At the outbreak of hostilities, as P. R. Earle observed:

> *there was no reference to the Second World War in any part of the* Journal. *One senses the chill of a horror which should not be visited on the young.* [13]

The *School Journal* underwent an almost palpable transition during wartime. Between 1940 and 1942, a new awareness of New Zealand culture began to reshape the publication, reflecting a growing confidence in, and curiosity about, life in this country. At the same time, the perfunctory non-fiction material that had all but swamped the *Journal* during the 1930s was scaled back or diverted into stand-alone Bulletins.

With the war in Europe winding down, the year 1945 began with a series of covers that could have been produced by the Tourism Board – airy vistas of local countryside with billboard-like mastheads adrift on them. In May 1945, the month of Germany's surrender, the *School Journal* Part 3 cover featured a native pigeon flying high over the Kapiti Coast, at once a nationalistic emblem and a localised dove of peace. The Part 2 *Journal* for the same month featured a weka by E. Mervyn Taylor, striding forth surrounded by native ferns. Physical aspects of the *Journal* were changing as well as the thinking behind it. Wartime paper restrictions were soon lifted, and new printing technologies were just around the corner. Within a decade, the *School Journal* would have coloured covers.

John Drawbridge, cover artwork for *Hilltop* 2, ed. J. M. Thomson, Literary Society of Victoria University College, 1949

E. Mervyn Taylor, cover illustration for *School Journal*, Part 2, May 1945
Courtesy of the E. Mervyn Taylor Estate

Under the capable art editorship of Cliff O'Malley a team of good contributing illustrators has been assembled [by School Publications]. Russell Clark is the most experienced, witty and sophisticated. Juliet Peter's distinctive style is childlike and charming. Others who help to maintain the high standard are Conrad Frieboe, Sam Williams, Mervyn Taylor, George Woods, S. B. Maclennan, Joan Smith, Yvonne Bendall, J. W. Bowie, Joan Dukes. This is one of the encouraging signs that the Education Department are thoroughly alert to the importance of good design.

Howard Wadman, *Year Book of the Arts in New Zealand*, no. 3, 1947

Another remarkable aspect of this post-war period for the *Journal* was that it was not only contemporaneous with, but also umbilically linked to, exciting developments in New Zealand art. While Colin McCahon was reinventing cubism, his wife Anne was producing emblematic drawings for School Publications (see page 119). The work of an emerging generation of painters and writers was characterised by a melding of local realities with international trends, an identical formula to that prescribed for the contents of the *Journal* by key figures such as Stuart Maclennan and, a little later, Roy Cowan.

Many of the regular *School Journal* artists were, indeed, part of the vanguard of New Zealand art. During the seven years that it was published (1945–51), every issue of the prestigious *Year Book of the Arts in New Zealand* featured artists on the School Publications payroll – among them Maclennan, Cowan, George Woods, E. Mervyn Taylor, Russell Clark, May Smith, Juliet Peter, and Rita Angus. In the 1951 issue of the *Arts Year Book*, the *School Journal* was the subject of an extended essay by J. C. Beaglehole, and surveys of design and graphic arts featured work from the *Journals*.

E. Mervyn Taylor, cover illustration for *School Journal*, Part 2, August 1945

"Reality and Immediacy", a display of School Publications books from J. C. Beaglehole's "A Small Bouquet for the Education Department", *Arts Year Book*, no. 7, 1951

The relationship between the Wellington literary periodical *Hilltop*, which published three issues in 1949, and the *Journal* was a close one. Among the *Hilltop* contributors who would later make a significant contribution to the *School Journal* were the artist John Drawbridge; the young poets James K. Baxter, Alistair Campbell, Louis Johnson, and Pat Wilson; Brian Sutton-Smith (whose "Our Street" serial appeared in the *Journal* the same year as he was publishing fiction in *Hilltop* 2); and *Hilltop* editor J. M. Thomson, who contributed stories and essays to the *Journal* on a wide range of topics.

E. Mervyn Taylor, cover illustration for *School Journal*, Part 3, May 1945

It is obviously most important that the opening eyes of the young should not be debauched by bad design and slovenly typography.

Howard Wadman in *Year Book of the Arts in New Zealand*, no. 3, 1947

Joy Miles, Form 2, Waitoriki School, cover for "Children's Number", *School Journal*, Part 4, October 1946

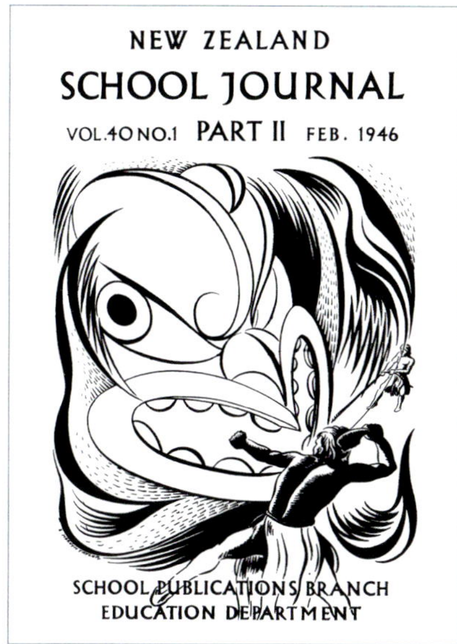

E. Mervyn Taylor, cover drawing, *School Journal*, Part 1, February 1946

Daisy Ngan, Standard 3A, Te Awamutu Primary School, cover for "Children's Number", *School Journal*, Part 4, October 1946

Immediately after the Second World War, a number of issues were devoted to writing and art by schoolchildren. The children's work felt surprisingly at home in the context of the *Journal* at the time. Certainly by the 1950s, the work of artists such as Anne McCahon, Jean Angus, and Evelyn Clouston reflected an awareness of, and responsiveness to, children's art. In recent years, Learning Media has published an annual *Journal of Young People's Writing*, illustrated by children, carrying on this tradition.

S. Emery, Form 3, Rangitahi Native School, illustration for "Children's Number", *School Journal*, Part 4, October 1946

By the late 1940s, the sense of New Zealand as a country independent from England had further consolidated. The 1948 *Revised Syllabuses* upheld "love of one's country, willingness to serve it, and faith in its future" as something which "should begin to evolve in the primary-school child's own emotional life." [14] Importantly, rather than telling children what exactly to think, in the "best" colonial tradition, the *Journal* was now expected to present materials that might inspire children, by the "discovery method", to reach their own conclusions.

Life in the Pa

A landmark both in the history of the *School Journal* and in the artistic careers of Mervyn Taylor and Russell Clark, a book-length feature about traditional Māori life appeared in 1948. Written by *Journal* editor Ray Chapman-Taylor (whose name was absent from the *Journal* publication), *Life in the Pa* presented an unromanticised account of what life prior to European contact might have been like. Eclipsing even Chapman-Taylor's fine writing, the illustrations were eloquent and sympathetic depictions of ordinary life and customary practices. *Life in the Pa* told the story of a boy who was taken from his Northland village by a pillaging war party and subsequently raised by another tribe. The series was rich in historical detail, evoking not only warfare but also fishing, bird catching, and children's games.

LIFE IN THE PA

NEW ZEALAND SCHOOL JOURNAL

VOL. 42 NO. 8 PART III SEPT., 1948

SCHOOL PUBLICATIONS BRANCH EDUCATION DEPARTMENT

LIFE IN THE PA

NEW ZEALAND SCHOOL JOURNAL

VOL. 42 NO. 7 PART III AUGUST 1948

Published as three consecutive issues of the *School Journal*, Part 3, 1948, *Life in the Pa* contained over 150 drawings by Russell Clark and E. Mervyn Taylor – in all probability the largest illustrative assignment in the history of the *Journal*. While Clark drew the action scenes and group compositions, Taylor contributed images of birds and of Māori implements and weapons that he had studied extensively in the Dominion Museum, Wellington. After appearing in the *School Journal*, the series was published in book form by Paul's Book Arcade.

At daybreak the kumara-planting began. A carved stone was carried to the field from the tapu place in the pa and set in the soil at the end of the field. Because this stone belonged to the gods, the field in which it stood would certainly grow many kumaras. The tohungas, the men who knew many things difficult to learn, chanted the proper prayers to make the kumaras grow.

A party of men lined out along the field, each with his ten-foot ko, or digging stick, ready to begin the work. At once a young man famed for his fine voice began to sing a working song and all the men pushed their pointed sticks into the ground. At the place where each plant would grow they pushed in the ko three times and loosened the soil with a pull of their sticks three ways, one to the left, one to the right, one straight ahead, and then stepped back to the next place.

When the looseners had passed on a little, another party, each man armed with a small wooden grubber called a timo, began to beat and break up the lumps and to work in the ashes left from great bundles of manuka which had been burnt there the day before. At one side of the field the soil was black and sticky. There the pinaki men added to the soil coarse sand and gravel brought in flax bags by sweating slaves.

Life in the Pa by Ray Chapman-Taylor, *School Journal*, Part 3, August, 1948

Two female portraits and stone kūmara god by E. Mervyn Taylor.
Other images by Russell Clark.

"Our Street" by Brian Sutton-Smith

Well, Brian and Smitty and Gormie and Horsey would all sit on Gormie's front porch on a Saturday morning "bagzing".

"I bagz we go to the zoo," Horsey would say.

"Aw, no. I bagz we go to the pictures," Gormie would say. He always made this bagz because he always had plenty of money. Whenever he was short, he would just go and ask each of his brothers and sisters for something and soon he would have several shillings. But Brian and Smitty, though they would like to have gone to the pictures, didn't make this bagz because it meant they would have to ask their Dad for the money, and he would probably say, "No." Their Dad said they should play out in the fresh air all day, but they usually grew tired of the fresh air by the afternoon.

"I bagz we go to the football," said Smitty.

"Aw, no," said Gormie.

"Why not?" asked Brian.

"Because," said Gormie.

"Because what?" asked Smitty.

"Because I bagz we go to the pictures."

"I bagz we don't," said Brian.

"I bagz the zoo," said Horsey.

"I don't bagz the zoo," said Smitty.

"Well let's see which two we bagz most out of the three," said Smitty.

"The flicks and footy," said Gormie.

"Yes, I bagz the flicks and footy too," said Brian.

"I still bagz the zoo, and I'm going by myself, anyhow," said Horsey.

"Brian and I won't be allowed to go to the pictures," said Smitty, "so we'll have to go to the football. Anyhow, Old Boys are playing. It'll be good."

"There's a Technicolour Hop-along Cassidy in the Bar 20 Range, at the flicks," said Gormie.

Then nobody said anything for a long time, and the sun poured down and it was hot and lazy. Trams went backwards and forwards a few streets away, sounding sort of dull in the dazzling sun. It was very bright and, though they didn't feel sleepy, they didn't feel they could move from the hot sun pouring onto their bare arms and legs. Gormie was chipping bits of hard dirt and dust from out between the porch boards with a bit of stick. Smitty and Horsey were just sitting, and Brian had his finger-nail under a paint blister and was slowly picking it out. The edge of the dry paint was hard under his nail and it hurt now and again if he pushed his finger too hard. He had picked about six inches of paint off the porch wall in the last three weeks. The porch was the only part of the house wall which looked as if it had been painted at all, and Brian was slowly making the porch look like the rest of the house. If he sat there for enough Saturday mornings there would be no paint left. But he didn't think of that. He just thought of the nice hard sharp feeling under his middle-finger nail.

"I bagz we go to the zoo," said Horsey again.

Illustrations by Juliet Peter, *School Journal*, Part 3 Number 6, 1949

While, by present day standards, the "Our Street" stories seem innocuous and benign, the series made newspaper headlines around the country in 1949 and was discontinued after only three of the projected ten episodes. The first instalment appeared in *School Journal*, Part 3, prefaced by an explanatory note from the author asking that young readers analyse the behaviour of the mildly dissolute group of protagonists and consider the fundamental question of whether it is possible to have a good time without harming or inconveniencing other people. The note concluded, "Well, that's for you to work out for yourselves." A textbook case, you could say, of the "discovery method" in action.

Author Brian Sutton-Smith (born Wellington, 1924) also contributed an article to the periodical *Education* to coincide with the *Journal* publication and, presumably, to stave off criticism. The serial was intended, he wrote, to be a means of making "closer moral contact" with a Standard 3 class he was teaching.

In "Our Street" a gang of boys find themselves in various situations that are familiar and real to many New Zealand children. The gang is not really tough, but its activities often border on the antisocial. [15]

Ideally, the stories would prompt discussion of moral and social issues among the young.

The use of slang in "Our Street" was at least as controversial as the antisocial behaviour of the gang – see the letter from the President of the Headmasters' Association, H. H. Hawkins (following page). The *Journal's* side of that argument was articulated in a memo from the Education Department to the Minister of Education dated 20 August 1949.

The literary standard of the author's work should surely be judged by the veracity with which he portrays his characters and situations. If children's reading is to be limited to so-called "standard" English, it becomes necessary to debar them from any acquaintance with such books as Oliver Twist, David Copperfield, Tom Sawyer, Huckleberry Finn, Alice in Wonderland ... [16]

The stories were accompanied by drawings of suburban Wellington by staff artist Juliet Peter, who went out sketching the precise locations in Sutton-Smith's narrative to give it authenticity. Even these charming, informal illustrations were dragged into the controversy. An article in the *Hawera Star* (18 August) reported a meeting of the Taranaki Education Board at which a fuming Miss V. I. Curtis accused Peter's drawings of evoking "a mean and sordid atmosphere".

In the third and last instalment published in the *Journal*, the evil-doing of the band of vagabonds reaches a crescendo when the boys accidentally break a cat's milk saucer with a cricket ball and a policeman is called. Before the policeman leaves the scene of the crime, he explains to the youngsters how to play French cricket "by holding the bat in front of his legs while the boys tried to hit his legs with a tennis ball". This was clearly too much for the moral guardians and whistle-blowers of the country at the time, particularly those in Dunedin and Taranaki, where opposition was most vocal. With no sign of the hoopla dying down, the Education Department withdrew the stories, the official reason being on account of "misunderstandings about the purpose for which they were written". This, despite a statement from the Acting Director of Education supporting the publication and pointing out that:

it remains the professional responsibility of all teachers to select from all education publications those sections which they desire to study with their own classes. They are free to reject anything which they personally may consider to be educationally unsound, or which they feel would have no appeal to the children they teach. [17]

Upon the termination of the series, the *Taranaki Daily News* struck a smug, triumphal note, its headline of 31 October 1949 reading, "Articles Cut from *School Journal* Issue – Result of Protest Begun in Taranaki". Not only was the "Our Street" incident a flashpoint in the history of School Publications, it was a curtain-raiser for the wider moral arguments of the 1950s about comics and the erosion of youth morality in Lower Hutt and elsewhere.

The entire sequence of "Our Street" stories was published by Reed, with illustrations by Russell Clark, in 1950. Two years later, Brian Sutton-Smith left New Zealand after being awarded a Fulbright Fellowship. In November 2006, Sutton-Smith wrote:

I am forever grateful to the School Journal *for having the guts to do what they did and publish my innocently drawn "Our Street" kids. As for the withdrawal of the series from publication, that was in the hands of the usual, sometimes child-traumatised, Board members.* [18]

The Acting Director of Education,
Wellington.

Dear Sir,

On behalf of the Headmasters' Association of the Dunedin Primary Schools, I wish to protest most emphatically about the low standard of English and some of the content matter of the School Journals published recently.

The reading matter coming into the schools, especially when we are handicapped by lack of text books, should be on a very high plane.

We have been for many years fighting the lowering influence of comics, 'penny dreadfuls', American language in pictures and every-day speech, the questionable language used over the radio, and the ordinary laziness of children to speak correctly.

We have for many years used the Journal as a substitute for an English book, relying on its standard of English for examples of what we wanted in Composition work, and for correct speech. We feel however that this standard has dropped very considerably and we find frequent examples of very bad grammar, and numerous examples of slovenly and lazy construction.

We realize that the modern tendency is not to have the flowery elaborate sentences of 'our' day, but we deplore the Journal's extreme opposite view as exampled in Part III, pages 162 - 170. In those 8 pages there are only 2 Periodic sentences but -

9	sentences beginning with	But
11	" " "	Then
7	" " "	And
6	" " "	Now
5	" " "	So

Again on Page 47, we have 10 sentences. 7 of these are simple sentences. On Page 123, we have "so she says" 3 times in 8 lines and "says he" 8 times in 9 lines. For variety the ninth time we have "said he", in spite of grammatical correctness.

\- 2 -

We maintain that variety has a very necessary place in our language but we find on the same page no conjunction but "and".

The following too are examples from the same Journal -

There's no more dances.
The cook she set about it.
I haven't nowhere to go
\- who the sheep belonged to -
Near enough for him to creep out at night and steal down on them.
Always and always with nothing but a hut to sleep in and only meat to eat.
Beautifullest lady
But come the evening -
she offed
slipt
The master's son was rarely glad.
Bagz
Aw
Flicks
And there he laid
He appeared for to be
He won't send his cat on board for no one
etc. etc.

The glamourizing of dishonesty as expressed in 'Our Street' even although the author safeguards himself by asking the class to discuss the principles involved, is in our opinion to be deplored.

There are on the other hand many good articles, but we wish to bring to your notice those to which we take exception. We would appreciate your interest in this matter.

Yours truly,
H.H. Hawkins
President, Headmasters' Association.

Letter from H. H. Hawkins, President, Headmasters' Association, to the Acting Director of Education, 15 August 1949. Courtesy of Archives, New Zealand

In his reply to the above letter, the Acting Director of Education wrote, "It has always been the policy of the *Journal* to introduce children to books and poems which may be considered a part of the national culture ... It is also part of the policy of the *Journal* to introduce children to the best work of New Zealand writers who can give them an understanding of their own experience and environment ... If the *School Journal*, or any other of the School Publications, is to have a policy planned to implement the purpose of the new curriculum – to help each child to understand himself as a person and in relation to society – there must be a certain amount of carefully planned experiment."

Rita Angus, cover illustration, *School Journal*, Part 2, August 1955

As the 1950s progressed, the *Journal* increasingly commissioned work from local artists and writers. Alistair Campbell, one of the stalwarts of the *School Journal* editorial staff, made a point of shoulder-tapping established writers around this time:

> *I tended to look at writers who were experienced in writing adult fiction, and ask them to try writing stories for children. Most of these people hadn't written for children before, and they seemed to think it was a special skill. But I told them that most of us remain quite childlike at heart – you never really lose the side of you that has a sense of excitement in quite ordinary things – and I asked them to make contact with that side of themselves.* [19]

If writers for the *Journal* were often co-opted in cafés or pubs in the vicinity of the School Publications office, visual artists were even closer at hand. During the 1950s, the School Publications office was just down the corridor from the Arts and Crafts Branch, which was headed by occasional *Journal* contributor Gordon Tovey. A mover and a shaker in educational matters, Tovey lectured extensively on childhood creativity and the importance of imagination; his ideas, doubtlessly, struck a chord with *Journal* staff.

> *The imaginative process, as I see it, is a natural birthright of children that enables them to transmit to objects and creatures apart from themselves a consciousness similar to their own. And this is one of the fundamentals in education, because, in using this ability, children go out and meet the world in a way they can understand. Then to them the trees whisper; the waves laugh; the wind sighs; and so they proceed through a whole series of self-identifying patterns through which they become part of the environment, and the environment becomes an organic part of them.* [20]

Tovey's daughter, Carol Henderson, recalls School Publications editor Cliff O'Malley and Tovey forming a close working relationship. In her book *A Blaze of Colour*, she quotes John Drawbridge on the interconnectedness of the two departments:

> *The intermixing of our groups saw kinship built up – friendships developed that were important personally and professionally. Several of us got commissions to do illustrations for School Publications, that gave recognition and an outlet for our own art work.* [21]

Farming Crossword

CLUES.

ACROSS.

1. Cattle will use this to cross a stream or river.
5. Enclosures for sheep.
8. May be seen on all plants. (Two words.)
10. When these come to high country runs, shepherds are busy.
15. — and haws.
17. Short for lieutenant.
19. Girl's name.
20. "I did but see her — by."
23. Sheep.
24. Exclamation of surprise.
25. Monster.
27. A farmer might plough his way through his monthly account, but a calculating machine would do it more quickly.
32. Grass for grazing.
34. Seen in a farmyard. (Two words.)
35. "— light, — bright."

DOWN.

1. This kind of lamb brings the highest price.
2. Pieces — eight.
3. Initials of Scottish author.
4. A Spanish title.
5. Seat in a church.
6. Short for Emergency Relief Service.
7. Her name was Susannah.
9. Buildings on a sheep farm.
11. "The mountain — are sweeter."
12. You can't see far when it is this.
14. Containers for wool.
16. Short for South Africa.
18. Seventh note of scale.
21. "When they said it was —, He replied, 'yes, I know'."
22. "— safe jump for a failing horse."
26. May be either flower or vegetable.
27. The noun is an animal, the verb means to imitate.
28. A good name for boy and dog.
29. "— a long way to go."
30. Add another and the result is a mild scolding—too mild for sheep dogs.
31. By means of.
33. Short for Royal Academy.

Published by the School Publications Branch, Education Department. Printed by Hutcheson, Bowman & Stewart, Ltd., Printers, Wellington.—July, 1950. 75,000.

John Drawbridge, decoration for a Farming Crossword, *School Journal*, Part 4, July 1950

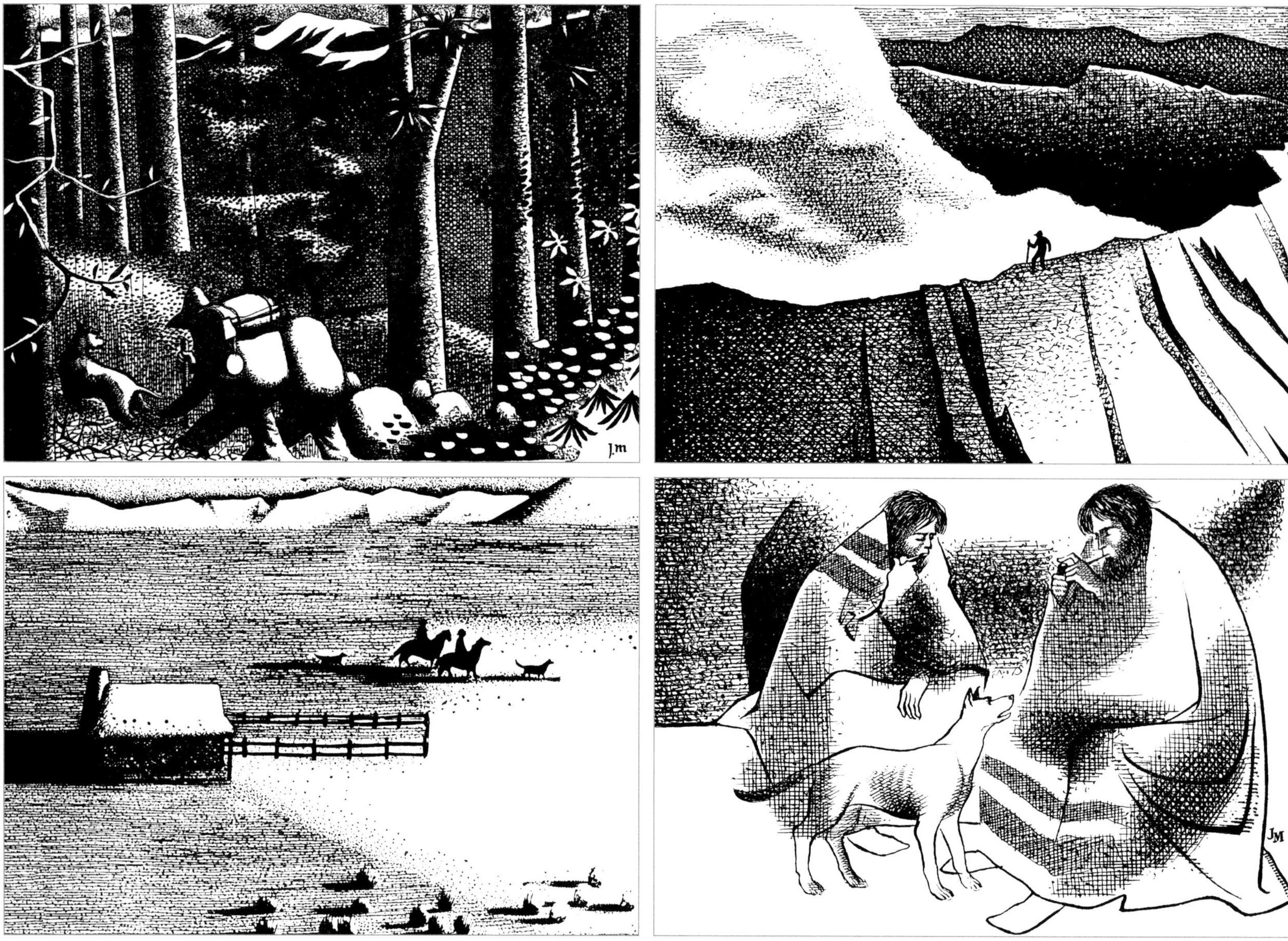

Jill McDonald, illustrations for "Four Explorers of New Zealand", by John Pascoe, *School Journal*, Part 3, Autumn 1956–Summer 1956–7

The explorers profiled by Pascoe were, clockwise from top left – Thomas Brunner, John Carne Bidwill, Arthur P. Harper, Samuel Butler

A major acknowledgment of the *School Journal* came in 1957, when UNESCO in Paris published a report on School Publications praising the way the New Zealand government had "found a particularly interesting solution to its publishing problems – the establishment of a highly efficient School Publications Branch, within the Department of Education."[22] A seminar in conjunction with the report, to discuss aspects of the programme, was held in Wellington that same year, with representatives of thirty countries attending. Alistair Campbell recalls how, when the Afghan delegate came to speak, an earthquake shook the building: "Beaming at the audience he said, 'You see, ladies and gentlemen, the power of my words.'"[23]

Beeby contributed an introduction to the UNESCO document in which he outlined what he believed to be the reasons for the *Journal's* success. He highlighted the importance of the publication remaining responsive "to the deep undercurrents that run through the education system as a whole."[24] Of the decade 1935–45, he observed that "the country was no longer satisfied with a primary school system that still had much of the aridity of its nineteenth century forbears." Following two world wars and the Great Depression:

> *New Zealand was beginning to feel the steady pressure of a new sense of nationhood ... Her social experiments had attracted attention in the world, and her own writers were beginning to attract attention in New Zealand.*[25]

He stressed the need for an organisation like School Publications to have some creative distance and freedom from the governmental and departmental powers that be. It needed long-range aims but at the same time had to give writers and artists room to move "within the broad framework of a vigorous educational policy."[26] Lastly, he maintained that genuine experts should be employed to write on their topics and that high standards be imposed at every stage of the production.

"Good educational theory and our new sense of nationhood both demanded that we should begin the child's education from his own world immediately surrounding him,"[27] Beeby noted, echoing the statements Allen Curnow, M. T. Wollaston, and others of that time were making concerning the necessity of creating an art deeply rooted in the local and familiar. By the early 1960s, the *School Journal* had gone a long way towards achieving Beeby's objectives. It had become almost entirely local in its content, for a start.

Mary Roberts, cover design, *School Journal*, Part 1 Number 1, 1960

Lizard-like, the *Journal* has changed its skin many times since the mid-century. Just as the content has changed, design and layout have had to keep pace with technological developments as well as responding to changes in taste. Initially the typography was as conservative as the *Journal's* contents – printed by lead type with spartan illustrations. Through the 1940s and 50s, the *Journal* was elegant and not dissimilar to the literary quarterly *Landfall* (many of whose contributors it shared). Line drawings by E. Mervyn Taylor, Russell Clark, and others were the perfect counterpart to the spacious, refined typography of that period. Through the 1960s and 70s, as colour printing became increasingly viable, the *Journal* became infused with colour – at first two- or three-colour printing and then, incrementally, the pages inside became multi- and then full-coloured. Art editor Terence Taylor recalls the arguments within the organisation regarding the introduction of colour printing. It was about the same time that colour televisions were moving into homes around the country and commercial publishers were beginning to mass-produce full-colour picture books. The *Journal* had to keep up.

With the advent of flower power, *Bullshit and Jellybeans*, and the *Whole Earth Catalogue*, things were destined to unravel somewhat in the *Journal* art department. By the mid-1970s, unorthodox typefaces were being incorporated. In fact, the colour that now saturated the illustrations was taking over type-design as well – as a contents page from 1975 attests.

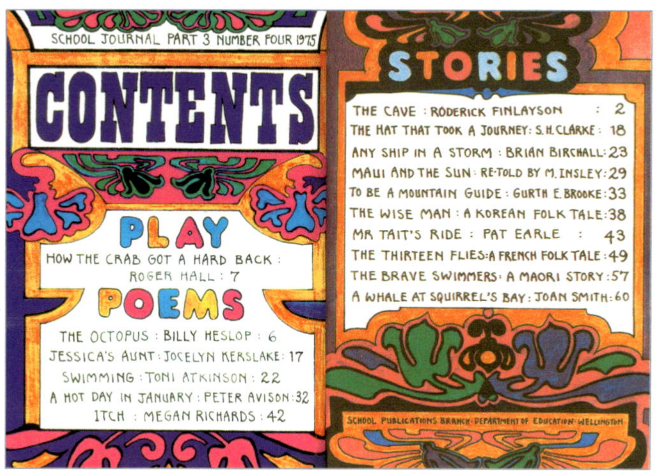
SCHOOL JOURNAL PART 3 NUMBER FOUR 1975

CONTENTS

PLAY

HOW THE CRAB GOT A HARD BACK : ROGER HALL : 7

POEMS

THE OCTOPUS : BILLY HESLOP : 6
JESSICA'S AUNT : JOCELYN KERSLAKE : 17
SWIMMING : TONI ATKINSON : 22
A HOT DAY IN JANUARY : PETER AVISON : 32
ITCH : MEGAN RICHARDS : 42

STORIES

THE CAVE : RODERICK FINLAYSON : 2
THE HAT THAT TOOK A JOURNEY : S. H. CLARKE : 18
ANY SHIP IN A STORM : BRIAN BIRCHALL : 23
MAUI AND THE SUN : RE-TOLD BY M. INSLEY : 29
TO BE A MOUNTAIN GUIDE : GURTH E. BROOKE : 33
THE WISE MAN : A KOREAN FOLK TALE : 38
MR TAIT'S RIDE : PAT EARLE : 43
THE THIRTEEN FLIES : A FRENCH FOLK TALE : 49
THE BRAVE SWIMMERS : A MAORI STORY : 57
A WHALE AT SQUIRREL'S BAY : JOAN SMITH : 60

SCHOOL PUBLICATIONS BRANCH · DEPARTMENT OF EDUCATION · WELLINGTON

Contents page, *School Journal*, Part 3 Number 4, 1975

It was an era of jam-packed page layouts, pink and purple colour schemes, and swirling doodle-like decorations. Taylor recalls a surge of creative energy in the design department at the time, which he largely attributed to a very energetic young designer-artist, Vanya Lowry, who embraced the new possibilities and pushed the limits. "In a design studio, you tend to get fireworks when you introduce new technology," he notes. [28] The 1970s in the School Publications office were a case in point.

Vanya Lowry, illustration for Peter Bland's poem "Wings", *School Journal*, Part 4 Number 1, 1977

The new informality of the *Journal* was aimed at dispelling the notion that the publication was an instrument of the status quo and of a moribund education department. In stark contrast to E. Mervyn Taylor's soaring birds of the 1940s, which embodied an ideal of art as something poised, refined, and complete in itself, the *Journal* during the 1970s was quirky, hyperactive, and even, at times, optically challenging (witness Graham Percy's cover design for the 1976 reader, *Stories for You*). Since the 1970s, art editors have recognised

Graham Percy, cover artwork, *Stories for You*, *School Journal*, Part 3, 1976

the need for covers to be attention-grabbing in order to compete with other publications and media in a cluttered and competitive world.

By the late 1970s, the reinvigorated and boisterous *Journal* had arrived at close to its present format, with colour covers and usually full-colour pages throughout. In recent years, new printing and design processes have given the *Journal* the ability to perform tricks that were unimaginable previously. Yet, as ever, it is the quality of the writing and the attentiveness of the writer and illustrator to the story and the world beyond that matters in the end. As the 1994 *A Guide to the School Journal* states:

> *The best* Journal *items are popular because they cater for deeper and more permanent impulses shared by all children – their curiosity, their imagination, their sense of humour, and their attempts to make sense of the world they live in.* [29]

In recent years, the contents of the *Journal* have tended to be more grounded in the everyday experiences of children, skirting cautiously around the edges of the mystical and mysterious. Possibly as a result of the "Our Street" controversy and a further ruckus fourteen years later concerning the School Bulletin *Washday at the Pa*, the *Journal* has trodden carefully and, arguably, erred on the side of caution when it comes to matters of social or political sensitivity.

Perhaps the most significant development in recent decades was the 1989 merger of the School Publications Branch with the former Department of Education's Audio and Visual production units to form the Learning Media Group – a part of the new Ministry of Education. Four years later, Learning Media Limited Te Pou Taki Kōrero was incorporated as a Crown-owned company under the Education Amendment Act. In January 2005, Learning Media became a state-owned enterprise. While these were far-reaching administrative changes, the restructuring did not alter the *School Journal* itself in any noticeable way. The *Journal* was both robust enough as an institution and sufficiently valued in governmental circles that, to put it plainly, the ship was left to sail on.

Geoffrey Nees, cover artwork for *School Journal*, Part 2 Number 6, 1961

It is debatable at which points in the *Journal's* history it has been most responsive to the needs and desires of children. Certainly the art and literary editors of recent decades are confident that the *Journal* at the outset of the twenty-first century is inviting, exciting and, necessarily, educational. From the present vantage point, it might be argued that the "artistic" excellence of the post-war years was in fact tailored to adult ideas of what was good for children, at the expense of the children themselves – a point we will return to. Yet, given the austere production values of the 1940s and 50s, the images of Russell Clark, E. Mervyn Taylor, and Juliet Peter seem to have been remarkably effective in reaching a broad, young audience and making an impression they have taken with them into their adult lives.

In recent years, the *School Journal* has had to work twice as hard to reach and edify its readership because "of new ghosts, like television and film, haunting society and taking away part of the time traditionally given to reading" (as Margaret Mahy wrote in 1982).[30] Computers and digital media have now joined those new ghosts. While the stated role of the *Journal* has, at least in recent decades, been to reflect society rather than to shape it, the extent to which the publication leads, follows, or coincides with developments in the culture at large remains a matter of some complexity.

Art editor Penelope Newman believes that it is the job of the editors to stay abreast of trends while keeping in mind a sense of the *Journal's* past.

To stop absorbing new styles and ideas would be the quickest way for the Journal *to lose its relevance. We can't afford to ignore the influences that come from other publications, computer games, and the media. At the same time, we have to incorporate the things that go along with sound literacy practice – like getting an accurate picture–text match, organising the page so the reader knows where to start and how to negotiate their way around it, using appropriate fonts for different audiences. In the future, the* Journal *will continue to change and adapt, just as it always has.* [31]

Ruth Paul, cover illustration for *School Journal*, Part 4 Number 3, 1995

Given the present cultural and technological environment, it is unlikely that the *School Journal* will ever occupy the singular position for today's readers that it did for earlier generations. Yet its influence remains immense. Each year, 715 700 *Journals* are distributed to schools, and these are often accompanied by audio CDs and electronic storybooks. The basic purpose of the *School Journal* is as constant as ever – to foster a love of reading, to inspire and enlighten, and to help children steer a course through an often perplexing world.

Donna Cross, cover design for *School Journal*, Part 3 Number 3, 1994

The World as We Know It:

New Zealand, nature, and the School Journal

Euphoric meditations on the New Zealand landscape were commonplace in early issues of the *School Journal*. Unlikely as it might seem, until well into the 1920s such conservationist outbursts were often presented alongside enthusiastic accounts of tree-felling, burn-offs, land clearance, and the construction of homesteads and towns. For example, in the 1923 Arbor Day issue of the Part 3 *Journal*, Shelley's archetypal "Green" poem, "Recollections of the Forest", was followed by "Felling a Forest Giant" – an article that evoked the idyllic New Zealand bush – before shifting into settler/land clearance mode:

> Like the grand column of some ancient temple the grey-blue trunk of this king of the forest rises sixty feet from the ground to the lowest branches. It was probably growing proudly here when Julius Caesar first landed in Britain, and for hundreds of years has stood supreme, braving the terrors of storm and tempest. Beneath its shade long-vanished members of ancient native tribes have sheltered in the far-distant past, and gigantic moas have searched for food.
>
> But today its splendid history avails it nothing. Timber is needed for building houses and for a thousand other things, and so the great tree is doomed. The bushmen have come with axe and saw to cut it down ...
>
> A stalwart bushman takes one end of the saw, his mate goes to the other, and, bending to their work, they swing the keen steel blade with a long, steady motion. Deeper and deeper it cuts, but the task of sawing through this great mass of solid timber is a heavy one. Tiny wrens and fantails, attracted by the strange sound, flit about the workers and settle on the fallen trunk, while the tuis, whose voices were silenced by the thunderous crash of the mighty tree, burst into song from the topmost boughs of other giants near by.

THE FALL OF A GIANT.

Juliet Peter, illustration for "Sheep-dogs", *School Journal*, Part 3, May 1946

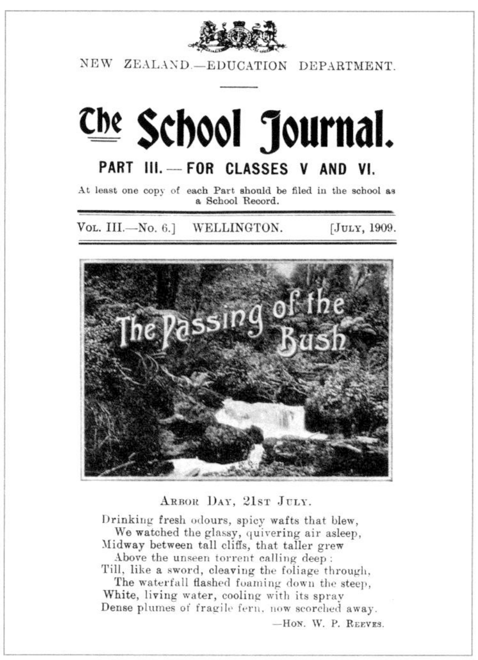

NEW ZEALAND.—EDUCATION DEPARTMENT.

The School Journal.

PART III.—FOR CLASSES V AND VI.

At least one copy of each Part should be filed in the school as a School Record.

VOL. III.—No. 6.] WELLINGTON. [JULY, 1909.

The Passing of the Bush

ARBOR DAY, 21ST JULY.

Drinking fresh odours, spicy wafts that blew,
We watched the glassy, quivering air asleep,
Midway between tall cliffs, that taller grew
Above the unseen torrent calling deep:
Till, like a sword, cleaving the foliage through,
The waterfall flashed foaming down the steep,
White, living water, cooling with its spray
Dense plumes of fragile fern, now scorched away.

—HON. W. P. REEVES.

(on left)
Jill McDonald, cover illustration, School Journal, Part 3, Spring 1958

Mountains, as well as forests, have served to define the New Zealand of the colonial mythmakers. Robert Burns's great poem of Highland Scotland, "My Heart's in the Highlands", chimes like an adopted anthem from numerous early issues of the *School Journal*. The same sentiments were later rephrased in the *Journal* by local poets such as Basil Dowling and Denis Glover and echoed in the visual art of Russell Clark and Juliet Peter. Until relatively recently – the 1960s, at least – an overseas reader of the *School Journal* might have assumed New Zealand was a country without any cities at all. Even if our hearts remained well and truly in the Highlands, as the century progressed, the *Journal* began to reflect the fact that the vast majority of its readers now lived, for better or worse, in cities. Yet stories with rural settings continued to dominate until relatively recently.

Editor Tricia Glensor has suggested that, particularly during the 1940s and 50s, outdoor adventure stories set in the country offered a means of escape from the suffocating blandness of life in small-town New Zealand and, increasingly, suburbia. Attempts to locate high-spirited adventures within urban society took a huge setback with the "Our Street" debacle in 1949. For the time being at least, icy mountaintops, rocky crevasses, and windblown plains were a safer territory than the street corner or neighbourhood cinema.

Summer Afternoon

Through drowsy stillness drifts a sound of mowing.
A crested quail from the hedge-top is crowing.
A cricket sets his midget motor going.

Over the hill white clouds in prosperous masses
Shepherd their shadows on the sunburnt grasses
While summer day to summer evening passes.

Basil Dowling
School Journal, Part 4, Summer 1965

Juliet Peter, illustration for Helen Wilson's "High Country Childhood"
School Journal, Part 4, Summer 1956

Some men would never feel happy in our bush country. Others would make it their home and move about in it as freely as though it was their back-yard. You know how it is, when you are out walking in the bush. Sometimes you feel as though you could turn somersaults in the undergrowth – supplejacks, ferns, and all – just because you are bouncing with energy.

John Pascoe, "Heaphy was a Bushman", *School Journal*, Part 4, Spring 1956

Writing in 1992, editor Alistair Campbell believed the rural emphasis during the 1950s was consistent with the broader aims of the *Journal.*

An important part of our job was to implant in the minds of kids a love of the land, the resources that we have here, and the people who work those resources whatever they may be – farms or rivers or beaches or factories. [1]

In recent *Journals*, forests, mountains, and coast have continued to figure as sites of quintessential New Zealandness – places of spiritual replenishment as well as high excitement. Yet, in an effort to remain relevant to its readers, the vast majority of present-day *Journal* stories have urban settings – in schools, parks, suburban homes, streets, and backyards.

In recent decades, respect for the environment has been an inherent value in the *School Journal* – witness Witi Ihimaera's "The Pupu Pool" (page 75). Discussion of nature is often tempered by an awareness of conservation, recycling, and sustainable industries. In a Part 4 *Journal* from 1996, Andrew Crowe's article "Shifting Sands" examined coastal erosion, its natural causes, and the ramifications for those living nearby. Instructive in tone, the piece highlighted planting initiatives, the laying of boardwalks, and other measures to limit the problem.

Pat Quinn's article "The Motorway Debate" (Part 4 Number 1, 1992) examined the arguments for and against a motorway extension in Wellington. As well as exploring the environmental repercussions of motorway building, the article highlighted the planning process, lining up the arguments for and against so that readers could make up their own minds. "The debate goes on," Quinn concluded: "convenience versus conservation".

Two years later, Diana Noonan wrote an article about pupils from Kaikorai School, Dunedin, and their campaign to stop the chopping down of a sixty-year-old lime tree in their neighbourhood. The pupils wrote letters and faxes to the council. It became a lesson in the democratic process as well as in conservation. They "got involved", and the tree was saved. The children were acting very much in the spirit of William Pember Reeves, who had written a century earlier that the modernising world can leave you with "a bitter price to pay", the end result of progress being "beauty swept away".[2]

On the cover of a 2000 *Journal,* Wellington artist Nic Marshall offers a contemporary New Zealand rural idyll, with a few imaginary interlopers: an elephant, a monkey, a mule, and a procession of giant ants (see below). Like many other recent *Journal* illustrators, Marshall presents New Zealand as an immensely fertile imaginative ground. Whereas fifty years earlier, dairy farms and high country were where the nation's soul was supposedly formed, here the land is a point of departure, a leaping-off place for dreamers as well as adventurers.

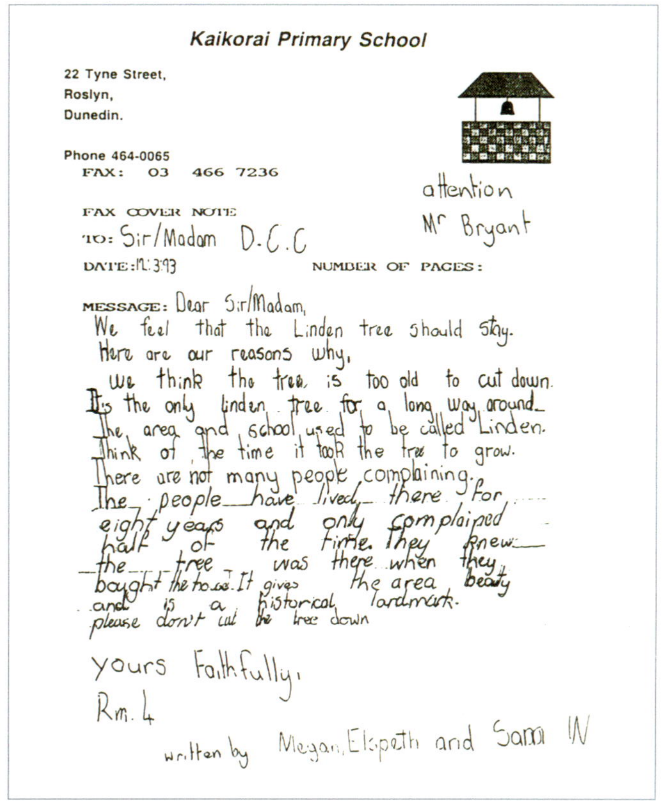

Kaikorai Primary School

22 Tyne Street,
Roslyn,
Dunedin.

Phone 464-0065
FAX: 03 466 7236

attention Mr Bryant

FAX COVER NOTE
TO: Sir/Madam D.C.C
DATE: 11:3.93
NUMBER OF PAGES:

MESSAGE: Dear Sir/Madam,
We feel that the Linden tree should stay.
Here are our reasons why,
We think the tree is too old to cut down.
It's the only linden tree for a long way around.
The area and school used to be called Linden.
Think of the time it took the tree to grow.
There are not many people complaining.
The people have lived there for eight years and only complained half of the time. They knew the tree was there when they bought the house. It gives the area beauty and is a historical landmark.
please don't cut the tree down

yours Faithfully,
Rm. 4
written by Megan, Elspeth and Sara W

The fax to Mr Bryant, *School Journal,* Part 3 Number 2, 1994

Nic Marshall, cover artwork, *School Journal,* Part I Number 3, 2000

A Literary Perch:

Writers in the School Journal

While an extraordinary array of New Zealand writers drifted in and out of School Publications from the early 1940s onwards, a core of them found full-time employment in the office. Poet and *Journal* editor from 1955 to 1972, Alistair Campbell recalls his classics lecturer, Professor H. A. Murray, describing School Publications as "a nest of singing birds" – referring not only to Campbell and the three other poets involved at the time, James K. Baxter, Louis Johnson, and Peter Bland, but also to

> *a variety of other gifted people, some of whom came with established reputations, or developed them later. [They included] Eric Schwimmer (anthropologist), Michael Turnbull (historian), Hugh Price (publisher), Roger Hall (playwright), Bob Brockie (political cartoonist), Pat Earle (playwright), Evelyn Clouston and Jill McDonald (artists), and Anthony Alpers (biographer).* [1]

According to Campbell, the employees "flourished – editors, art editors and clerical staff – in an atmosphere where genuine creativity was encouraged". [2] The *School Journal's* contributors extended well beyond its Wellington offices – writers and artists from much further afield were producing commissioned work or submitting material. Contributions came from Pat Wilson in London, from Ruth Park in Sydney, from Ruth Ross and Barry Mitcalfe (both living in Northland), and from Ruth Dallas in Dunedin.

This upturn in activity was a flow-on effect from the formation of School Publications in 1939. As a result of the Beeby-driven reforms, a publishing programme of longer Bulletins was initiated alongside the *School Journals*. These focused on single topics and provided writers with an opportunity to explore a theme at a length the *Journal* could never accommodate. James K. Baxter wrote two of these longer Bulletins, *Oil* (1957) and *The Trawler* (1960). For the most part, these Bulletins dealt with history, social studies, and geography, and as Brent Southgate points out, they were:

> *written with skill and authenticity, but in a form that was readily accessible to children. Some took a notably independent line:* Te Tiriti o Waitangi, *by Ruth Ross, challenged the then-received view of the Treaty; and Roderick Finlayson's series of bulletins on Māori history, later reprinted as* The Springing Fern, *was similarly adventurous.* [3]

(left) Jill McDonald, detail from cover illustration, *School Journal*, Part 1 Number 5, 1965

Oil, A Primary School Bulletin by James K. Baxter, illustrated by William Jones; diagrams by Roy Cowan, 1957

Much as you would imagine the editorial discussions in the offices and adjacent premises, the written correspondence between School Publications editors and authors tended to be relaxed and collegial. The fact that so many of the editors were writers or artists themselves would certainly have been a factor in this respect.

Writing to Ruth Dallas about her first script, a Bulletin about sawmilling in Northland, Baxter mentioned a recent visit he had made to the Hokianga region: "An extraordinary country: quite unlike any part of New Zealand I had seen before … mangroves like hair along the estuaries, and the whole great sluggish sea invading the land." [4] In a letter to Alistair Campbell shortly before Christmas 1956, Maurice Duggan concluded on a personal note, describing the festive season as "a sufficient excuse to discover in oneself chasms of exhaustion, really as inexplicable as a well in the dining room". [5]

The Rock Pool, a *Primary School Bulletin* by Arthur Torrie with art by Roy Cowan, 1960

Frank Sargeson and the Beginning of the Century

Frank Sargeson with girl
Courtesy of the Alexander Turnbull Library

Among the many writers with established reputations who contributed to the *Journal*, Frank Sargeson (1903–82) produced a series of reflections in the early 1950s, reminiscing about what New Zealand had been like half a century earlier. Looking back to his own childhood, he noted the change from gas lamp to electric street-lighting, from horse and cart to car. In the Part 4 *Journal*, April 1953, Sargeson lamented some of the things that had disappeared – among them the silkworms children used to keep as pets, Punch and Judy shows, and the cries of people in the streets.

> There are still the newspaper boys, certainly, and sometimes I hear "I Buy Bottles"; but not for many years now have I heard "Rags Bags Bones and Bottles"; or "Clothes Props"; or "Fish, All Alive-o"; or "Ices", which was short for ice-cream, and always sounded like "I Sez." You bought it from a handcart that was shaded from the sun by a sort of little tent, made of cloth that was gaily striped with all the colours of the rainbow, and fringed with a row of silken tassels. Instead of eating the ice-cream from a cone, you ate it like a sandwich, between two biscuits.

Sargeson also contributed an essay about the early days of cinema in New Zealand, "The Arrival of the Films". In "The Beginning of the Century: Games" (*School Journal*, Part 4, June 1953) he quoted no less an authority on the seriousness of sport than the French writer Montaigne. "He wrote a wonderful book of Essays," Sargeson chimed in a footnote, "which I hope many of you will read when you are older." Among the childhood games he recalled were The Farmer Wants a Wife and Poor Jenny's A-weeping, singing and clapping games, My Mother Said, skipping, French knitting, marbles, and tops. You can sense Sargeson's delighting in the names of the pastimes as much as in the games themselves. Moving Statues, Tip the Finger, Hoops, Hide and Seek, Tig, Buttons, Knifey, and Cowboys and Indians.

> The games Mr Sargeson describes were played in New Zealand because our great-grandparents and great-great-grandparents had played them in England, Scotland, Ireland and Wales when they were children.

So the *Journal* editor commented at the end of the piece, seemingly oblivious to the possibility that *Journal* readers may have been Māori or from other ethnic backgrounds.

M.K.Joseph

Having served in the Royal Field Artillery in World War Two, poet and academic M. K. Joseph (1914–81) contributed two memoirs of his childhood in Europe based on memories rekindled during his recent posting there. Published in 1953, Joseph's contributions, like many around this time, seem aimed at an adult readership as much as a twelve-year-old one. There is some truth in the observation that, during this period, editors deemed any writing about childhood to be invariably suitable reading for children. That said, Joseph's "Times to Remember" is a splendid example of literature that straddles both childhood and adult worlds. Ruminating on his upbringing in England, Belgium, and France, Joseph revisited these locales with a certain wistfulness and introspection – a mood enhanced by the subtle line-drawings of Yvonne Bendall.

M. K. Joseph, c.1950s
Courtesy of the Joseph family

Just after New Year 1944, I was in the Ardennes, the hilly country in the eastern corner of Belgium. One of the last big battles of the war was petering out in a country deep under winter snow. We had seen very little of this battle. On New Year's Eve we had moved there, with a blizzard driving the snow right against the windscreens of our trucks. Now cold was the real enemy. It turned the fields into frozen feather-beds, and iced the roads like skating rinks. It hung the trees with heavy masses of snow which would slide off at night with a soft *ploof*, making the sentries jump.

It so happened that a very happy year of my childhood had been spent in another little village not so very far from here. How long ago? Let me see - yes - nearly twenty-five years. One winter afternoon, as the short day came to an end I stood outside the farmhouse where we were billeted. As I looked out over the white fields and the bare trees and the foggy hills, the past came back to me very vividly.

The first thing I remembered was the garden. It had seemed vast to me, but then, I had been a very small boy. A park it seemed, where the grass grew long in summer for mowing. There were old trees to climb, or to sit under in hot summer afternoons. A kind of mound - I think it had once had a summerhouse on it - was my castle. Along the top of the garden, which sloped gently down to the road, was a cool, tree-shaded avenue. Off the path, among the moss, were wild violets and tiny wild strawberries. These tasted so much better than the big ones that grew in the kitchen-garden behind the house. Above the avenue were great clumps of blackberry bushes, with the biggest, juiciest fruit I had ever tasted.

M. K. Joseph's "Times to Remember",
illustrated by Yvonne Bendall,
School Journal, Part 4, April 1953

Imagine that we are setting off together for school at eight in the morning, walking up the cobbled street. We are wearing short black smocks, which look drab, but keep our clothes clean. Under one arm, each of us carries a folding leather satchel, holding all our books. It is a fine, clear day, with a touch of frost.

M. K. Joseph's "Times to Remember",
illustrated by Yvonne Bendall,
School Journal, Part 4, July 1953

Roderick Finlayson

Photograph of Roderick Finlayson published in *Landfall*, no. 53, March 1960

A prolific contributor to School Publications during the 1950s, Roderick Finlayson (1904–92) produced ground-breaking stories and articles, many of them about contemporary Māori life. As well as writing the series "In Auckland, Fifty Years Ago" and "Toi and Wiki" for the *Journal*, he composed six Bulletins between 1955 and 1960, focusing on Māori communities during the period after the arrival of the Europeans. Married into a large Māori family, Finlayson sought to

> *reconcile the nobility of the Māori of legend and tradition, and the great mana of an ancient ariki, with the humble estate of the people I had known and lived with … outcast and dispossessed on the fringe of the Pākehā world.* [6]

According to critic Bill Pearson, the aim of Finlayson's stories was "to discover the springs of life that might save us from the spiritual sickness that hangs like exhaust fumes on a sultry day at every corner of the industrial city". [7] This was as true of his *Journal* contributions, such as "The Cave", as it was of his books for adults, notable among them *Tidal Creek* (1948) and *Brown Man's Burden and later stories* (1973). "The Cave" was reprinted a number of times in the *School Journal*, and in 1975 an abridged version appeared with illustrations by Dick Frizzell, which eloquently captured the warmth as well as the gravity of Finlayson's parable about biculturalism.

The Cave

Toi, Wiki and Tom were walking home from school. Toi and his sister, Wiki, were Maori children. They lived on a farm with their grandparents. Tom was a Pakeha boy who lived on the farm next door.

Tom picked up a pretty stone with gold lines all over it.

"Look at that goldie," said Tom.

"It isn't real gold, is it?" asked Toi.

"No. I'm going to take it home though. I've got lots of nice stones at home," said Tom.

Toi wanted to know why Tom kept old stones.

"I like it," said Tom.

They were nearly at the quarry. The quarry men had gone home, so the children began to play slides down the grassy hill.

Suddenly Tom shouted, "What's that over there – that white thing?"

The children ran over the stones and up a hill to see.

"It's a skull," cried Tom. He held up a human skull. It looked very old.

Then Tom found two bones. He crossed them over and put the skull on top. "That's the pirate's sign," he said. "A skull and crossbones. This must be an old Maori burying place. Let's dig. We might find some greenstone. I'd like some to put with my other stones."

Toi looked frightened, and said something in Maori to Wiki.

"What are you saying?" Tom asked.

"We'd better go home and help with the milking. You'd better come too," said Toi.

Tom said, "Don't go home. Here's the start of a cave. See if we can make the hole bigger and get inside."

Toi ran back down the hill. He shouted. "You leave those old bones alone, Tom, and come with us. It's very bad to touch bones!"

Tom kept on digging, and shouted. "Toi's a scaredy cat!"

Just then, Tom fell down the hole. Toi and Wiki climbed back up to where Tom had been, to see what had happened. They looked down into the hole. There, at the bottom, was Tom – looking very scared.

Toi remembered that there was a rope by the tool shed. The quarry men must have left it there. He ran and got the rope, and let it down into the hole. He told Tom to tie the rope around himself.

Slowly, Toi and Wiki pulled Tom up. Tom climbed some of the way.

As he came out of the top of the hole, Wiki cried, "Look at all the blood! What a mess he is in!"

Tom's leg was cut, and was covered with blood.

Toi said, "You'd better come home to our place."

Toi and Wiki helped Tom to walk to their grandparent's farm. Their grandparents were milking. "We've got a sick man here!" Toi called.

"A sick man?" said Toi's grandmother. She came and looked at Tom's leg. She cleaned it and bandaged it.

"What happened, Tom?" Toi's grandfather asked.

Tom told him. "I thought I might find some greenstone to put with my other stones. I shouldn't have done it. Toi told me to leave the bones alone."

Toi's grandfather said, "You know, Tom, those old Maori burial grounds are tapu. They are just as sacred as a new pakeha cemetery. You wouldn't dig up a grave in a churchyard, would you, Tom?"

Tom shook his head. He felt like crying.

Toi's grandfather didn't want Tom to be sad. He said, "Wait a minute, Tom." He went and looked in a cupboard. He brought back a piece of greenstone for Tom to put with his other pretty stones.

Toi's grandfather said, "Hold the greenstone up to the light, Tom. See how the light shines through it like clear green seawater?"

Tom couldn't think of anything to say. He said, "Thank you" very quietly.

Then Toi's grandmother brought out home-made cake and lemonade. She told the children to help themselves.

When Tom had finished eating. Toi's grandfather said, "Come on, Tom. I'll take you home. There's plenty of time for milking. Anyway, Toi and Wiki might have finished the milking by the time I get home. Toi's grandfather laughed.

Roderick Finlayson, illustrations by Dick Frizzell
School Journal, Part 3 Number 4,1975

Ruth France at Sea

An extensively published poet under the name Paul Henderson, Ruth France (1913–68) contributed a number of articles and stories to the *School Journal* using her own name. These included "The Men Who Lived with Moas" (*School Journal*, Part 3, Winter 1960, and subsequently reprinted) and a series of pieces about yachting. France's reputation beyond the *School Journal* is largely based upon her 1958 novel *The Race*, a storm-tossed tale based on the real-life nautical adventures of her husband and her own experiences as the shore-bound spouse.

France's experience of sailing was fortuitous as, after World War Two, the *Journal*, for reasons hard to gauge, published a plethora of stories about sailing and ocean voyages. France, along with G. D. Jensen, Adrian Hayter, Pat Wilson (writing as John Bates), and Maurice Duggan, was amongst those with the requisite knowledge (or the fictional prowess) to write convincing nautical tales. Illustrators Russell Clark, Conrad Frieboe, and Juliet Peter in particular were kept very busy during this period, drawing rippling seas and mainsails.

"Hullo, Leda. I've got your tin opener for you. I will make a bombing run over you and drop it. Stand by."

Then the giant flying-boat came swooping overhead, so low that we thought she was going to hit Leda's mast. A tiny white package fluttered out from the rear door and hit the water just ahead.

"Leda" by W. A. Wilson, illustrated by Russell Clark, *School Journal*, Part 4, November 1953

Helen Shaw

Helen Shaw, photographed by Frank Hofmann, c.1943 Courtesy of the Hofmann Family Estate

Like Joan Smith and a number of other contributors in the mid-century *Journal*, the poet and short story writer Helen Shaw (1913–85) produced both writing and artwork. A suitably bushy drawing of hers accompanies her story "Aunt Janey Hunts a Rabbit" in the September 1951 *Journal*. Shaw's writings reflect a European sensibility – somewhere between Eileen Duggan and Janet Frame – which makes her a difficult author to place in the local literary scene. Her reputation no doubt suffered on account of her writing being considered decorative and mannered at a time when New Zealand literature for both adults and children seemed fixated on realism.

Helen Shaw, illustration for her story "Aunt Janey Hunts a Rabbit", *School Journal*, Part 3, September 1951

"We're right near where the swans are, Renny," Rory said. "Leave the billies here and we can get them on the way back."

"Do you think we ought, Rory?"
"I won't take you where the bull is, cross my heart, and then it'll be all right."

"What if Papa's cross?"
"Come on, Renny, come as far as the swans."

Helen Shaw's "Come as Far as the Swans", illustrated by Joan Smith, *School Journal*, Part 3, June 1953

Ruth Park's Shaky Island

Brought up in the King Country, Ruth Park (born 1922) spent much of her adult life in Australia, apart from a period on Norfolk Island from 1973 to 1985. She is best known on both sides of the Tasman for the two volumes of autobiography *A Fence around the Cuckoo* (1992) and *Fishing in the Styx* (1993). Between the 1940s and the 1960s, Park frequently contributed to the *Journal*. First published in the *School Journal*, Part 2, May 1947, her story "The Shaky Island" is an evocation of an imaginary rather than a real place.

Once there was a tiny island off the coast of eastern Australia. It lay in the warm, blue sea like a brightly painted ship at anchor, all its palm trees blowing like flags.

Living on this island was like living on a merry-go-round. Your house was on a hill one day, and in a valley the next. Sometimes the roof fell down, and sometimes a great wave came roaring in and washed you out into the ocean. It was very exciting, but a great nuisance.

Park's "Shaky Island" is a South Seas fantasy rather than an imagined version of her homeland. It was only some time later that New Zealand became commonly, and usually condescendingly, referred to in Australia as the "Shaky Islands" or the "Shaky Isles". (Economic realities and, possibly, seismic factors were to blame for the real-life label, rather than the giant turtle that rattles Park's fictional island.) It is not impossible, however, that the title of Park's oft-reprinted story might have influenced the later moniker.

A subsequent story by Park, "The Little Stone Axe" (Part 2, April 1953), offers the opposite viewpoint: a view of Australia from New Zealand. Drawing on Aboriginal mythology, the story begins in Park's characteristically musical style.

Australia is a great square country lying in the hot blue seas west of New Zealand. "Wish-wash!" says the sea all day long; it's just like a piece of music with the chorus sung over and over again.

As well as contributing many stories, Ruth Park wrote a novella, *Ring for the Sorcerer*, which was published as an entire issue of the Part 2 *Journal* in 1965. A tale of two New Zealand children in Rome, it melds light-hearted travel writing with an unfolding drama about a missing cat. Searching for their lost pet, the protagonists ring the doorbell of a wise man – the "sorcerer" of the title – to procure advice that will lead them towards the story's happy conclusion. Although living in Australia at the time she wrote the story, Park tailored it for a New Zealand audience, linking the children's new and strange situation with memories of home.

The palace stood just inside the great Wall of Rome. Its windows looked upon the River Tiber. The Tiber was not as big as the Clutha, or the Waikato, or the Wanganui. It was not much wider than the stream which ran through the children's home town in New Zealand. It was shallow and brown as tea.

Later in the narrative, Park commented on the linguistic echoes between Italy and New Zealand, her observations clearly drawing on her experiences of growing up in the King Country during the Depression.

The children were already beginning to understand Italian. Dad said they were lucky they were New Zealanders because New Zealanders are used to Italian sounds. Maori has many Italian sounds. If a Roman tried to say Waikato or tui, or Rotorua, or weka, he would say it just as a Maori does.

William Stobbs, cover artwork for *Ring for the Sorcerer* by Ruth Park, *School Journal*, Part 2 Number 6, 1965

Maurice Duggan and the Water Boy

Falter Tom was old. He had been given his nickname because of his stiff leg which gave a peculiar style to his walk. At one stride he would seem to be setting off on some far journey; at the next, drawing his stiff leg up to his good leg, he would falter and frown, pause, and stride out again. The look on his face matched his walk. When he was striding out, his face was bright and his eye was lively; when he faltered, his face became angry and sad. Falter and frown, stride and smile; so he went along.

If he had another name it had been long forgotten. It might even have been forgotten by Falter Tom himself. Once, many years ago, someone had come to the town inquiring for a Mr. Thomas Kevin O'Hennessy; but no one had heard of such a man and no one thought it could be Falter Tom. So the man went away. And whether it was Falter Tom or not, who could say?

Falter Tom once told the postmaster that he was eighty-four years of age. "And fifty or more of those years were at sea," Falter said. "Where I got my game pin, you should know, striking at whales. A good deal south of here, I don't mind telling, and in colder water."

But he looked too young to be eighty-four. His eyes were too bright, his tongue too quick. The postmaster looked at him and wrote down, on the form he was filling out, Falter Tom: aged seventy-one years.

Why seventy-one and not seventy? Because the postmaster was a man who thought all round figures looked too much like a guess.

From his brogue you would know that Falter Tom was Irish; though you wouldn't be able to tell just what part of Ireland he was from, north, south, east, or west. And from his talk you would know him for a sailor: he talked all day of ships and the sea.

Maurice Duggan

Maurice Duggan on a fishing excursion, Lake Taupo, 1965, photographed by Marti Friedlander. Courtesy of the photographer

First published in 1956 as two instalments in the Part 3 *School Journal*, Maurice Duggan's children's novel *Falter Tom and the Water Boy* won the Esther Glen Award, an occasional prize for excellence given by the New Zealand Library Association, and later appeared in book form from Paul's Book Arcade (New Zealand), Faber and Faber (London), and Criterion (New York). It is certainly one of the most remarkable literary works to ever come through School Publications. According to Maurice Duggan's biographer, Ian Richards:

> Falter Tom and the Water Boy *was in fact a work of conscious artistry which Duggan chose to present in the form of a children's tale. [Alistair] Campbell [Duggan's commissioning editor] asked for some small changes to the ending, and was pleased at how accepting Duggan was of any editorial suggestion that might improve the work. To Campbell the sophistication of the story was impressive, and he saw immediately in Falter Tom's depiction something of Duggan's own life.* [8]

Limiting his cast to the youthful water boy and the seadog Falter Tom, Duggan created an atmospheric narrative, full of sub-aquatic details – echoing the classics of children's literature, with some tonal devices borrowed from the poetry of T. S. Eliot and Dylan Thomas. (Ian Richards argues, convincingly, that the character of Falter Tom, with his white goatee and his limp, is modelled on Duggan's one-time mentor and fellow *School Journal* contributor, Frank Sargeson.) The tale also contained much poignant speculation about youth and old age.

Peter Campbell, illustration for "Falter Tom and the Water Boy", *School Journal*, Part 3, Spring 1956

Cover artwork by Kenneth Rowell, *Falter Tom and the Water Boy*, London: Faber and Faber, 1962

The sea was rich: in the calm depths there was a wealth of wonder, and Falter Tom, swimming hard on the green heels of the water boy, saw much to surprise and delight him. They swam, by round-about ways, towards the Cave of Voices.

They swam slower in the deep water and the boy's green skin gave off a shining, milky glow, so that Falter Tom had no difficulty in following him.

"Falter Tom" was followed by a four-part serial, "The Fabulous McFanes", in 1957, and "The Sailor on the Hill", which appeared in three episodes during 1958. (Duggan described the latter story as "a parable of the situation of the artist" – a remark worth dwelling upon.) His final contribution to the *Journal*, "On the Wild Harbour", appeared in 1961. Ian Richards observed:

> *Appreciation of children's literature was not widespread among adult readers at this time, but Duggan felt justifiably proud of all the children's stories he wrote. "*Falter Tom and the Water Boy*" was widely praised, not only by the children who read it in class, but also by such sensitive adult readers as Sargeson, [Keith] Sinclair and [Charles] Brasch.* [9]

The story had an adept illustrator in Peter Campbell, a Wellington-based artist who later transplanted to England, where from 1979 until 1994 he designed the typographical covers for the *London Review of Books*. Since then the watercolour cover designs he has produced for every issue have become a trademark of that leading literary periodical. Peter Campbell produced drawings for School Publications between 1955 and 1960, six months of which he spent on the full-time staff. He came to be employed, like many artists and writers around this time, as a result of personal connections. (In fact, his maternal grandfather, F. L. Combs, was the first editor of the *Journal*, and his father, A. E. Campbell, worked in the Department of Education and was Director of Education from 1960.) Peter Campbell recalls that, around the mid-1950s:

> *apart from* The Listener, *the* Journal *was the most important regular New Zealand employer of writers and illustrators. As they commissioned illustrators from abroad (Richard Kennedy, William Stobbs) you could feel that you had matched up to (or tried to match up to) English professionals.* [10]

In hindsight, Campbell notes his growing awareness, since leaving New Zealand in 1960, of "the extent to which the *Journal* was forming a native way with narrative and illustration". [11]

Peter Campbell, cover illustration for *School Journal*, Part 1, October 1945

Prior to working professionally for the *School Journal*, Peter Campbell made his first appearance in the publication in 1945 when, as a schoolboy at Wadestown School in Wellington, he produced a drawing of horses galloping across the volcanic plateau.

Peter Campbell, cover illustration for the *London Review of Books*, 24 June 2004

Ruth Dallas's "Children of the Imagination"

Photograph of Ruth Dallas, published in *Landfall*, no. 53, March 1960

Poet Ruth Dallas (born Invercargill, 1919), began her involvement with School Publications in 1957, when editor John Kelly asked her to write a Bulletin entitled *Sawmilling Yesterday*. "I don't know why he thought I was knowledgeable on that subject," Dallas recorded in her 1991 memoir, *Curved Horizon*. She did, however, proceed with the commission and followed it shortly after with a memoir, "Guy Fawkes Night in the 1920s" (Part 4, Summer 1958). Another three stories were accepted in 1959 and, from that time, Dallas was a regular contributor.

> *Occasionally a schoolchild writes to me and asks, "Are the children in your stories real?" To that I can only reply, "They seem real to me while I am writing the story, and real to you while you are reading it, but they are fiction, children of the imagination."* [12]

Looking back on the books of her childhood – all of them by overseas authors – Dallas wrote, in *Curved Horizon*, of how she would like to have been able to "people the countryside" of her childhood reading "with New Zealand children who had New Zealand adventures …" It was this desire that not only led her to write stories set in this country but also, she recalled, to set all of her stories out of doors:

> *because that was much more interesting than indoors, and even later, when I was grown-up, for a long time I preferred books where the characters were out of the houses, under the sky, and cooked their food on driftwood fires.* [13]

Betty Gilderdale has written of Dallas' quintessentially New Zealand stories, with their recurring images of sea and coast and the insight they offer into "the delicate balance between loneliness and independence". [14]

When Karen came home from school, she could not find her dog.

"Where's Ben?" she asked Mum.

"I don't know," Mum said.

Karen went out to look for him.

First she went down to the beach.

Ben was often there. She could see where a dog had been running along the sand.

She called, "Ben! Ben!" and whistled as loudly as she could. Then she saw Ben out on the rocks across the bay.

She saw Ben turn to run back over the rocks. Suddenly, he was gone. Karen heard him bark.

"Ben!" Karen called. "Come on!" Ben barked again, but he didn't show his head.

Karen could see the tide was coming in fast. If Ben didn't get off the rocks soon, he would be drowned. The rocks were covered with water at high tide. The sea came right up to the cliffs.

Already, there was only a little room at the foot of the cliffs. Soon there would be no way to get across.

"Ben! Ben!" Karen screamed. "Hurry up!" Nothing happened. So she began running as hard as she could.

She found Ben behind a big rock. His leg was caught in a crack. He was wet from the waves which had splashed over him.

Karen tried to pull the leg out, but it wouldn't come. Ben cried. She had to go around and pull him from behind. At last, the leg was free.

Then a big wave came and hit both of them. Ben was nearly swept out of Karen's arms.

She was afraid to put him down in case another big wave swept him away. She put the dog on her shoulders.

He was shivering and scared. Karen was scared too. She didn't know how they were going to get back. The waves were coming right up to the cliff now.

Karen waded through them. She kept as close to the cliff as she could. Some waves came nearly up to her middle. But she got to the other side.

She put Ben down, and walked home, with the dog limping behind her.

Mum was wild when she saw Karen's wet clothes. She said, "I've told you not to go down on the rocks when the tide's coming in."

"You'd better tell Ben, too," said Karen, and Ben wagged his tail.

Published in *Now for a Story* 2, *School Journal*, 1977

Janet Frame and "The Friday Night World"

In the first volume of her autobiography, *To the Is-land*, Janet Frame (1924–2004) recalled her experiences of growing up in Oamaru during the 1930s and being reliant on the *School Journal* for literary nourishment, which the publication provided, but only in part.

> *Much of the* School Journal *dealt with celebrations of the British Empire, with articles and photographs of the royal family, chiefly the two little princesses, Elizabeth and Margaret Rose. There was a description, too, of their life-size dolls' house, with photographs. In contrast to the factual prose of the* School Journal *and the praise of the Empire, the king, the governor general, the Anzacs at Gallipoli, Robert Falcon Scott at the South Pole, the poems were full of mystery and wonder, with Walter de la Mare, John Drinkwater, and Christina Rossetti as the editor's first choices, followed by Alfred Noyes and John Masefield, to give the rollicking touch.* [15]

In the mid-1950s, while living in a shed on Frank Sargeson's property in Takapuna, Frame submitted two stories to School Publications after hearing that editor Alistair Campbell had ready cash to pay for writing on any topic. Sargeson, in a letter to C. K. Stead, later reported that Frame knocked out both stories during one twelve-hour stint. Quoted in Michael King's biography of Frame, Sargeson, with good reason, felt "chagrined all morning to hear her typewriter going hell for leather while I've been tentatively pencilling six lines of dialogue". [16] The first of these whirlwind stories, "The Wind Brother" appeared in the *School Journal*, Part 3, Autumn 1957, the same year that Frame's *Owls Do Cry* appeared.

The old man told his story – how he had wakened from a wind-sleep of a thousand years to find the seagulls grown to huge metal birds that rushed and roared up and down the roads of the sky ...

Margaret and Colly listened with sympathy to the old man. They were anxious to help him. It is strange, they thought, he thinks we are birds, and we think he is a man.

Colly thought the best thing to do would be to explain what "Air Mail" really meant. "It is for aeroplanes," he said, glad to show his knowledge. "People travel in them. The letters are meant for them. We have never asked the wind to deliver letters for us."

"Oh no," said Margaret. "Why, you have so many other tasks. You have to carry the seeds and guide the birds. And who would talk to the trees on a hot day? Oh no, we do not ask you to deliver our letters."

"The Wind Brother" manifests the traits of her greatest writing for adults – a preoccupation with the interplay between the linguistic and physical worlds. There are echoes of the later novels in the closing passage of that story, when the two protagonists are back in the classroom after meeting the Wind Brother.

... Then one day at school in the social studies lesson the teacher and the children were looking at the map of the world. The teacher showed them where lay a great white mountain away in the far south.

"Nothing grows there," the teacher said. "It is covered with – well now, Margaret and Colly, what would a mountain be covered with?"

"With letters, hundreds and hundreds of letters," Colly and Margaret said together.

"Nonsense!" the teacher said. "You mean snow."

But Colly and Margaret smiled at each other, for it was their secret of the post office and the Wind Brother.

From Janet Frame, "The Wind Brother", illustrated by Evelyn Clouston, *School Journal*, Part 3, Autumn 1957

The Friday Night World

by JANET FRAME

ONCE upon a time (and it happens to this day) there was Late Night in the city, or Friday Night Shopping. On Late Nights the streets and shops, as you know, are filled with people hurrying and scurrying and buying things. Now in the middle of one city stood a large store which was crowded with people every Friday night; for it sold everything, or nearly everything – soap and peppermint cushions and handkerchiefs and electric light bulbs and clothes and skeins of wool and dahlia seeds. Now one night when so many people were trampling and shoving over the floor, one of the floorboards said in floor-language, ''Squirk'' which meant ''Oh dear, Oh dear''.

Another board replied with ''Squeak'', which meant ''Oh dear, Oh dear, Oh dear''.

And the third board said ''Squawk'', which meant fifteen ''Oh dears'', one after the other!

Then together they said, still in floor-language, ''We are tired of holding people on Friday Night. We are tired of feet treading on us, toepeeper shoes and sandals and high heels and long feet and fat feet and feet with corns and bunions. We shall ask the King of Friday Night to rescue us.''

The King of Friday Night who reigns in every town and every shop in the land, and whose palace had been built directly under *this* shop, was listening. He has eleven and a half eyes, one for each hour of Friday that a shop is open. Sometimes it changes to ten eyes, sometimes to eight. His eyes are brighter than an electric light bulb, and cleaner than soap, blank as writing paper, striped like peppermint cushions, round as a dahlia, and almost everlasting as a skein of wool. He was idle this evening, and heard the floorboards go squeak and squirk and squawk, and he promised he would try to help them. Not that he was always a good king. Oh no! He happened to be in the mood for promising.

59

Opening pages of "The Friday Night World" with illustration by Evelyn Clouston, *School Journal*, Part 3, Autumn 1958

Janet Frame's moody, twilit fable "The Friday Night World" appeared in the Autumn 1958 *School Journal*. While the piece was, in some respects, typical of the *Journal* around that time finely written, beautifully illustrated, and well edited – its dreamy, nocturnal world and verbal pyrotechnics were less than characteristic. For the most part, stories published during the 1950s and earlier were infused with the light of day – they were shaped by and addressed the conscious rather than the subconscious mind. From the time of its inception, the *Journal* was essentially a vehicle of enlightenment, offering sense, order, and knowledge, yet the inclusion of fables and fantastical tales like this one presented, on occasion, a darker, more elusive element.

"The Wind Brother" has aspects of a traditional children's story, only the construction and wordplay are too oblique and elaborate for it to be entirely successful as such. In the case of Frame's two *Journal* stories, the broader literature of the country has arguably gained more than the young readers of the time.

At the outset of her second *Journal* contribution, "The Friday Night World", a typically Frame-esque disappearance takes place, in which:

> the floorboards began to sink down and down, and all of the people standing on them, and the whole shop sank down, down to the palace of the King of the Friday Night World.

As in Frame's later novels *Living in the Maniototo* and *The Carpathians*, the story is at once a dream narrative and a critique of the material world – more specifically of consumer society. Accompanied by a swarm of bees and a viola, a prince from a distant land sets out on a journey to save the sunken shop and its entranced shoppers. Like "The Wind Brother", "The Friday Night World" is alive with imaginative play, more Lewis Carroll than Walt Disney, and some delightfully metaphysical slapstick:

> While the prince stood wondering what to do next, he noticed a triangular-shaped clock hanging on the wall. It showed only four hours – five o'clock till eight o'clock. It seemed there was no morning or mid-day or afternoon in this world. Time passed from five o'clock to eight o'clock or half-past eight, then returned to five o'clock, and every day was Friday.
>
> Suddenly the clock struck the eighth hour. There came a roar like the jingling of a million cash registers and the shuffle of a billion feet, and the King of Friday Night appeared.

By the time "The Friday Night World" appeared in Autumn 1958, Frame was living in London and had moved on to another phase in her literary life. No further stories for the *Journal* were forthcoming, although in 1969 a novella for children, *Mona Minim and the Smell of the Sun*, was published in North America. Despite Sargeson's remarks about the hurried composition of her *Journal* contributions, which have never been reprinted, the pieces are vintage Frame.

James K. Baxter and the Wellington Group

James. K. Baxter c. 1960s, photographed by Theo Schoon
Courtesy Alexander Turnbull Library

Not surprisingly perhaps, the poets who came to be known as the "Wellington Group" – James K. Baxter, Louis Johnson, Alistair Campbell, and Peter Bland – published in and edited for School Publications. Arguably New Zealand's greatest poet, James K. Baxter (1926–72) was a School Publications editor between 1956 and 1963, the only significant period of his life that he spent in paid employment. This was at a time when, on account of the UNESCO report, the organisation was receiving international attention and, as a result, in 1958 Baxter was awarded a fellowship, to live for six months in India. The poet's first-hand experiences of communal living and urban poverty there galvanised his radical views on social reform and probably sowed the seed for his eventual departure from School Publications in 1963. While Baxter's years at School Publications were pivotal for him as a poet – with the publication of *In Fires of No Return* (1958) and, three years later, *Howrah Bridge and other poems* – holding down a full-time job was always in conflict with his poetry.

Frustrated by bureaucratic preoccupations, Baxter would later capitalise on his experiences at School Publications in *The Bureaucrat*, a satirical play that presents a kind of parallel universe to School Publications, in which grand thoughts and tawdry behaviour jostle for the audience's attention. The name of the main character, Tom Fireman, may well have its origin in a near-disaster while Baxter was working at School Publications. Art editor Jill McDonald related how, on one occasion, she heard a loud scream emanating from the poet's office. On entering, she found Baxter dancing around the room, one leg stuck in a blazing wastepaper basket. He had thrown a cigarette butt into the bin and, when it burst into flames, tried to quash the blaze with his foot.

Rising to his feet early in the play, Tom Fireman sums up the vocation of the *Journal* editor.

It's not just a job. Not just a way of getting by. It's more than that. We're the fire-bringers. The Fire-bringers! Like Martin Luther. Can't you see what I'm getting at? All this monotony – semicolons even – committees at your elbow – piles of waste paper – that's only the outward shell of what we're doing. Somewhere a child picks up a bulletin – reads about – Gambia! – and suddenly his world is enlarged … All over the country. Knowledge. Just like the replacing of the kerosene lamp by the electric light. [17]

If there is irony and overstatement in Fireman's speech, there is a residue of genuine idealism. He continues:

Knowledge is a blessing in itself. Sanitation. Good housing. Art galleries. A merciful humane attitude to other people. We're helping make it possible. [18]

Throughout the play, Baxter appears to be sending himself up as well as the organisation in which he found himself.

You realize, there are two main categories under which my duties fall, as Head of the Branch. One is to implement the production of written material for the schools – the other is – (He smiles and speaks jokingly.) – to keep the staff in order. [19]

It was not until 1967 that *The Bureaucrat* was premiered at the Globe Theatre, Dunedin, and the following year in Wellington, where the reception may well have been muted.

Baxter's biographer, Frank McKay, observed that the group of poets employed by the Branch were considered by the rest of the staff as having "something of the character of wandering minstrels". Yet if Baxter's work habits were, according to some sources at least, erratic, he later maintained that he had ably filled the valuable role of "an amiable donkey who occasionally excreted lumps of gold". [20] Pointing to a more conscientious side of the poet, McKay observed how he would go through submissions:

page by page and indicate to the writer what parts needed to be pruned or reshaped … Baxter's tone was friendly and he sweetened his reservations with humour. He told the author of an outsize manuscript: "See if you can put it in the Turkish bath." [21]

Artist Peter Campbell, writing in 2006, recalled that for Baxter and other writers, employment at School Publications was:

more an income and a useful perch than a literary spring board for them. The atmosphere was only mildly bohemian. Jim was by then off the booze. I remember many empty pop [soft drink] bottles in his office. [22]

THE FIREMEN

"Clang! Clang! Clang!"
Says the red fire bell –
"There's a big fire blazing
At the Grand Hotel!"

The firemen shout
As they tumble out of bed
And slide down the pole
To the fire engine shed.

The fire engine starts
With a cough and a roar,
And they all climb aboard
As it shoots from the door.

The firemen's helmets,
The ladders and hoses,
Are brassy and bright
As a jug full of roses.

"Whee! Whee! Whee!" –
You can hear the cry
Of the siren shrieking
As they hurtle by.

At the Grand Hotel
There is smoke and steam,
Flames at the windows
And people who scream.

The biggest fireman
Carries down
A fat old lady
In her dressing gown.

When the fire is finished
The firemen go
Back through the same streets
Driving slow.

Home at the station
The firemen stay
And polish up the nozzles
For the next fire day.

James K. Baxter, Published in *School Journal*, Part 2 Number 1, 1969 (reprinted from Part 1 Number 1, 1960) Illustrations (unattributed), *School Journal*, Part 1 Number 1, 1960.

Resigning from School Publications in 1963, Baxter became a postman, a job he believed would free up his mind for poetry. In a letter to Charles Doyle, dated June that year, he harked back to his time in the hold of "the educational boa constrictor that moistens you so lovingly before it swallows you".[23] However, his verse for children continued to appear in the *Journal* through the 1960s, and a selection of these poems was published as *The Tree House* in 1974. Of the *Journal* poems, "The Firemen", "Spring Heeled Jack", "The Tree House", and "The Seagull" are among those often reprinted.

Juliet Peter, illustration, *School Journal*, Part 4, May 1949

The Seagull

"Seagull, seagull,
Riding high,
What do you see
With your bold, bright eye?"

"I see the sun
On a winter morning
Over the edge
Of the broad sea burning;

"I see the boats
On the harbour smoking;
I see an engine
With the stoker stoking;

"I see the town
And a church with its steeple,
And the pavements full
Of hurrying people.

"The men and women
And girls and boys
Look far, far smaller
Than painted toys.

"I like to glide
On my wings and stare;
I like to ride
On the pillowy air;

"But if you'll throw me
A crust or two,
I'll come right down
And eat with you."

James K. Baxter, Published in *School Journal*, Part 2 Number 1, 1969

Rhymes

Let's start with jelly.
It's a wobbly word
that rhymes with belly
and smelly, of course,
and my old Aunt Nelly,
who's also wobbly
and works in a deli
when she's not at home
in front of the telly
being wobbly and eating jelly
and thinking of her brother Kelly,
who ran away with a girl called Shelly,
who worked – small world –
in the very same deli
as wobbly, telly-loving
old Aunt Nelly.

Rhymes run around
as light as a feather.
Think of a few
and put them together.

Peter Bland

"Rhymes", by Peter Bland, illustrated by Peter Campbell, *School Journal*, Part 2 Number 2, 2005 (Note: The illustrator of this poem, Peter Campbell, is not the Peter Campbell whose work is discussed in chapter 2 and appears elsewhere in this book.)

Pat Wilson's "spuds in a boiling pot"

In 1960, James K. Baxter wrote to a New Zealand writer based in England, Pat Wilson, encouraging him to send further work to the *Journal*. As it was in his communications with other writers, Baxter's manner was collegial rather than domineering. A letter to Wilson, dated 27 September 1960, ended on a note typical of Baxter.

> *You must have a vast fund of New Zealand themes jolting just under the lid, like spuds in a boiling pot – at least I hope the pot is boiling. Verse too, if you have it, with that dry lucid quality, like sacking spread out in the sun. Drop me a note anyway. One goes on living; but it seems surprisingly less difficult in the thirties.*[24]

Wilson (born 1926) published poems in the *School Journal* under his own name as well as prose under the name of John Bates. (A memoir, using that pseudonym, about sailing on Tauranga Harbour appeared in the *School Journal*, Part 4, Spring 1958 and an eeling saga, "Fair Exchange", the following year.) Writing as John Bates, Wilson continued to publish stories in the *Journal* until the 1970s. His poem "The Anchorage" has been reprinted many times in the *Journal*.

Alistair Campbell

Alistair Campbell c. 1955
Courtesy of the Campbell family

As well as being a very active editor at School Publications between 1955 and 1972, poet and novelist Alistair Te Ariki Campbell contributed a number of stories to the *School Journal*. Nine of these interconnected stories were subsequently collected in *The Happy Summer*, published by Whitcombe and Tombs Limited in 1961, accompanied by the *Journal*-commissioned drawings of celebrated British illustrator Richard Kennedy. Of Cook Islands and Pākehā descent, Campbell (born 1926) studied during the 1950s at Wellington Teachers' College, where he associated with Barry Mitcalfe, who taught there and was later to become a regular contributor to the *School Journal*.

As official correspondence shows, Campbell, like Baxter, was a thoughtful and sympathetic editor, who made a point of travelling the country to meet writers. He was also instrumental in increasing the quantity and quality of Māori and Pacific content within the *Journal*. Prior to the 1960 Māori Issue (over page), Campbell wrote to the Inspector of Māori Schools about the publication.

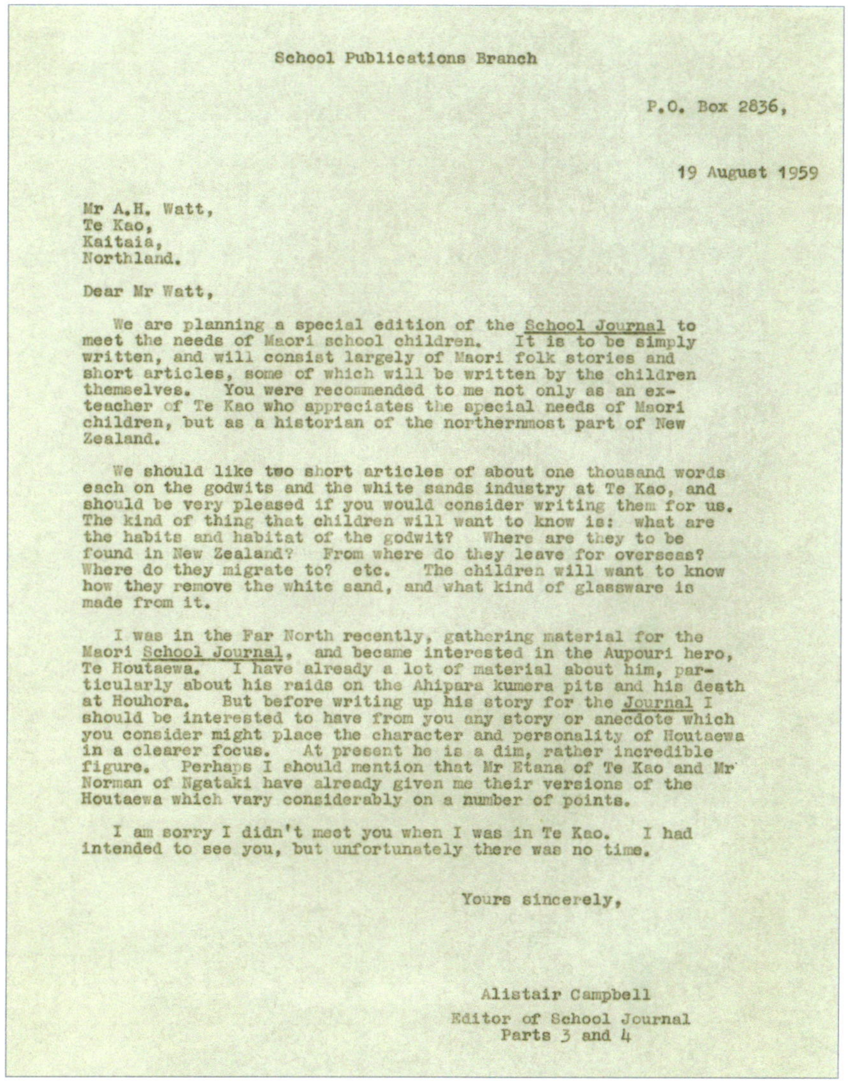

School Publications Branch

P.O. Box 2836,

19 August 1959

Mr A.H. Watt,
Te Kao,
Kaitaia,
Northland.

Dear Mr Watt,

We are planning a special edition of the School Journal to meet the needs of Maori school children. It is to be simply written, and will consist largely of Maori folk stories and short articles, some of which will be written by the children themselves. You were recommended to me not only as an ex-teacher of Te Kao who appreciates the special needs of Maori children, but as a historian of the northernmost part of New Zealand.

We should like two short articles of about one thousand words each on the godwits and the white sands industry at Te Kao, and should be very pleased if you would consider writing them for us. The kind of thing that children will want to know is: what are the habits and habitat of the godwit? Where are they to be found in New Zealand? From where do they leave for overseas? Where do they migrate to? etc. The children will want to know how they remove the white sand, and what kind of glassware is made from it.

I was in the Far North recently, gathering material for the Maori School Journal, and became interested in the Aupouri hero, Te Houtaewa. I have already a lot of material about him, particularly about his raids on the Ahipara kumera pits and his death at Houhora. But before writing up his story for the Journal I should be interested to have from you any story or anecdote which you consider might place the character and personality of Houtaewa in a clearer focus. At present he is a dim, rather incredible figure. Perhaps I should mention that Mr Etana of Te Kao and Mr Norman of Ngataki have already given me their versions of the Houtaewa which vary considerably on a number of points.

I am sorry I didn't meet you when I was in Te Kao. I had intended to see you, but unfortunately there was no time.

Yours sincerely,

Alistair Campbell
Editor of School Journal
Parts 3 and 4

Letter from Alistair Campbell to Mr A. H. Watt, 19 August 1959
Courtesy of Archives New Zealand

While Campbell did not end up writing most of the Māori Issue himself, his guiding hand can be seen in the contents. In a letter to Barry Mitcalfe, at the time a resident of Ahipara in Northland, Campbell demonstrated a sound knowledge of protocols when gaining approval for the use of customary materials:

> *The Maori Journal should be out in a week or two. Did I tell you that the Aupouri people who saw the galley proof of the Te Houtaewa story were very enthusiastic? On receiving comments from them and from you I revised the story so that it should now be more acceptable to all parties, e.g., I armed some of the Aupouri warriors at Hukatere with muskets.* [25]

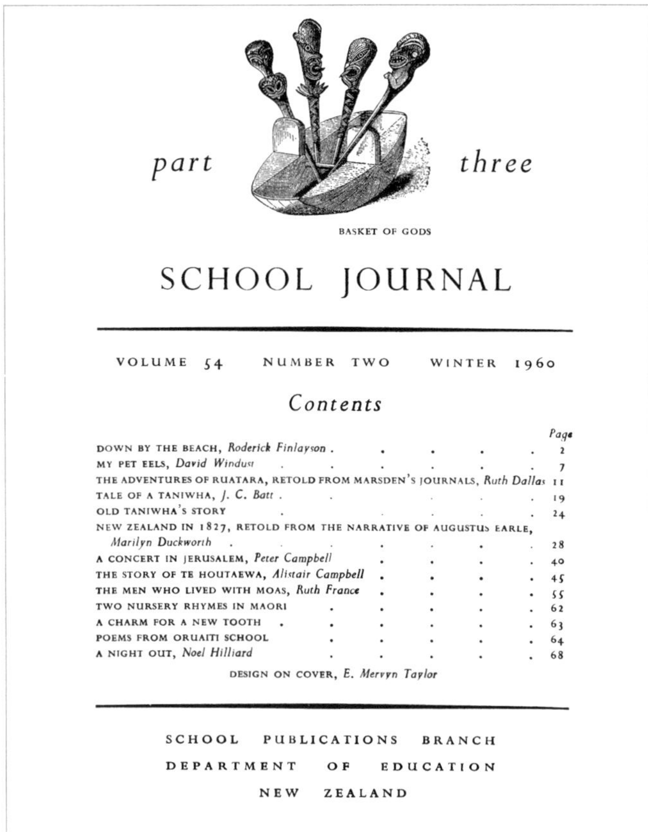

part three

BASKET OF GODS

SCHOOL JOURNAL

VOLUME 54 NUMBER TWO WINTER 1960

Contents

DESIGN ON COVER, *E. Mervyn Taylor*

SCHOOL PUBLICATIONS BRANCH
DEPARTMENT OF EDUCATION
NEW ZEALAND

Contents page of Māori issue, *School Journal*, Part 3, Winter 1960
(The cover of this *Journal* is reproduced on page 104.)

Alistair Campbell c. 1950s. Courtesy of the Campbell family

Te Houtaewa and the Kumaras

Te Houtaewa used to camp with his mother at Kahokawa at the northern end of the Ninety Mile Beach. One day when she went to prepare a meal she found they had nothing to eat but dried fish and shellfish. She went to her son and told him the bad news.

"Do not worry, Mother," said Te Houtaewa, "we shall have kumaras with our fish. Yesterday a war party returned from the south with the news that on the hillsides of Ahipara are kumara pits that are left unguarded. Our enemies have so much they can surely spare us some."

His mother pleaded with him not to be so rash as to go alone into enemy territory, but he laughed at her fears and said, "Light up the fires, Mother, and before the stones are hot enough I shall be back with the kumaras."

He told her to fetch him the two largest kits she could find and, with one in each hand, he set off. He took no weapon because he meant to rely entirely on his speed to get him out of trouble; and he ran naked so that the wind would not catch at his clothes and hold him back.

The beach stretched ahead of him, gleaming in the morning sun. He ran where the sand was firm, just beyond the reach of the breakers, his legs a blur as they devoured the miles as if they were mere chains.

Te Houtaewa's heart was full of joy. He liked nothing better than running on the beach with the sea beside him. He loved the slight give of the sand beneath his toes and the breeze whistling through his hair. Even the thought of the danger ahead of him did not reduce his pleasure. Instead it seemed to put steel springs into his legs so that each stride he took measured more than fifty feet. For mile after mile he ran tirelessly, slackening speed only when his feet became so hot with friction that he had to run into the sea to cool them off.

Within an hour he had reached Ahipara and hid in the sand-hills so that he could spy out the land. It was noon and the sun was very hot. The whole village seemed to be sleeping, apart from a few dogs that were too busy tearing at a carcase to be interested in him.

In a dozen giant strides Te Houtaewa reached the kumara pits on the hillside, tore away the wiwi covering, and began filling the first of his kits. He had half-filled it when a Rarawa woman came out of a whare and happened to look up. She recognized him at once and screamed out the alarm: "Te Houtaewa – the thief! Surround and kill him!"

Immediately the whole village was in an uproar. The children wailed, the dogs barked, and the men shouted and cursed as they ran for their weapons. They planned to surround Te Houtaewa as quickly as possible, then rush at him and kill him.

What a prize had fallen into their hands! The man who struck him down would be famous as the slayer of Te Houtaewa! Each man gripped his weapon more firmly as the long line moved quickly and cautiously up the hillside.

Halfway up the beach, at a place called Ngatamarawaho, he saw a flock of godwits, and he decided to catch some to take home to his mother. He put his kits down, crept as close as he could, and waited for the waves to break, for he knew that godwits always faced the breakers and were then off their guard. When that happened he swooped on them and gathered up an armful before they were aware of their danger. Satisfied with his morning's work he hurried home to his mother, who was relieved that he had come to no harm and had brought back the kumaras with him.

It is said that the two kits of kumaras weighed forty pounds apiece, but such was Te Houtaewa's strength that his journey home took only a little longer than his journey to Ahipara.

Alistair Campbell, illustrated by E. Mervyn Taylor,
School Journal, Part 3, Winter 1960

What was Te Houtaewa doing meanwhile? When the old woman cried out he had almost panicked and fled, but he reminded himself that he was Te Houtaewa who feared no man, least of all the Rarawa. Keeping an eye on the advancing men and ignoring their fierce taunts and insults, he filled his first kit and began on the second. They were now less than fifty yards away and were hurrying to encircle him. It would be very dangerous to delay any longer.

Te Houtaewa picked up the full kits, one in each hand, and looked for a gap in the cordon. He pretended to start his run and when the Rarawa scattered he jeered at them. He then gathered his strength and with a shout he hurled himself down the hill with the speed of an avalanche. No man could have stood in his way and lived. The cordon gave way, and in a flash Te Houtaewa was through it and speeding towards the beach.

Louis Johnson

Louis Johnson c. 1955, Courtesy of the Alexander Turnbull Library

An irrepressible enthusiast for all things literary, Louis Johnson (1924–88) established the *New Zealand Poetry Yearbook* in 1951. Later that decade, he worked alongside Campbell and Baxter as an editor at School Publications, where he wrote many poems and stories for the *School Journal* as well as three book-length features, of which two, *Holiday in the Capital* (1964) and *The Circus Comes to Town* (1965), were illustrated with photographs by Ans Westra.

After leaving New Zealand in 1968, Johnson continued to contribute stories and poems. "The Postman", his "day-in-the-life" narrative about a Wellington postie, with photographs by Warwick Teague, appeared that same year. That issue feels distinctly like a homage to Johnson's friend James K. Baxter, who had resigned from School Publications to take up the mail satchel.

The Liftman

I'd like to be a liftman –
To push the button then
Go whizzing through the building
Up to the floor marked ten,
Then push another button
And whizz right down again.

I'd polish all the mirrors
And keep the buttons bright;
I'd be so proud of my own lift
I'd sleep in it at night.
I'd go so fast that all the mice
Would scamper off in fright.

When all the office people
Came in to start the day,
I'd whizz them to their offices
Before they'd time to say
"Jack Robinson," or tell me that
"Today's a lovely day."

And when the boys came after school
To ask for rides, I'd be
The jolliest sort of liftman
That ever you could see –
I'd whizz them up and down again
Till they went home for tea.

Louis Johnson
Published in *School Journal*, Part 1, November 1955

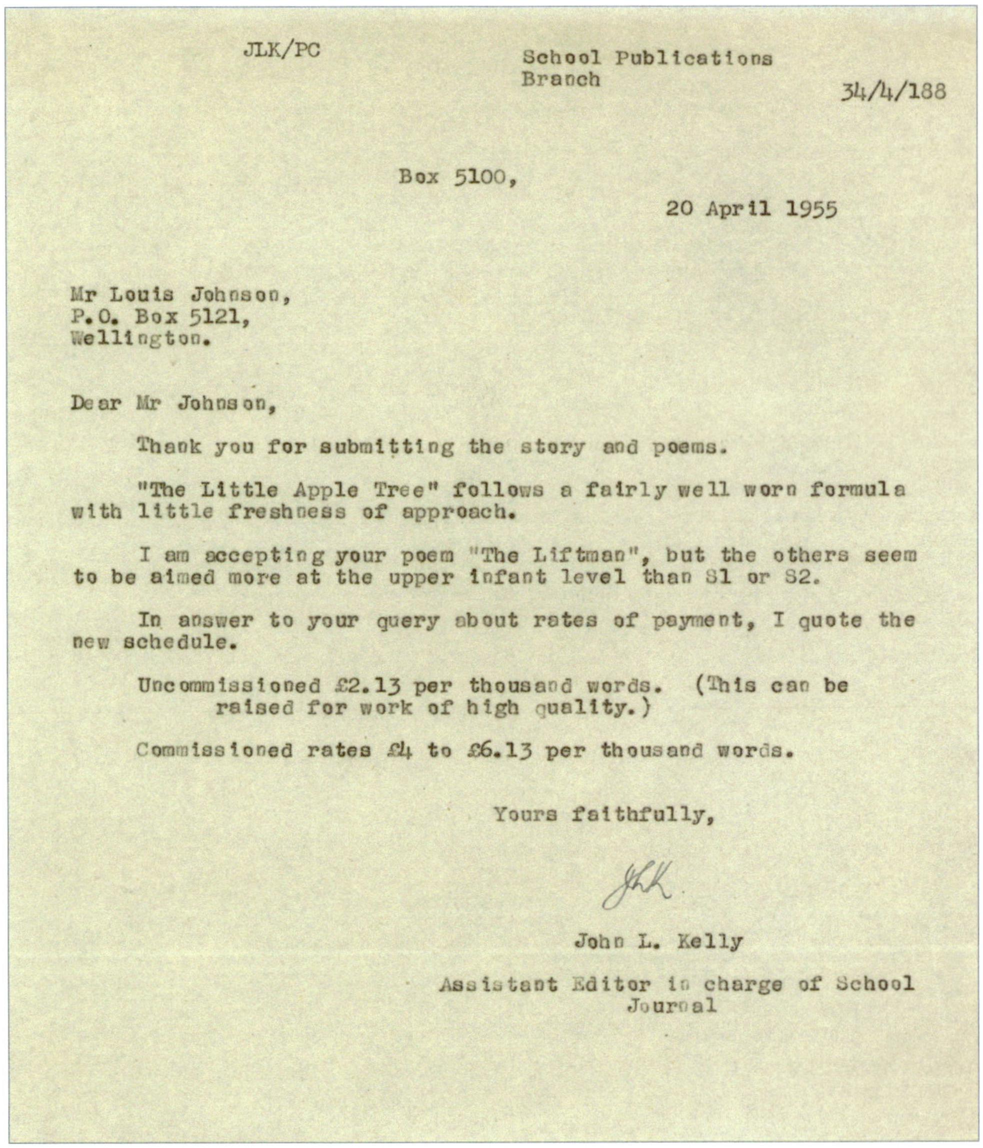
JLK/PC

School Publications
Branch

34/4/188

Box 5100,

20 April 1955

Mr Louis Johnson,
P.O. Box 5121,
Wellington.

Dear Mr Johnson,

Thank you for submitting the story and poems.

"The Little Apple Tree" follows a fairly well worn formula with little freshness of approach.

I am accepting your poem "The Liftman", but the others seem to be aimed more at the upper infant level than S1 or S2.

In answer to your query about rates of payment, I quote the new schedule.

Uncommissioned £2.13 per thousand words. (This can be raised for work of high quality.)

Commissioned rates £4 to £6.13 per thousand words.

Yours faithfully,

JLK

John L. Kelly

Assistant Editor in charge of School Journal

Letter courtesy of Archives New Zealand

From Letter to John L. Kelly

by Alistair Te Ariki Campbell

And who can forget Cliff O'Malley, our
chief art editor, with his high bald dome,
fringed with wiry hair, his flushed complexion,
and a grand Episcopal manner, belied
by his fund of indelicate stories,
and worse – and all endlessly recycled?
He was delightful company, full of gossip,
a loyal colleague, but in the end
something of a mystery ... John, you had
a run-in with Pat Hattaway – remember?
I can still see your red face going
a brick-red at the injustice of her rebuke,
because, after all, you hadn't gone
to the pictures in office hours, but just
to place a bet, or something – and where's
the harm in that? Deeply humiliated,
biting your lips, without saying one word
in your defence, you turned and left the room;
whereas James K. Baxter, who'd made an art
of riding the gravy train, was only
mildly reprimanded for yet another
of his extended absences, which he
received with bowed penitential head,
the very attitude that he adopted
when he knelt before the little crucifix
in the cell-like office on the ground floor.
Then he ran all the way back to the Picasso
Coffee Bar where a game of chess awaited
his next move ... "A nest of singing birds,"
that's how Professor Murray, my old Classics
teacher, quoting, as you know, Dr Johnson,
described us – and he was right, what with
Baxter, Johnson, Peter Bland, and myself
in editorial chairs, providing a headache
for Pat Hattaway and subsequent chief
editors. It was while John Melser was
in charge that Peter Bland took time off
to establish with Martyn Sanderson,
what was to become our leading theatre
company, Downstage. Singing birds, maybe
but disinclined to sing any song
except their own. I'm being unfair. I think
of Baxter who, when on a job, could visit
an unfamiliar place, and write a Bulletin
for schools about it and a poem, At Akitio,
both turning out to be excellent ...

... Evelyn Clouston also
comes to mind, who, even in her sixties,
had the mind and the light step of a girl.
I worked for seventeen years at School Pubs,
and in that time the offices of the branch
were shifted several times, from one end of
the city to the other, and Evelyn always
turned the tiny room allotted her into
a studio, with hanging flowers and pictures
on the wall by Chagall, the artist she most
admired, a child-like spirit like herself.
When I first met her, she painted my portrait,
and to my surprise I became a long-necked,
gentle creature with doe-like eyes –
not at all the sophisticated image
I had of myself. At any time you could
find Evelyn at her favourite coffee bar
at Roy Parsons', and this is where Pat Hattaway
happened to find her one afternoon during
working hours. "I'm not very happy to find
you here," she said. "And I'm not very happy
to see you here," said Evelyn ...

... As for you, John, I can't chart all your
movements. I only know you left before
I did, and then returned to end your career
at School Pubs, but what you did after that,
what you died of, and where, I do not know.

Previously unpublished poem

Illlustration by Evelyn Clouston, *School Journal*, Part 1 Number 1, 1960

Beyond the Wellington Group

A famous writer once said – "With twenty-six soldiers of lead I will conquer the world." He did not mean toy soldiers but the letters of the alphabet, set up in type, which could take his ideas into every country of the world.

So begins J. M. Thomson's "The Story of Printing" in *School Journal*, Part 4, Summer 1958. A year later, he offered a companion piece, "The Story of Numbers". In a cracking twenty-four pages, the latter article began with a description of people counting on their fingers and ended with that very latest of inventions – the computer. An authority on the history of music as well as a writer and editor, Thomson covered a wide range of topics for the *Journal*, including "The Exploration of Australia", and in 1968, he produced a special issue devoted to "The Red Cross in the World Today" (Part 4 Number 3). In his essay "The Gay Dolphin" (Part 3 Number 3, 1967), he made good use of his musical background when writing an illuminating piece tracing the history of dolphins from Ancient Greece to Hokianga Harbour, which had been frequented, only a few years earlier, by the famous Opo.

Arion's music was supposed to have attracted the dolphins in ancient times and somebody remembered this and tried it out on Opo. A man played his bagpipes for over an hour along the shore but Opo took no notice. Yet when another man took a portable radio out in his boat Opo danced excitedly around and under and almost over the boat ...

Another regular contributor during the 1950s and 1960s, Barry Mitcalfe (1930–86) later became well known for his anthologies of traditional Māori poetry and *Boy Roel: Voyage to Nowhere* (1972), an account of sailing to Mururoa to protest against French nuclear testing. Importantly, in the Winter and Spring 1960 issues of the Part 4 *School Journal*, he profiled sympathetically and in some detail "Two Maori Prophets" – Te Kooti and the Parihaka leader, Te Whiti. These illustrated accounts were ground-breaking and attracted the attention of adult as well as young readers.

David Cowe, illustration for Sonia Mulheron's "Ivan and the Dolphin", *School Journal*, Part 2 Number 3, 1968

Elsie Locke (1912–2001), a writer with deeply held political convictions, published her first story *School Journal* story, "The Secret Rescue", in 1958, and her final contribution, "A Present from Pudding", appeared in 2001, shortly after her death. Between times, her contributions often reflected her deeply held views on social justice and human rights. She wrote unabashedly political pieces (at least by School Publications standards), among them an article for the Part 4 *Journal* in 1968, which was designated Human Rights Year by the United Nations. In her "Every Child Should Have a Chance – Human Rights", she used true stories from around the world to illustrate a list of fundamental human rights:

Everyone has the right to food, clothing, housing and social services.

No one shall be held in slavery or servitude.

Everyone is entitled to these rights and freedoms without distinction of sex.

Everyone has the right to freedom of thought, conscience and religion; to freedom of speech and opinion, and of peaceful assembly and association.

Elsie Locke also wrote a Part 4 *Journal*, *The Long Up-Hill Climb – New Zealand 1876–1891*, in which a sequence of stories and articles dealt with historical issues as various as workers' rights and the "rabbit invasion". Among the many books of fiction and non-fiction Locke published, her novel *The Runaway Settlers* (1965) is the best known and is still widely read.

Through the 1950s and into the 1960s, stories appeared from a diverse group of writers, including the young novelist Marilyn Duckworth (born 1935) and her poet sister, Fleur Adcock (born 1934). Adcock wrote a variety of non-fiction pieces including a dutiful account of "The Children's Crusade" (Part 3, Summer 1959) and, in the Part 3 *Journal*, Winter 1958, a brief biographical sketch of the English explorer David Livingstone (of "Dr Livingstone, I presume" fame). More in keeping with her literary sensibilities, Adcock also contributed "The Story of the Alphabet" in the *School Journal*, Part 4, Autumn 1958, having just knocked off, in recent months, "A Day in Ancient Rome" and "A Day in Elizabethan London". Adcock and Duckworth would have been familiar with the workings of the *School Journal* as their mother, Irene Adcock (1908–2001), was a prolific and accomplished contributor over many decades, writing poems, plays, and stories.

Sunday Shoe Shop

"It's Sunday today," said the shoe-shop man,
And drove away in his big red van.
All the shoes came out of the shelves.
"Now we're going to enjoy ourselves."

The gumboots looked through the window pane.
"We're going outside to splash in the rain."
The slippers were blue and green and red.
"We'd rather sit by the fire," they said.

The marching boots formed into a row
"Come on, you chaps! It's time to go."
"I want to dance," said a slim black shoe.
"I'll make some music while you do,"
Said the shoehorn, tapping time on the door.
The baby shoes toddled round the floor.

All of a sudden, the clock struck ten.
With a rush, they got on the shelves again.
The gumboots got back just before the van.
"It all looks fine," said the shoe-shop man.

Irene Adcock
School Journal, Part 1 Number 1, 1989

David Cowe, cover artwork for Elsie Locke's "The Hopeful Peace & the Hopeful War", *School Journal*, Part 4 Number 3, 1968.

Kirsty Lillico, cover illustration for Elsie Locke's "A Present from Pudding", *School Journal*, Part 1 Number 3, 2001

The choice of Kirsty Lillico, one of the liveliest of the recent *Journal* artists, to illustrate Elsie Locke's last published story was marvellously apt, bringing together one of the *Journal* stalwarts and a bright, new talent.

Dennis Beytagh, cover illustrations for *School Journal*, Part 4, Summer 1959

In this *Journal*, the sixth in the series about life in New Zealand in earlier times, you will read about things that are well-remembered by many people still alive. These may include your grandparents, or uncles, or neighbours, or family friends.

I have spent many interesting hours listening to the stories told by these "old-timers," and I know they have enjoyed telling them to me.

Elsie Locke

Brian Sutton-Smith

Book cover for the 1950 edition of *Our Street*, published by Reed

Following the 1949 "Our Street" debacle, Brian Sutton-Smith studied in the United States and, in 1956, took up an academic position at Bowling Green State University, Ohio. Based in the United States since then, he is presently Emeritus Professor at the University of Pennsylvania. His life's work as an educationalist has been, he says, shaped by a desire "to discover what the meaning was of what I had said in 'Our Street'". He considers his career as an author and editor – producing around 50 books and 350 articles – an attempt to explore issues raised in "Our Street". Furthermore, Sutton-Smith considers both his academic career and the books he has written to be investigating the fundamental idea of "play" – the concept at the very heart of the 1949 serial.

While Brian Sutton-Smith's association with the *School Journal* in the late 1940s was a brief one, it was significant, not only for him as a writer in the decades that followed but also in the history of the publication (see pages 24–26). Like the writing of his contemporary J. M. Thomson, Sutton-Smith's stories were shaped by the intellectual preoccupations of the time as they were by his passion for educational matters.

> *In the 1940s I had become acquainted with the spirit if not the detail of existentialism. "Our Street" and "Smitty Does a Bunk" [a subsequent series of stories including many of the same characters] probably owe more to Albert Camus than to Karl Marx. My stories seemed to escape the moral and politically correct tendencies of the day and find pleasure in just what the kids were finding relevant for themselves. I remember now that the most immediate influence on my writing was* The Book of Wiremu *by Stella Morice. The kids in my standard three class enjoyed that so much that I thought I could do it as well. I loved the roughness …*[26]

In 1954, Sutton-Smith's interest in children's vernacular caused another round of trouble when he submitted his doctoral thesis to Victoria University:

> *It included some of the obscenities that I had collected from the children while amassing my 900 page thesis on the games of New Zealand children. I was told if such matters were in the thesis in the library there could be a general Educational Board reaction against allowing such research to take place.*[27]

Regardless of the opposition, Sutton-Smith became the first PhD in Education from that institution.

Margaret Orbell and Legends of the Māori

Editor of the Māori Affairs Department bilingual quarterly *Te Ao Hou* (The New World) between 1961 and 1965, Margaret Orbell (1934–2006) contributed many retellings of Māori legends to the *Journal* during the 1960s and 70s. In the *School Journal*, Part 4, Summer 1961, she wrote an essay about Māori carving, highlighting the ways traditional Māori carving had accommodated and adopted European imagery and techniques – a ground-breaking area of research for that time. (It was not until Roger Neich's comprehensive study of such Māori figurative art in the 1990s that these carvings were given the acknowledgment they deserved.)

> Carving is not always easy to understand at first, because it is quite different from anything that we are used to. Maoris were not trying to imitate the appearance of things. Like all good artists, they liked making patterns. Most of these patterns are based on the human face and figure. These figures are sometimes quite realistic, but often they are nothing at all like real figures. The features of the face and the limbs of the body have been turned into a pattern, which, when you look at it carefully, has its own kind of beauty …
>
> After the Europeans came, Maoris still went on carving. There are still some carvers today, though only a few. Carving changed in a number of ways, and it became more realistic. The man with gun and dog [on right] is called Agnew Brown. He was a European farmer who lived near Gisborne in the 1870s. Some Maori friends of his were building a meeting house, and they were having a hard time finding the last pieces of timber they needed. 'I will give you the timber,' Agnew Brown told them, 'if you will put me in your meeting house.' So there Agnew Brown still is today, with his gun and with the dog which used always to be at his heels.
>
> If there is a meeting house near your home, you may find, especially if it is fairly old, that it has some very surprising things inside it.

Margaret Orbell, "Maori Carving", *School Journal*, Part 4, Summer 1961

E. Mervyn Taylor, illustration for *Life in the Pa*, *School Journal*, Part 3, August 1948

(a)

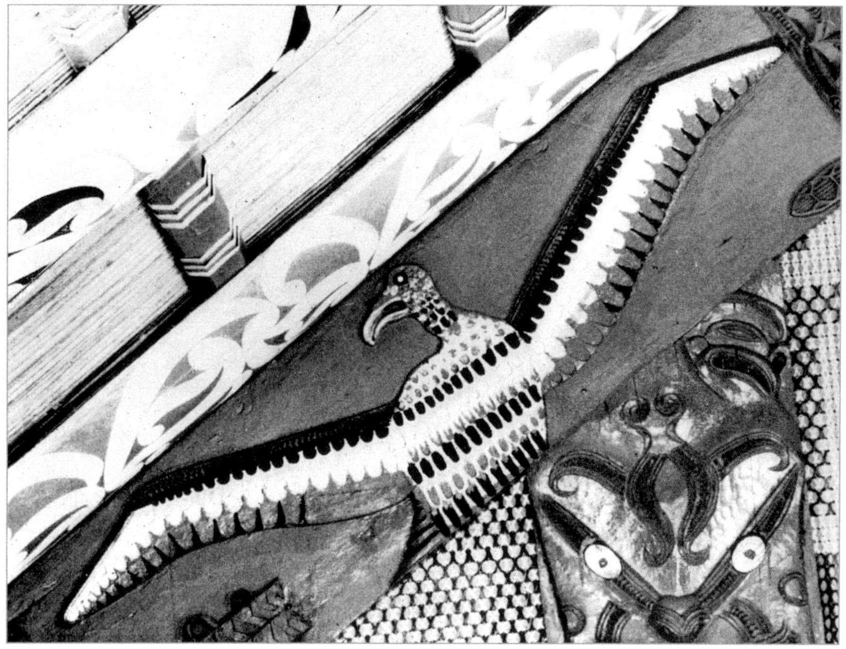

(b)

(c)

(a) Agnew Brown and his dog.

(b) This carving is in Te Mana o Turanga. It is different in many ways from older work. For example, the carved and painted bird is quite untraditional.

(c) These figures, with meres, painted in imitation of carvings, are in the house, Te Poho o Tamaterangi near Wairoa.

Photographs of Māori carved and painted panels, with their captions, *School Journal*, Part 4, Summer 1961

Margaret Mahy Takes Flight

Margaret Mahy's first appearance at the School Publications office, sometime around 1960, has become almost legendary. "One day in came this woman who told me that she had a yen to write," recalled John Kelly, *Journal* editor from 1955 to 1962.

> *She told me that she lived in a very strange, dark, damp house under the pine trees in Ohariu Valley, where wolves howled in the night and owls moreporked, and she wouldn't have been in the least surprised if witches flew around, and there was the odd bubble of cauldrons here and there, and, all in all, a very fey woman was she.* [28]

Margaret Mahy photographed by Robert Cross, 1987
Courtesy of the photographer

The first two Mahy stories to appear were "Teddy and the Witches" and "The Procession", both in 1961 – "a year polished and gilded, that shines in my memory," as Mahy recalls. (It was also the year her daughter Penny was born.) Two poems, "The Witch, My Sister" and "Witch Poem", also appeared that year. The next "polished and gilded" year for Mahy as a writer was 1965 when the *School Journal* devoted two issues solely to her work – *A Lion in the Meadow* and *The Midnight People*. These were followed in 1966 by *The Wind between the Stars* which, like *A Lion in the Meadow*, was illustrated throughout by Jill McDonald. McDonald's dreamlike designs were the perfect match for Mahy's bustling cast of animals, humans and, very often, witches. Tricia Glensor has commented on this miraculous series of Mahy issues.

> *In the world of New Zealand in the early 1960s, what could be more liberating, even revolutionary, than to see the drab suburbs of post-war New Zealand populated by creatures of the imagination. The vibrancy of Jill McDonald's layout and illustrations and the zany imaginative creativity of Margaret Mahy's prose seem to gust like a great, joyful, rumbustious Wellington wind through the* Journals *of the mid-60s, blowing away the stuffiness and drabness of post-war New Zealand life.* [29]

Evelyn Clouston, illustration for *The Midnight People* by Margaret Mahy,
School Journal, Part 2 Number 5, 1965

Evelyn Clouston was the last person to hold the position of staff artist at School Publications. She worked full-time on the *Journal* 1951–73. (Since then, all artists have been employed on a contract basis.) Clouston produced delicate, rhythmical suites of drawings to accompany major work by Frame, Baxter, Mahy, and many others.

When Mahy began writing in the early 1960s, local publishers resisted her work on the grounds that it was not set in New Zealand. Yet, as readers would discover in the ensuing years, Mahy's world was one in which elements of the local, the global, and the cosmic were constantly overlapping and transforming one another. Between 1961 and 1986, Mahy published over seventy-five stories and poems in the *School Journal*. When her work for the *Journal* was featured in a School Publications display in the United States in 1969, it was seized upon by publishers in that country and, soon after, in England and elsewhere. From there, her stories began appearing around the globe and in many languages. "I owe the *Journal* a great deal," [30] Mahy says.

"Countries of the Mind"

by Margaret Mahy

Among the places where I did make some contact with an indigenous literature was the *School Journal*. All the way through primary school I had contact, in this magazine, not only with stories that deliberately tried to promote New Zealand as an arena for family adventure, but with poetry, too. There was one poem I remembered for years after I had left school – a poem that began:

The farther the little girl leaped and ran,
The farther she longed to be;
The white, white fields of jonquil flowers
Danced up as high as her knee
And flashed and sparkled before her eyes
Until she could hardly see.
So into the wood went she.

Apart from that beginning and a memory of the plot, and one or two haunting phrases (including the evocative one "the town between the hills") the poem was lost to me for many years until *These Islands: a collection of New Zealand verse for young people* was published, and there it was, quite unchanged, as magical and mysterious as ever, with the same lilting simplicity in its first few lines. It constituted a true encounter. Another more enigmatic meeting was with Denis Glover's *Threnody*, the title of which intrigued me, and the verses of which puzzled me. I was, even at primary school, pretentious enough to want grand meanings easily available and I was scornful of something that announced:

In Plimmerton, in Plimmerton,
The little penguins play,
And one dead albatross was found
At Karehana Bay.

I came to realise, of course, that part of the meaning of this poem was that I remembered it, said it to myself regularly over many years, and always think of it when I find myself going by Plimmerton. It took on the nature of a jingle I had been born knowing. It was through poetry in the *School Journal* that I made my most real contacts with my own country and the dry, driving presence that language could give it. The first poem does not really speak of New Zealand, even though it was by Katherine Mansfield. What makes me still think of it as a New Zealand poem is not the author but the *Journal* in which I first read it. Perhaps that is why, when I first submitted stories to the *School Journal*, I deliberately tried to make them New Zealand stories, feeling that they would gain favour over and above others. The editors, however, correctly detected that, when I wrote, I did not entirely belong here. I could not conceal that my natural writing landscape was not Whakatane and the Bay of Plenty which I loved dearly, but another mongrel country where the Wild West and forests of wolves and lions melted into each other.

There are many stories I write now, which I see as being set in New Zealand, though I do not always say so. I live in New Zealand and do not wish to live anywhere else, for I am a true New Zealander, marked as one by attitude, accent, and by the way in which I feel completely part of the hills I live among. However, the old disjunction is still there – an imperfection, I suppose. The most "New Zealand" stories I write seem to be about suburbia – about libraries, councillors, supermarkets, accountants, and so on, even though the suburbs are populated by dragons and witches as well as people. A step beyond this, and I am really in patchwork land – the land I built for myself out of my childhood reading and writing, by rewriting for myself my favourite reading. As long as I am silent, the two countries exist side by side, sharing certain features. It is when I try to talk or write that I am obliged to declare for one or the other, and am astonished when sometimes someone asks me, "Do you ever write about real life?" because I think I always write about real life, though sometimes indirectly – whereas something as direct and visible as a team of marching girls never quite manages to seem like real life to me.

Published in *Education*, vol. 31 no. 1, 1982, on the occasion of the seventy-fifth birthday of the *School Journal*

Illustrations (unattributed), *School Journal*, Part 2, November 1945

A lion in the meadow

The little boy said:
"Mother, there is a lion in the meadow."
The mother said:
"Nonsense little boy."
The little boy said:
"Mother, there is a big yellow lion in the meadow."
The mother said:
"Nonsense little boy."
The little boy said:
"Mother there is a big, roaring, yellow, whiskery lion in the meadow."
The mother said:
"Little boy you are making up stories again. There is nothing in the meadow but grass and trees. Go into the meadow and see for yourself."
The little boy said:
"Mother I'm scared to go into the meadow because of the lion which is there."
The mother said:
"Little boy you are making up stories so I will make up a story too. Do you see this match box? Take it out into the meadow and open it. In it will be a tiny dragon. The tiny dragon will grow into a big dragon. It will chase the lion away."
The little boy took the match box and went away. The mother went on peeling the potatoes.

Jill McDonald, illustrations for *A Lion in the Meadow and other stories and poems* by Margaret Mahy, *School Journal*, Part 1 Number 3, 1965

Suddenly the door opened.
In rushed a big, roaring, yellow, whiskery lion.
"Hide me!" it said. "A dragon is after me."
It hid in the broom cupboard.
Then the little boy came running in.
"Mother" he said. "That dragon grew too big. There is no lion in the meadow now. There is a DRAGON in the meadow."
The little boy hid in the broom cupboard too.
"You should have left me alone," said the lion. "I eat only apples."
"But there wasn't a real dragon," said the mother. "It was just a story I made up."
"It turned out to be true after all," said the little boy. "You should have looked in the match box first."
"That is how it is," said the lion. "Some stories are true and some aren't. But I have an idea. We will go and play in the meadow on the *other* side of the house. There is no dragon there."
"I am glad we are friends now," said the little boy.
The little boy and the big roaring yellow whiskery lion went to play in the other meadow. The dragon stayed where he was and nobody minded.
The mother never ever made up a story again.

Then suddenly, at his very feet, a cave opened in the silver sand and out came a tall woman dressed in a dress of seaweed and shell, with ropes of pearls around her neck and a wonderful magical cap made of crayfish shell. All Jack could do was to stare in admiration and say ...

"What a fine figure of a woman my eyes do now behold!"

"You may well say so," she replied. "My name is Jones, Miss Emily Jones, one of the famous submarine family of Jones. Our most famous member is my Uncle David, who has a well-known locker. But there are others of us too, as you may see. And who are you, sailor Jack, and what are you doing on my island?"

"Sailor Jack", in *A Lion in the Meadow and other stories and poems* by Margaret Mahy, illustrated by Jill McDonald, *School Journal*, Part 1 Number 3, 1965

Jack Lasenby

Jack Lasenby, photographed by Robert Cross, 1995.
Courtesy of the photographer

A hugely important figure in the development of the *School Journal* in recent times, Jack Lasenby (born 1931) brought to his role as writer and editor, from 1969 to 1972, a love of language and an imagination that was grounded in a strong embrace of New Zealand land, history, and culture. Having spent ten years as a deer-culler in the Urewera Ranges, he was well versed in the rural habits and language of New Zealanders, both Māori and Pākehā. He was a close friend of Maurice Duggan from the late 1950s – both writers had lost a parent while very young (Lasenby's father was killed in a hunting accident) – and his stories have something of the elder writer's richly nuanced language and comic sense.

In the *Oxford Companion to New Zealand Literature*, critic Paul Millar notes Lasenby's audacious imagination with its "travelling asparagus beds, fast grass, and giant kauris with a view of the South"; he then goes on to describe the writing as "observant, erudite, witty, often caustic, scathingly anti-bullshit [and] alert to fit the fable to the moral (and vice versa)". [31] Rural stories had been a mainstay of the *Journal* over previous decades, but the arrival of Lasenby upped the genre's imaginative and comedic ante. Since the 1960s, Lasenby has published retellings of ancient stories (see page 129) as well as contributing fiction, poetry, plays, and articles to the *School Journal*. In a 1982 interview, he stressed the importance of myths and fables:

> *The scientist who takes the great steps always takes them imaginatively rather than through more logical reasoning processes. And I think that sort of power in the imagination is actually developed through the child's reading fiction, especially fantasy, which is at its most powerful in the myths and legends. I think a child growing up in New Zealand should hear the Māori folk literature, that of Northern Europe, and the Greek – and work out from there. That seems to me an almost essential basis for the imagination to work from.* [32]

Next time he called in, I gave him a hand to put the hogget in the school horse paddock.

"That dog-scoffing boar pig has finished rooting up my back paddock," he said. "He's started on the hay paddock now. He's made a nest out of last year's old haystack, and he sleeps in there with the tips of his tusks sticking out like white knives."

You couldn't let me have a couple of pumpkins for the street stall next week, could you?" Mum said. "The Institute's got to pay for the hall, for the flower show."

"I'll bring you a load of pumpkins," said Uncle Trev. "They're growing wild on my silage heap. You might as well have them as that dog-scoffing boar pig."

"Do wild pigs eat pumpkins?" I asked.

"A boar pig that size will eat anything," said Uncle Trev. "I've moved the hoggets nearer the house, just in case."

Jack Lasenby, "Uncle Trev and the Dog-scoffing Boar Pig", illustrated by Dick Frizzell, *School Journal*, Part 3 Number 2, 1989

Among his most loved and acclaimed contributions is the series of Uncle Trev stories, which found the perfect illustrator in Dick Frizzell. Since leaving School Publications, Jack Lasenby has published many novels including the Seddon Street Gang trilogy: *Dead Man's Head* (1994), *The Waterfall* (1995), and *The Battle of Pook Island* (1996).

Then one night that old pig kept me awake, rubbing himself against the tree, trying to shake me down like a ripe apple, so he could crunch me up between his dog-scoffing jaws, but he got so thirsty, I saw him go down in the moonlight to have a drink from the creek, from the deep pool under the bridge. He stuck his head in, gulped, and I saw the level of the water go down a couple of inches.

46

"An eel as big as a crocodile stuck his head out of the pool. He had tusks as big as the boar's, and they locked them together and fought till daylight, shrieking and splashing. Sometimes the pig dragged the eel out on the bank; sometimes the eel dragged the pig into the water.

"Then, the eel threw a row of coils around the pig, each coil glistening like wet tar as the sun came up and shone on them. The boar pig tried to get up the bank, but the eel threw a few more loops around him and rolled down into the pool like a big ball. They disappeared under the bridge.

"About midday, a giant bubble came to the surface, burst, and the water was still. I reckon that's the last of the dog-scoffing boar pig of Waharoa."

"What about the eel?" I asked Uncle Trev. "Won't it try to eat you?"

"A big eel like that will eat somebody young," said Uncle Trev, "say a girl, or boy about your age, but he's not going to bother about me, so long as I don't go bothering him. I'm probably a bit tough, and I've smoked all my life. Eels don't like the taste of tobacco."

47

From "Uncle Trev and the Dog-scoffing Boar Pig", illustrated by Dick Frizzell, *School Journal*, Part 3 Number 2, 1989

Uncle Trev, Old Tip, and Old Toot

by Jack Lasenby

WHEN Old Tip lost his bark, Uncle Trev had to teach his horse, Old Toot, to bark and chase the cows up to the shed for milking. That's what he told me, though my mother said it was nonsense.

After she went to Institute, Uncle Trev called in, and I asked him how Old Toot was getting on with his barking lessons.

"He's turning out a handy horse," said Uncle Trev, "you know, like a handy dog. He'll head or hunt both sheep and cattle."

50

He held up what he was putting into the food safe. "Gee!" I said. "Where'd you get it?" But Uncle Trev put his finger to his lips.

"You know how Old Tip used to run across the sheep's backs?" he asked.

"Yes."

"Well, Old Toot can do that. You'll never see anything like the look on a sheep's face when Old Toot's run across its back barking."

"He'd squash them!" I said.

51

Illustrations by Dick Frizzell, *School Journal*, Part 3 Number 1, 1992

Joy Cowley

Joy Cowley, photographed by Rob Kitchin
Courtesy of the *Dominion Post*

Born in Levin in 1936, Joy Cowley is one of New Zealand's most prolific and widely read children's authors. Among her prodigious output are many readers, as well as stories, plays, and poems for the *School Journal*. One of her most enduring commissions for School Publications was the Ready to Read story *Number One*, which appeared in 1982, illustrated with gusto by Jill McDonald. This was to be McDonald's final illustrative project as she died in 1981, having completed only the black and white preliminary artwork for Cowley's story. The subsequent decision to publish the book in this stark black and white format was an inspired one. It went on to become one of the most popular and most often reprinted publications in the history of School Publications/Learning Media.

Jill McDonald, artwork for Joy Cowley's *Number One*, Ready to Read, 1982

My Tiger by Joy Cowley

My tiger had a bad tooth. I went with him to the dental nurse.
"Please nurse," I said, "will you fix my tiger's tooth?"
"Is he dangerous?" said the nurse.
"No," I said. "He only eats cake."
"Tell him to sit in the chair," she said.
Tiger sat in the chair. He didn't like the drill.
When it hurt him, he cried.
"There," said the nurse. "All done. Tell him he's not to have cake again."
"But he always eats cake," I said.
"It's bad for him," she said. "No more from now on. Do you hear?"
"Then what can he eat?" I said.
"The same as other tigers," she said.
So my tiger ate the dental nurse.

Illustrated by Robyn Belton
Now For A Story 1, *School Journal*, 1979

Then the strangest thing happened. The piano, which had been standing quite still, suddenly moved. It shivered all over and bent in the middle. Its keys jiggled up and down. Its legs wobbled,

"Oh my goodness!" said the woman. "Why did it do that?"

"Bless me if 1 know," said Mr Miggs. "Would you like to try it again?"

The woman in the red gown tried a different note this time. "La-la-la," she sang and down came her finger.

The same thing happened. The keys jiggled up and down like chattering teeth and the piano bent in the middle as though the wood had turned to rubber.

"How odd!" said Mr Miggs. "I've never seen a piano do that before."

The woman was angry. "I'm afraid it's of no use to me," she said, putting on her red gloves. "I want a good piano," and she walked out of the shop.

"Well, well, well," said Mr Miggs as he shook his head at the piano. "I don't think you're worth three hundred dollars after all." He took the ticket off the piano and put on a new one that said: "Piano $160", and he moved the piano back from the window.

The next day a man in tight trousers came in.

"Can I help you?" said Mr Miggs.

The man bowed. "I'm the great Frankio," he said "You must have heard of me."

"Yes, yes I have," said Mr Miggs. "You have a jazz band."

The great Frankio bowed again. "That's right. It's the best jazz band in the land, only I need another piano. One with more life in it. You know what I mean?"

From Joy Cowley, "The Second-hand Piano", illustrated by Clare Bowes,
School Journal, Part 2 Number 4, 1969

Jill McDonald, cover illustration,
School Journal, Part 3, Summer 1958

Evelyn Clouston, illustration for "The Fire of the Gods", a play by Margaret Watson, *School Journal*, Part 4, Summer 1957

As early as the 1940s, key positions at School Publications were held by Māori, notably art editor Roy Cowan (Ngā Puhi) and Alistair Campbell (Cook Islands Māori) who, as we have seen, was instrumental in the 1960 Māori Issue of *School Journal*, Part 4. In the 1960s and 70s, the publication had an important role to play in the upsurge in Māori writing, a wave of creativity that placed Patricia Grace, Witi Ihimaera, and others at the forefront of New Zealand literature.

From its outset, the *School Journal* paid a dutiful amount of attention to Māori culture. In her essay "The Maori in the *School Journal*: 1907–1981", Diana Beaglehole suggests that the high incidence of Māori material in the fledgling *Journal* reflected a conscious effort to create "historical myths for a new nation". [33]

Athol McCredie has noted how, during the 1940s and 50s, Māori content in the *Journal* – and in the Bulletins which appeared alongside it – tended to be:

> *mythological or historical tales or … stories set in the backblocks about barefoot Maori farm children. These latter stories, such as the Dennis Knight Turner illustrated Bulletin* East Coast Village *(1962), were usually highly sympathetic and sensitive, but the genre came to grief with Ans Westra's 1964* Washday at the Pa. [34]

While the 1948 series *Life in the Pa* and the 1960 Māori Issue of the *Journal* had been largely produced by Pākehā, the significant shift during the 1960s and early 70s was the upsurge in Māori contributors. During that period, Witi Ihimaera and Patricia Grace became prominent names in the *School Journal*, their writing deliberately setting out to fill the void they had personally felt as young Māori reading the *Journal*. Both contributed first-hand accounts of Māori experience in the contemporary world.

Patricia Grace, photographed by Robert Cross, 1987. Courtesy of the photographer

Born in Wellington in 1937, of Ngāti Raukawa, Ngāti Toa, and Te Āti Awa descent, Patricia Grace began publishing in the *School Journal* in the 1960s while working as a school teacher. Her 1975 collection, *Waiariki*, was the first book of stories written by a Māori woman. In the 1970s, some of her best stories – among them "Huria's Rock", "Beans", and "Drifting" – appeared in the *School Journal*, where they found an avid readership among both children and adults.

FIREWOOD BY PATRICIA GRACE

Tony was the first to wake on the day that they were to go for firewood.

"Get up," he yelled at Hughie who lay sleeping beside him. He kicked out sharply under the blankets, then jumped out of bed as Hughie lunged at him with his fists.

"Think y' smart," he growled, but Tony was already well out of reach.

"Get up," he shouted to his elder brother, Rana, as he prepared to dive at him on the other bed. But he was too late.

"Yow." He hit the floor with Rana's shoulder firmly pinning him by the chest.

"Get off. Mum, look at Rana," he called.

"Ya ha. Serve you right," roared Hughie. "Thinks he's smart just 'cause Dad said he could put the chains on Blue Pony."

"You boys go and catch the horses," called their father from the next room. "Punch, Jack, and Blue Pony. Don't be long."

Breakfast was ready when the boys returned with the horses. They slipped the reins over some fence posts in the yard and ran into the warm kitchen. Tony hurried through his porridge, gulped the warm, sweet tea and buttered himself two thick slices of Maori bread.

"Come on you fellas," he called as he ran outside to prepare his horse for the day's work.

In the shed at the other end of the yard his father had sorted out collars and chains. Tony selected what he wanted from the piles, unhooked a pikau bag from a nail, picked up the slasher and went out to where Blue Pony was tethered.

"You fellas are slow," he called at Hughie and Rana and then his father crossed the yard to the shed.

"You got the slasher?" his father asked.

"Yes."

"O.K. That's your job when we get up the hill."

They were ready at last. Tony looked proudly at his horse. It had a big leather collar in place, hames with the long coils of chain hooked to them, and the pikau bag with the slasher in one pocket and ropes in the other. He gripped the reins with one hand and the horse's back with the other, bounced upwards and lay across his horse, then swung himself upright and tucked his legs into the pockets of the pikau bag.

"Hurry up you fellas," he called.

"You go over by the bank," called his father. "I'll double up with you."

Tony slapped his legs against his horse's sides and rode to a small bank where his father would mount behind him. Soon they were on the way along the track which led down from the house towards the creek, then on up to the scrub-covered hills. The day was warm and still. The horses' hooves thudded softly on the grassed track as they began to climb, and the sweet smelling manuka trees rattled and whispered as they brushed past. Behind him Tony heard Rana and Hughie begin to sing softly.

19

"First load for me, Dad?" he asked.

"Yes, O.K."

"By myself?"

"Yes."

His father joined in the singing in his deep gentle voice, then Tony joined in too. Halfway up the hill, where a clump of manuka trees stood in a small clearing, they stopped, and tethered the horses. Tony watched his father walk round the stand of trees, select one and test his footing. He swung his axe back and chopped into the flaky manuka trunk. Ksss. Ksss. His father's breath fizzed through his clenched teeth as he sliced into the wood – under, over, under, over, under, over. And from the other side of the clump he could hear the slower rhythm of Rana's axe as he began to chop – under and, over and, under and, over and, under and, over.

The first tree fell, and Hughie dropped it down on to the track and returned for the next one. Tony gripped the smooth handle of the slasher and began to trim off the green tops and small side branches.

"Ksss, ksss, under, over, under, over, under, over," he said to himself as he worked. He cleared away the trimmed off pieces as he heard Hughie dragging the next tree down, and helped pull the new trunk level with the first. Once more he began on his task of slashing away leaves and small branches.

All morning they worked, and in that time they had cut, stacked and trimmed three loads which they bound with short chains.

"Get the horses," their father said. The boys led the horses down on to the track, one to the head of each load. Tony took one end of the long coils of chain at either side of Blue Pony's collar, and hooked the loose ends under the chain binding the wood.

"All set?" his father asked.

"Yes."

"O.K. Take off."

His father helped him on to the horse and he tucked his legs into the pikau bag and stretched them out over the chains at the horse's flanks.

"Get up," he said and slapped Blue Pony's rump with a small manuka switch. Blue Pony leaned forward taking the strain, then started off slowly down the track. Tony could feel his horse's muscles bunch and tighten under him as the blue roan mare felt the load running smoothly behind her. Hughie and Rana set their horses moving and their father started out behind the last horse so that he could watch the loads during the homeward trek.

Tony was hot after his morning's work and his arms were sore and tired. But there was a light breeze blowing and the green manuka boughs brushed his hot body coolly. He urged Blue Pony up a small rise, rested her there for a moment, then set her off on the downward track once more. It was good to be sitting there on Blue Pony, riding down the shaded track with a load of wood behind, and no one telling him what to do.

He began to sing. His high young voice rose and drifted back, and his brothers picked up the melody and joined in loudly. At the bottom of the hill by the creek's edge they rested the horses. Then the boys coaxed their horses down the bank, and urged them through the shingly creek and up the other side. It was a long straight run home now. The sun was hot there on the flat and already it was mid-afternoon. Tony looked towards the house. "They'll see us coming," he thought. "And they'll put a big pot full of mussels on the stove for us. And the new bread will be in the oven nearly cooked."

He took his feet out of the pikau bag and hooked them up behind him, then he lay forward and rested his head on Blue Pony's neck. He thought about the hot sun and the long pull home. He thought about the pot of mussels hissing and spitting on the range and the new bread wrapped in a damp towel steaming on the bench. Well, not far to go now. He closed his eyes as Blue Pony kept up her slow steady pace over the paddocks. "Wake up son," he heard his father say. "You went to sleep. Just as well Blue Pony knows the way home." He opened his eyes and looked around. There he was at home, and his two brothers were unhitching the chains from Punch and Judy. And there were his mother and his three sisters standing at the back door watching him. He waved to them.

"You fellas got some mussels on for us?" he called.

Illustrations by Jill McDonald,
School Journal, Part 2 Number 4, 1967

One Piece of Straw

One sparrow
With a piece of straw,
Another came along,
And then one more,
Then another
And that made four.
Four sparrows
And one piece of straw.
Cut it in half,
Divide by two,
Happy sparrows
Away they flew.

Patricia Grace
School Journal, Part 1 Number 3, 1967

While through the 1970s and 80s the number of stories about Māori in urban settings increased, stories and articles about customary practices such as flax weaving and eeling remained popular. The nineteenth-century explorer Elsdon Best's "Hopu Tuna" was retold by Jane Thomson in the *School Journal*, Part 2 Number 3, 1980; and *School Journal*, Part 3 Number 3, 1993 included four eeling stories gathered from kaumātua of the Manuel Jose family, Ngāti Porou, by Bob McConnell. In one of these tales, Ethel Tawhiri related:

> On one expedition with Harry, he got me to hold out my dress like a basket while he stood in the water. When he caught an eel, he would put it in the "basket". When there were several, he would pick me up, eels and all, and fling me up on to the bank above, with instructions where to leave the eels.

In "Tangaroa's Children at Wairewa" (*School Journal*, Part 3 Number 1, 1993), the children of Little River School tag along with George Skipper to learn traditional eeling methods in Wairewa or Lake Forsyth. Maybe the plethora of eeling stories was a concerted editorial effort to divert an appetite for smoked fish to an appetite for reading. Other contributors exploring Māori themes in recent years include playwright Hone Kouka, whose story "I Wanna Be" appeared in *School Journal*, Part 1 Number 1, 1992, and Paekakariki-based Apirana Taylor, who continues to reinvigorate traditional storytelling techniques in "The Dream of Aroha" (Part 1 Number 1, 1993).

Witi Ihimaera, photographed by Robert Cross, 1987
Courtesy of the photographer

Of Te Aitanga-ā-Māhaki descent, Witi Ihimaera (born 1944) has been a dynamic presence in New Zealand literature since 1972, when his often-reprinted collection of stories, *Pounamu Pounamu*, first appeared. Among his contributions to the *School Journal* was an abridged version of his 1973 novel *Tangi*.

In *Education* (Number 1, 1982), Ihimaera recalled his early exposure to the *School Journal*, "almost the only reading material we had at primary school" during the 1950s. "The pictures ... were all spidery and too delicate ... They weren't ideal, but better than comics – *School Journals* you could go back to again and again."

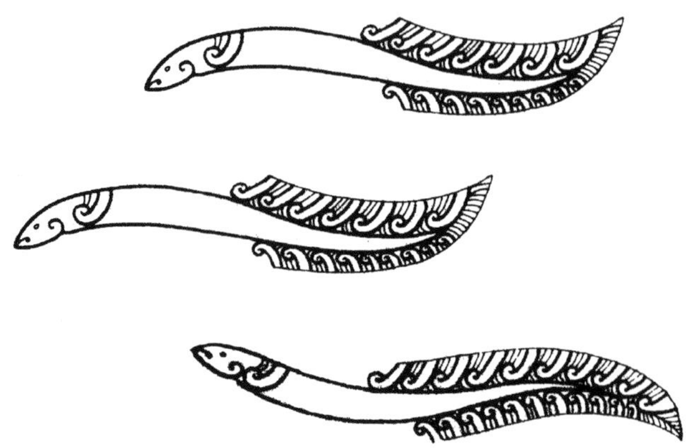

Cliff Whiting, illustrations for Jane Thomson's retelling of "Hopu Tuna" by Elsdon Best, *School Journal*, Part 2 Number 3, 1980

THE PUPU POOL BY WITI IHIMAERA

My sisters and I, we called them pupus. But the name they are given in the dictionary is: "winkle, *Lunella smaragda, Zediloma aethiops*".

What a mouthful! And they certainly were, those pupus. We would pop them in our mouths and roll our eyes around our faces. Mmmmmmm!

Pupus are sea food or kai moana. They are often known as "cat's eyes" and are shell fish which feed on seaweed. You can tell them easily because they have a shell like a snail's and a round green button at the hole of the shell which does look like a cat's eye.

My sisters and I looked for pupus in a very special place on the reef, which we called the pupu pool.

The reef was just outside the town where we lived. Just as well it was close by, because our father was always hungry for sea food. About every second Sunday, after our Sunday kai, he would rub his stomach and say: "Hey Mum! Those kinas are calling out loud to me today!"

Kinas are spiky sea food, also known as "sea urchins."

"These dishes are calling you too," Mum would reply. Dad would rub his puku even harder.

"Well, Mum!" he would say, pretending he hadn't heard her. "Those pauas are really singing out to me today!"

Paua are shell fish which live in beautiful shiny shells.

"These dishes are singing even louder," Mum would answer.

Again Dad would pretend not to hear her. He would rub his stomach harder than ever and say, "Pae kare, Mum! Those mussels can't wait for me to come for them!"

Mussels are kai moana also.

"Neither can these dishes," Mum would growl.

So Dad would make one last try.

"Well, Mum," he would sigh. "Those pipis are sure going to miss me today."

Dad, he knew that Mum loved a feed of pipis. For her, pipis was a magic word, as magic as abracadabra. And, sure enough, she would answer him: "What are we waiting for then! Can't disappoint those pipis today!"

"Nor the pauas," Dad would add.

"Or the pupus!" we would chorus.

So off we would go to the reef in our old truck.

My sisters and I rode on the back and by the time we got to the reef our mouths were already watering. Not for pauas or kinas or mussels or pipis – we didn't like them as much as Mum and Dad did – but for those delicious pupus.

If it was a sunny day, the reef would already be crowded with other people searching for kai moana. There they'd be, dotting the water with their sacks or kits in which they put their catch. They would wave and shout to us and we would hurry to join them, pulling on our shoes, grabbing our flax kits or sacks and running down to the sea. The shoes stopped our feet from being cut by sharp rocks as we waded into the water.

"Don't you kids come too far out!" Dad would yell.

He would already be way ahead of us, sack clutched in one hand and knife in the other. He used the knife to prise the pauas and kinas from the reef, because if you weren't quick enough they would hold on to the rocks really tight.

Sometimes, Dad would put on a diving mask. It made it easier for him to see underwater.

As for Mum, she liked nothing better than to wade out to where some women were. Then she would korero with them while she was looking for seafood. All the long afternoon those women would talk and talk and talk and talk!

For both Mum and Dad, going to the reef was a good excuse to meet our friends and relations. It was almost a family affair.

My sisters and I, we made straight for the pupu pool.

The pool was very long but not very deep. At its deepest the water was waist high. The reef around it was fringed with long waving seaweed. Small transparent fish swam among the waving leaves, and little crabs scurried across the floor of the pool. The pupus glided calmly along the sides of the reef. Once, we saw a starfish, inching its way into a dark crack.

But our most beautiful discovery was a delicate seahorse, magical and serene, shimmering among the red kelp and riding the swirls of the sea's current.

My sisters and I, we wanted to take it home.

"If you take it from the sea it will die," Dad told us. "Leave it here in its own home, for the sea gives it life and beauty."

And Dad went on, giving us our first lesson about treating the sea with aroha.

Vanya Lowry, illustration for "The Pupu Pool"

"Kids, you must take from the sea only the kai you need and only the amount you need to please your bellies. If you take more, then it is waste. Why waste food? Best to leave it in the sea for when you will need it the next times. The sea is good to us, it gives us kai to eat. As long as we respect it, it will continue to favour us. If you lift a stone from its lap as you search for shellfish, return the stone to where it was. Try not to break pieces of the reef, for it is the home of many kai moana. And do not leave litter behind you when you leave the sea ..."

Our father, he taught us to respect the sea and to have reverence for the life held in its waters. As we collected pupus, we would remember his words.

And whenever the seahorse peeked shyly at us from behind a curtain of kelp, we felt glad that we had left it in its pool to delight us.

As soon as we had filled our flax kit, we would return to the beach. We played together with other kids while waiting for our parents to return from the outer reef. One by one they would arrive: the women still talking, the men carrying their sacks on their shoulders.

Sometimes, we would have a small feed right there on the sand, sharing the kai between families. Then we would take the rest of the food home.

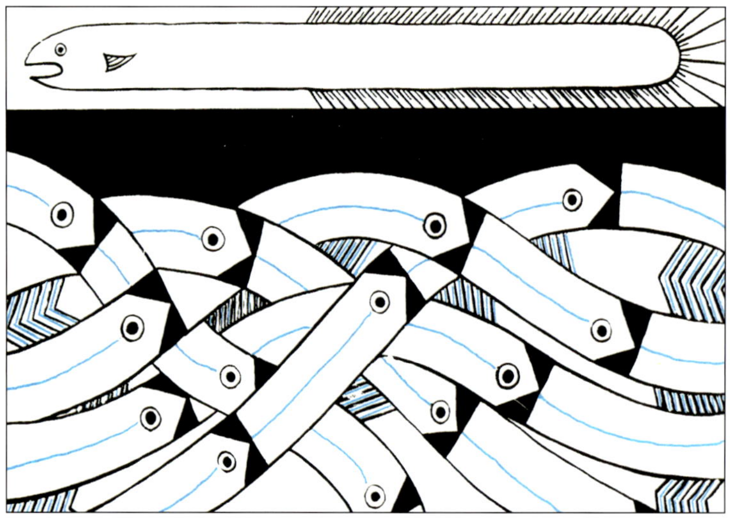

Cliff Whiting, illustrations for Jane Thomson's retelling of "Hopu Tuna" by Elsdon Best, *School Journal*, Part 2 Number 3, 1980

My sisters and I, we used to get very impatient waiting for the pupus to cook! They were put into a small pot of water and boiled on the stove. When they were heaped onto a plate, we had our safety pins ready.

To get the pupu out of its shell, you had to slip the pin under the green button of the cat's eye and twist it around. The pupu coiled easily out of the shell to curl into our mouths. Mmmmm. Pupu after pupu, until they were all gone and only a heap of empty shells was left. On the other side of the table, Mum would be eating her pipis and Dad his pauas and kinas.

"Isn't the sea good to us?" Dad would smile.

"Yes, Dad!" we would chorus.

And we would scrabble among the empty shells to make sure a pupu hadn't gotten away from us.

One day, we went again to the reef. We were in a happy mood. The sun was shining and skipping its beams like bright stones across the water.

But when we got to the reef, it was deserted. There were no people dotting the sea with their sacks, no loud calls of welcome from them.

Dad frowned. He saw our friends and relations clustered on the beach. There were many of them, staring out towards the reef.

"Something's wrong," he said.

He stopped the truck and we walked with him towards the people. They were silent and sad.

"The water too cold?" Dad asked, trying to joke.

Nobody answered him.

"Is there a shark out there?" Dad continued.

Someone pointed to a sign. It had been put up during the night. Dad elbowed through the crowd to read it.

"What does it say, Dad?" I asked.

His fists were clenched and his eyes were angry. Then his fists unclenched and his eyes became sad.

"It says that it is dangerous to take sea food from the reef."

"Why, Dad?"

"They've run a sewer pipe out there, son. The sea is polluted. If we eat the sea food we may get sick."

My sisters and I were silent for a while.

"No more pupus, Dad?"

"No more, son."

"And the seahorse, Dad? Will it be all right?"

He shrugged his shoulders.

We walked back to the truck. Behind us, an old woman began to cry out a tangi to the reef. It was a very sad song for such a beautiful day. While she was singing, Dad stopped and bowed his head. When the tangi was finished, he whispered: "We have been unkind to the sea. We have poisoned the land and now we feed our poison into the water. We have lost our aroha for the sea and our respect for its life."

He started the truck. We turned homeward.

In my mind I caught a vision of pupus crawling among polluted rocks. I saw a starfish encrusted with ugliness.

And flashing through dead waving seaweed was a beautiful seahorse, fragile and dream-like, searching frantically for clean and crystal waters.

School Journal, Part 3 Number 3, 1974

New Land, Old Stories

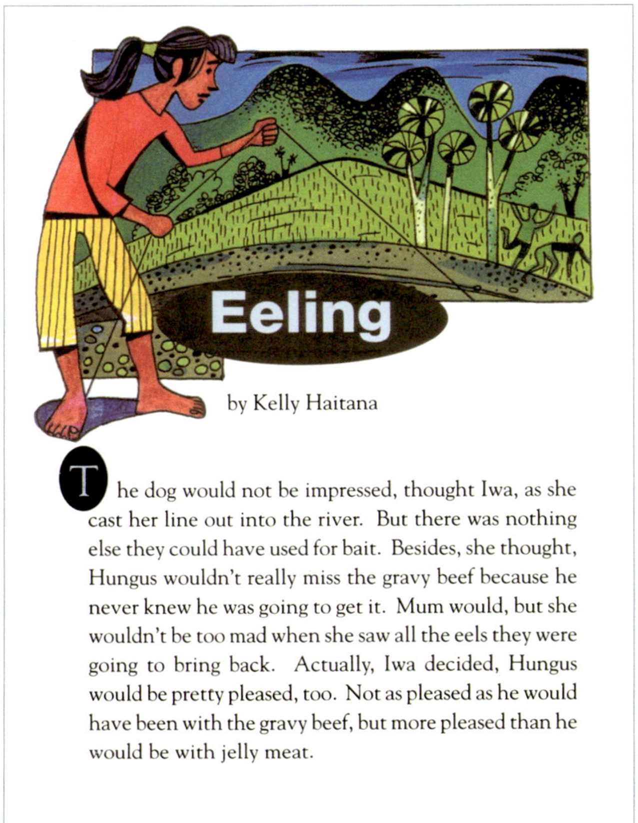
Eeling

by Kelly Haitana

The dog would not be impressed, thought Iwa, as she cast her line out into the river. But there was nothing else they could have used for bait. Besides, she thought, Hungus wouldn't really miss the gravy beef because he never knew he was going to get it. Mum would, but she wouldn't be too mad when she saw all the eels they were going to bring back. Actually, Iwa decided, Hungus would be pretty pleased, too. Not as pleased as he would have been with the gravy beef, but more pleased than he would be with jelly meat.

Murray Grimsdale, illustration for *School Journal*, Part 2 Number 4, 1990

Barry Clothier, cover photograph for *School Journal*, Part 3 Number 3, 1990

The confidence and diversity of Maori writing is reflected in this issue of the *School Journal* (Part 3 Number 3, 1990), which was entirely made up of Māori-related materials. As well as four stories with contemporary settings – "The Launching" by Lyn Taane, "Pinga Champ" by Donna Rapira, "Te Whakama e Patu" by Chris Szekely, and Kelly Haitana's "Sweet As" – the *Journal* included articles about kaimoana and fishing regulations, making piupiu, and a lively account of Te Mahia School entering a cultural festival.

As a response to increasing immigration from Europe after World War Two, the *School Journal* actively sought to help integrate recent arrivals into New Zealand life by describing their experiences and, at the same time, making New Zealanders aware of, and sympathetic to, the traditions they brought with them. Born in Dargaville in 1915, to Dalmatian parents, Amelia Batistich grew up in Northland, where she experienced first hand Dalmatian, Irish Catholic, mainstream Pākehā and, importantly, Māori culture. In the 1970s, she contributed a series about traditional Māori foods – fictionalised tales of gathering kōuka (cabbage tree leaves) on the East Cape and how to find out whether a kiekie is ripe for eating or not. But it was immigrant cultures she wrote most extensively about. In 1970, she contributed a two-part feature on "The Bohemians of Puhoi", which told the stories of immigrants who moved from what is now the Czech Republic to a small rural settlement north of Auckland. She also contributed much fiction to the *Journal*, often centring her stories on intercultural exchange.

The official *A Guide to the School Journal* (1994) states that a key aim of the *Journal* is to bolster a sense of identity and of belonging to a diverse society "by providing material that gives a sensitive interpretation of the children's own backgrounds".[35] The *Journal* was initially established to offset the amount of imported literature entering the country and offer something that was both alive to and affirming of the readers' place in the world. At the same time, over the years, the *Journal* has had to look outwards as well, to see New Zealand in relation to many other countries as well as on its own terms. In an immigrant society, it has had to meet the needs of recent arrivals in this country, be they from Europe or, increasingly in recent decades, the Pacific and Asia.

Unattributed illustration for "Fishing" by Albert Wendt, *School Journal*, Part 4, Summer 1961

Born in Western Sāmoa in 1939, Albert Wendt was a student in New Zealand at the time his story "Fishing" appeared in the *School Journal*. An important figure in emerging Pacific literature, Wendt went on to publish his first novel, *Sons for the Return Home*, in 1973. "Fishing" echoes Sāmoan traditional storytelling while exhibiting the writer's keen ear for dialogue. Like all Wendt's writing, the story is underpinned by his experience of Pacific culture as "a fabulous storehouse of anthropology, sociology, art, religion, history, dance, and music". [36] It would, however, be another two or three decades before a wave of Pasifika writers would be making a significant mark on the *Journal*, among them the Cook Islands writer Johnny Frisbie, who was profiled in a 1997 Part 3 *Journal*. Like Wendt, Frisbie added to the Māori/Pacific tradition of eeling stories. Her "The Moray Eel" appeared in the *School Journal*, Part 4 Number 3, 1994.

The spears were quivering no more. They took hold of their spears, pulled, and were surprised at how easily the eel came out. Then they surfaced quickly, dragging it behind them.

"She's big all right," laughed Sione.

They pulled it on board. Sione's spear had gone into its mouth and its point protruded from its belly. Pea's spear had sunk into its black slimy head and into its spine. The boys sat afraid to touch its body which was black and shiny. Yellow spots dotted its long black body.

From "Fishing" by Albert Wendt, unattributed illustration,
School Journal, Part 4, Summer 1961

A Pālāgi writer married into a Tongan family, Feana Tu'akoi produces energetic narratives melding mythology and contemporary life. In her story "Me and Jonah Lomu", (*School Journal*, Part 2 Number 4, 1999) a Sāmoan father explains to his New Zealand-born son how a battle between two giants made of stone was the origin of the punga rocks in the island lagoon:

"One of the giants, Punga, started to feel very tired. His arms and shoulders were aching. So the other giant saw his chance. He lifted Punga up into the air and heaved him right out there into the lagoon." Dad pointed out to where he and Sione had been swimming that morning. "When he landed, Punga broke into many pieces, forming the rocks we still call punga today."

From "Me and Jonah Lomu" by Feana Tu'akoi
illustrated by Greg Broadmore,
School Journal, Part 2 Number 4, 1999

Tom Coomber, cover artwork, *School Journal*, Part 3, Winter 1961

Tom Coomber's drawing of a puppet show (on the previous page) is, at one remove, a telling description of the *School Journal* and its function. On the back cover, we see the puppeteer adults working behind the scenes, putting on a performance for the group of entranced children on the front. It is an evening performance of "The Tortoise and the Hare", and the stage radiates brightness as the tortoise approaches the finish line. There is a sense of both work and play – and also of storytelling magic.

Plays have long been regarded as one of the most popular elements within the *School Journal*. According to the 1994 *A Guide to the School Journal*, they should ideally be:

> *enjoyed at various levels: as a simple shared reading, with parts being allocated; as independent reading; or as a production to be performed … Some are written with puppets in mind or can be easily adapted to include puppets.* [37]

In recent years, many of the most extravagant illustrative designs in the *Journal* have accompanied plays – as if page design has itself become a theatrical form. A high-octane example is Fraser Williamson's visual treatment of Bill Nagelkerke's "Words".

Fraser Williamson, illustration for Bill Nagelkerke's "Words", *School Journal*, Part 2 Number 2, 2002

The Action and the Word

Introduction to "Big House", a play by Allona Priestly

Big House is a mystery play. As you work over it, you'll realize that it is really very much the same type of play as *Beaten Gold*, which was a melodrama. In fact, this is a melodrama. The only difference is that more stress is laid on the working out of a problem and the solving of a mystery. Otherwise all the same rules hold good. The events are more important than the characters, the acting must be strong and fast, and the key points must be clearly made as the play goes along, so that the audience follows easily.

Costume: There is no difficulty about costume in this play. Wear whatever you can borrow from your mothers and fathers.

Setting: The settings should be fairly clear from the illustrations. There is no difficulty about the living-room scene. The beach is not so easy, but don't try to be realistic. A sea-scape on the blackboard or on a big piece of brown paper will make a good background. The jetty can be two tables put end to end, with cardboard rails fastened on with drawing pins. Leave the rest to the audience's imagination. But you must have some real wool caught in the end of your jetty for the manager to find. And you must have a step to get on to the jetty.

Props: Be careful about these. They supply a good deal of incidental action that helps the dialogue. Enough dishes for Mrs. Rainer to set a table, and some reasonable food for them to eat as a meal. It should be something soft and easily swallowed – mince or mashed potato. Practice the timing of Mrs. Rainer's trips in and out of the kitchen. Practise eating while the other person is speaking. Don't hold up dialogue while you swallow. And eat very small bits, or when your cue comes you'll be caught speechless.

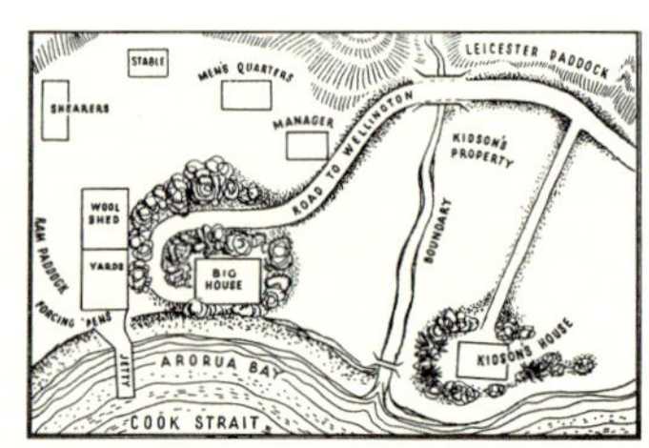

The scene is set in the living-room of the manager's house on Arorua sheep station. The station is on the coast, in a wide bay which looks across Cook Strait to the South Island. At the beginning of the play, Mary Rainer, the manager's wife, is setting the table. She is middle-aged, pleasant, and sensible, the sort of person who is never idle, but never in a hurry. There is the sound of the back-door opening and footsteps in the kitchen. Mrs. Rainer looks up and calls:

School Journal, Part 4, October 1950

New Zealand's most successful playwright, Roger Hall (born 1939), wrote numerous plays for the *Journal* during the 1970s and 80s, among them "Captain Scrimshaw in Space" (1975), in which a school group meet up with a hapless space-traveller. Working as an editor at the *School Journal* during the 1970s, Hall also adapted many literary works for the classroom stage, among them a West Indian folk tale, "How the Crab Got a Hard Back", and the classic "Jack and the Beanstalk".

GIRL. Where are we going?
SCRIMSHAW. To the moon. And when we get there we will be the first people from New Zealand to land on it.
BOY. What will it be like on the moon?
SCRIMSHAW. Great fun. Because when we walk about it will seem as if we are floating. And we will be able to jump up very high. Now, can anyone tell me why?
CLEVER BOY. Because the moon is smaller than the earth and so the gravity is less.
SCRIMSHAW. Oh, is that the reason? I've always wanted to know …

From Roger Hall's "Captain Scrimshaw in Space", illustrated by John Griffiths, *School Journal*, Part 3 Number 2, 1975

Suit the action to the word,
and the word to the action.
Hamlet, III, 2

Judith Shanahan, illustration for Roger Hall's adaptation of "Jack and the Beanstalk", *School Journal*, Part 1 Number 6, 1978

Many other writers have contributed plays, among them Irene Adcock, David Hill, John Parker, John O'Brien, Jane Buxton, Janice Leitch, Philippa Werry, and Diana Noonan, whose 2001 play, "The Ducks Dip Out", requires a cast of three picnickers, at least four swans, and as many ducks as you can manage. Janice Marriott's "Watching Wildlife", from the same year, requires an even more diverse avian cast.

From Janice Marriott's "Watching Wildlife", illustrated by Fraser Williamson, *School Journal*, Part 2 Number 3, 2001

TUI: Kiwi, get off the path! That path is for the humans so that they can freely wander around in their enclosure. Humans find it difficult to make their own paths. They tend to follow behind other humans.
DUCK. How boring.
TUI. When you were a duckling, you did exactly the same thing – you just walked along behind your mother.
DUCK. I never did!
KOOKABURRA. What will they do if they see us?
TUI. Humans are unpredictable and must be considered dangerous …

Diana Noonan, who, like Roger Hall, has been involved as both an editor and playwright for the *Journal*, notes that it is the interactive nature of drama that draws children to it.

> *Plays have to be fast, fun, easy to perform and stage in a classroom setting with few or no props. Largely, the text alone has to do the work and carry the "story". Children enjoy using plays because it's a chance to get together with their friends, even if it's just to read the plays aloud.* [38]

Gavin Mouldey, illustration for Philippa Werry's "A Dangerous Place", *School Journal*, Part 1 Number 1, 2005

Some of the most energetic verbal play in the *Journal* has surfaced in the drama section. One example is Stuart Payne's "Save or Delete" (Part 4 Number 1, 1997), which is set inside a computer with a cast comprising "the internal computer staff", with names like Cut, Paste, Insert, Copy, Virus Scan, and File Manager. A long way from the Shakespearean extracts that appeared in the *School Journal* during the 1930s, most recent plays are madcap affairs – see also Philippa Werry's kitchen disaster tragicomedy, "A Dangerous Place", illustrated in the most painterly of manners by Gavin Mouldey.

Moving On

If the plays tend to be irrepressibly funny, the emotional range of fiction in the *Journal* in recent decades has become broader than ever. Areas of childhood experience such as family break-up, loss, and grief are now dealt with directly, as in David Hill's "Moving On" – a story that had its origins in his own mother's death while he was still a child.

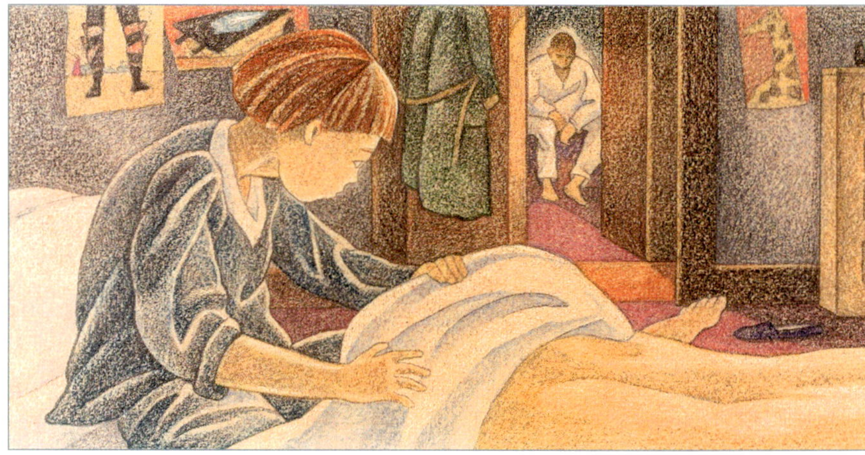

After his mother died, Todd sometimes woke in the night and heard his dad crying. Todd would cry, too. Or he'd pretend he had to go to the loo. His father would hug him and make them both a drink. Then they'd lie with the hall light on, talking to each other from their rooms till Todd drifted back to sleep.

From David Hill's "Moving On", illustrated by Caroline Campbell, *School Journal*, Part 3 Number 1, 1998

A significant and prolific contributor in recent decades, Beverley Dunlop (born 1935) didn't begin publishing until the mid-1970s but soon established herself as a writer for both adults and children. Norman Bilbrough is another prolific contributor established in the fields of adult and children's fiction. Other notable contributors include Bill Nagelkerke, Brian Birchall, John O'Brien, K. E. Anderson, Alan Bagnall, Dot Meharry, Anna Kenna, Roger Telenius, Gaelyn Gordon, and Bub Bridger.

Probably the biggest shift in the last ten years is that children's writing has become its own reputable genre, with national and international book awards, literary periodicals, newspaper and radio reviews, and specialist bookshops. It is no longer the moonlighting pursuit it was when Alistair Campbell was hitting up his writer friends for material fifty years ago. However, while children's writing has largely diverged from the "adult" publishing scene, a number of established "adult" fiction writers continue to make appearances in the *Journal* – among them Ingrid Horrocks, Jenny Pattrick, Elizabeth Smither, Vivienne Plumb, and Catherine Chidgey – carrying on the grand tradition of the walk-on part established by Sargeson and Frame fifty years ago.

Soon, Tiny and I were walking along the dusty road to school. Don barked and strained at the leash. He pulled so hard that sometimes Tiny nearly fell over.

Then Don saw another dog in a paddock. He gave a yell and pulled right away from Tiny. Off down the road went Don.

From Beverley Dunlop's "The Tail of the Smallest Piglet", illustrated by Deirdre Gardiner, *School Journal*, Part 2 Number 4, 1983

Squeaky Door

My bedroom door is a squeaky door. Sometimes I like to pretend that it's talking.

When I push it slowly, it makes a long deep sound like a sleepy "hello-o-o-o". If I push it faster, it squeals a quick "hi!"

Then I swing it back and forth at different speeds to make it groan, or laugh, or cry, or give long speeches.

A few weeks ago, Mum said, "Oh, I must do something about your door." She got a can of oil and squirted drops of it on the hinges. "That should shut it up," she said.

She was right. Suddenly, my door was horribly quiet. I swung it fast and slow, but it didn't make a sound. I really missed its voice.

Then, just this morning, when I opened my door I heard a tiny sound like a bird's chirp. I pushed the door back and it chirped again. The oil was starting to wear off the hinges.

Every time I've gone through the door today, the squeak's got louder and louder.

"Hello-o-o-o? Hello-o-o-o?"

My bedroom door is a squeaky door again. Not even Mum can keep it quiet forever.

Johanna Mary (Knox), *School Journal*, Part 1 Number 2, 1994

Ghost!

by Alan Bagnall

"Tomai! Tomai! Rawiri and me, we seen a ghost!"

"He kēhua, Tomai! He kēhua!"

"Yeah, a real ghost, eh, Rawiri? Old Miss Greenwood's ghost! It's her, standing in her sunporch! Just like she always used to. Scary, man!"

"We've run all the way back without stopping!"

Our big sister, Tomai, is hanging out the washing. She clips the pegs on slowly.

"Really, Taki!" she says. "Really, Rawiri! So you guys seen a ghost?"

"Yeah, man, staring right at us!"

"Old Miss Greenwood?" Tomai asks. "Old Miss Greenwood who stayed in the pilot's house? Old Miss Greenwood who died last week?"

We nod.

"She was a kind old thing. She wouldn't hurt anyone."

"You wanna see then, Tomai? She's scary, real scary!"

"Could you feel her?" Tomai asks. "Sort of feel her in the air?"

"Nah! She just stared at us!"

44

45

From "Ghost!" by Alan Bagnall, illustrated by Murray Grimsdale, *School Journal*, Part 2 Number 4, 1993

For a Song:

Poetry in the School Journal

Graham Percy, cover artwork for *Ten Tales*, *School Journal*, Part 1 Number 1, 1965

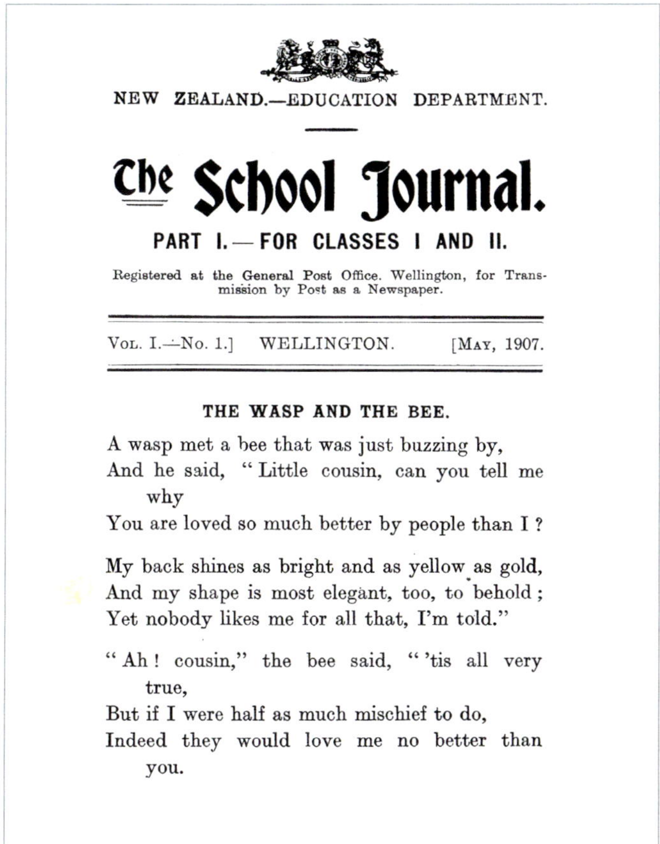
NEW ZEALAND.—EDUCATION DEPARTMENT.

The School Journal.

PART I. — FOR CLASSES I AND II.

Registered at the General Post Office, Wellington, for Transmission by Post as a Newspaper.

Vol. I.—No. 1.] WELLINGTON. [May, 1907.

THE WASP AND THE BEE.

A wasp met a bee that was just buzzing by,
And he said, "Little cousin, can you tell me why
You are loved so much better by people than I?

My back shines as bright and as yellow as gold,
And my shape is most elegant, too, to behold;
Yet nobody likes me for all that, I'm told."

"Ah! cousin," the bee said, "'tis all very true,
But if I were half as much mischief to do,
Indeed they would love me no better than you.

The first piece of writing of any kind to appear in the *School Journal* was a poem. In May 1907, the first issue of the first *Journal* – Part 1, Volume 1, Number 1 (above) – began with a nicely rhymed clasp of triplets in which a wasp and a bee get to talking about how it is that the former is so unpopular and the latter so popular. The conversation wraps up neatly with the following moral:

> From this little story let children beware,
> Because, like the wasp, if ill-natured they are,
> They will never be loved, if they're ever so fair.

Unattributed to any author, the poem manifests a sense of both play and purpose: music and morality in equal measure.

Also notable amongst the first poems in the *Journal* were those by the poet-statesman and *Journal* "godfather", William Pember Reeves, whose "The Passing of the Forest" and "The Passing of the Bush" would be frequently reprinted or excerpted until the 1960s. (A satirical poem Reeves co-wrote with George Edwards in 1885, "The Russian Scare", was selected by Elsie Locke for a special issue of the *Journal* devoted to nineteenth-century New Zealand in 1966.)

With a poet overseeing its origins, the *School Journal* was always going to give poetry some serious attention, at least in the short term. However, without a body of locally written literature to draw upon, the *Journal* had initially to rely largely on material imported from England. This situation would not change significantly for half a century – by which time, New Zealand literature was itself coming of age. And by the early 1960s, New Zealand could lay claim to its first genuinely great children's poet, Margaret Mahy.

Graham Percy, illustration for *School Journal*, Part 1 Number 2, 1965

A Witch Poem

> One of us said a magic word.
> Somewhere somebody must have heard,
> For smoke, like a thin green twilight came;
> And a witch jumped out of the candle flame.
> Shhh! Can you hear that secret laughter,
> And whispering footsteps following after?
> Nothing in life is ever the same
> When a witch jumps out of a candle flame.

Margaret Mahy
School Journal, Part 2 Number 3, 1961

Sam Williams, cover illustration, *Verse*, *School Journal*, Part 3, June 1948

Sam Williams was a stage designer (who trained in London during the 1930s) and graphic artist, whose work appeared frequently in the *School Journal* during the late 1940s.

According to *A Guide to the School Journal* (1994), between 5 and 10 percent of the space in an average *Journal* is devoted to poetry – about the same percentage as alcohol in beer or wine. Stories make up 40–55 percent, articles 15–20 percent, and plays 15–20 percent. "Appropriate proportions are maintained," the *Guide* continues, "in other categories, such as fantasy and realism, folk stories, and historical items." [1]

It is true that the *Journal* had thin pickings of New Zealand verse to draw upon in its first few decades. However, the poetry it did publish was to prove a potent element. Growing up in the 1930s, Janet Frame remembered the poems she encountered in the *School Journal* as being "full of mystery and wonder" and a dramatic contrast to the articles and stories, which she found mired in colonial rhetoric and thought. [2] Michael King, in *Wrestling with the Angel: A Life of Janet Frame* (2000), cited John Keats, Walter de la Mare, and Christina Rossetti amongst the poets Frame most enjoyed in the *Journal*. [3] Certainly Frame's writing career owed far more to the poetry she discovered there than to the prosaic articles, plodding histories, and clichéd adventures that dominated the 1930s *Journal* – a decade that must rate as a low point in the history of the publication.

The verse published in the *School Journal* during Frame's school years was, not surprisingly, a mixture of the good, the bad, and the indifferent. The index of poets featured in the Part 3 *School Journal* during the inauspicious year of 1933 includes, alongside a few ballads and some doggerel, pieces by W. B. Yeats, Shelley, and James Elroy Flecker. (Many of the better poems from these early *Journals* would be reprinted in subsequent decades.) A generation later, Margaret Mahy was able to write that "it was through poetry in the *School Journal* [in the 1940s and later] that I made my most real contacts with my own country and the dry, driving presence that language could give it". [4]

Poetry of an instructive nature went on and off the agenda over the years. Immediately after World War Two, the *Journal* featured a spate of safety-related items – as if the culture generally had grown into some new awareness of life and how it must be protected. In the *School Journal*, Part 1, July 1946, the topic of road safety was put into four-stressed lines and quatrains and punctuated by a brisk suite of drawings by Conrad Frieboe – an artist who could manage with equal dexterity a silly child and a car moving at speed. As well as being alert to poetry's information-bearing potential, the editors at this time were not averse to poetry's capacity as a sleep-inducing device – as Frieboe's cover drawing for a 1944 *School Journal* makes plain (see overleaf).

Juliet Peter, cover illustration, *School Journal*, Part 4, August 1950

E. Mervyn Taylor, cover illustration, *Verse School Journal*, Part 4, June 1951

Cover illustration, *School Journal*, Part 3, June 1949 (attributed to Russell Clark)

This *Verse* issue was the cause of the controversy noted on page 89.

Safety Rules

Dear Girls and Boys—

This month the Traffic Officers, who work to make the streets safe for children and grown-ups, are sending a special message to all readers of the *Journal*. They want you to be even more careful when you are going to school. They want you always to walk on the footpath or, if there is no footpath, on the side of the road ; to look both ways before crossing roads ; and not to play or ride your scooters or trolleys on the streets where traffic is passing all the time.

Here are some verses that may help you to remember these easy rules.

Yours sincerely,
Editor.

Every minute a car or tram
Passes the house of Paul and Pam ;
But though the twins are still quite small,
Mother doesn't worry at all.

When she sends them to the shop,
She knows that they will always stop,
While Pam looks left, and Paul looks right,
To see if there's a car in sight.

While it comes they stand and wait,
Then they walk across quite straight ;
And, watching traffic lights, they know
That RED says STOP, and GREEN says GO.

And always on the way to school
They try to keep each traffic rule.
'There's time to play at school,' says Paul ;
'The street is not the place for ball.'

At the corner soon they meet
Children from another street ;
There they wait and stand in line
For SCHOOL PATROL to give the sign.

And after school they think it jolly
To bring Mum's parcels home by trolley ;

But they NEVER COAST DOWN HILL
To meet a car would mean a spill.

On Saturdays they go for hikes
On country roads where cars and bikes
May travel fast, so on the right
They keep the traffic well in sight.

So this is why young Paul and Pam
Have no fear of car or tram.
From January till December
Traffic rules they both remember.

Conrad Frieboe, illustrations for "Safety Rules", *School Journal*, Part 1, July 1946

Conrad Frieboe, cover illustration, *School Journal*, Part 1, May 1944

Journal poems were not always soporific or instructive, however. They could, on occasion, be noisy and unruly. In 1949, the quality of poetry in the publication was drawn into the very public controversy about literary standards precipitated by the "Our Street" debacle. Referring to recent poems in the *Journal*, one protestor condemned Robert Burns's classic "Tam o'Shanter" as "a stark object lesson on the perils of intemperance" and the folkloric song "Steamboat Bill" as merely "a music hall song". In reply to such criticism, a memo to the Education Minister from the Branch pointed out that the issue of the *Journal* under attack on this occasion had also included:

> *passages from the Old Testament, and from Milton's "Samson Agonistes", four Shakepearean lyrics , and two of William Blake's poems, as well as poems by Browning, Moore, Scott, Wordsworth, Keats, Bunyan, Tennyson, and W. S. Gilbert, and a traditional song, "The British Grenadiers".* [5]

By the 1950s, a few unequivocally modern poems from Great Britain were appearing in the *Journal*: among them W. H. Auden's classic "Night Mail" and Dylan Thomas's "The Hunchback in the Park". The latter was prefaced, on its appearance in 1952, with some sound advice for poetry reading generally: "If you look at the poem too closely it is hard to follow; but if you can get the feel and sound of it, it comes into shape like a brightly coloured painting."

With local poetry claiming more and more of poetry's 5 or 10 percent of *Journal* space by the 1950s, Tennyson, Rossetti, and Burns were finally being edged out. A 1950 Verse *Journal* highlighted three New Zealand poets: Denis Glover (his much anthologised "Home Thoughts"), Cantabrian Basil Dowling, and Eileen Duggan – represented by "A Maori Lullaby" and one of the most reprinted poems in the history of the *Journal*, "The Kingfisher" (from Duggan's first collection, *New Zealand Bird Songs*, 1929):

The Kingfisher

Why do you sit, so dreamily dreamily,
Kingfisher over the stream,
Silent your beak, and silent the water,
What is your dream?

A falling, a flashing of blue and of silver,
Child, he is deep in the stream,
Prey in his beak and fear in the water
That was his dream!

Eileen Duggan,
School Journal, Part 4, August 1950

Illustration by Olga Volger, School Journal,
Part 3 Number 3, 1967

I Remember

Denis Glover, perhaps the finest New Zealand poet now writing, is also known as the founder of the Caxton Press, Christchurch; and was champion middleweight boxer in the New Zealand navy. This poem expresses Glover's attitude towards the country, and his memories of childhood. "Harry" is an imaginary person, a kind of spokesman for the poet. The poem is crystal clear, apparently casually written, and was probably worked over in the poet's mind for several years. What part of the country do you think the poem may have been written about?

I remember paddocks opening green
On mountains tussock-brown,
And the rim of fire on the hills,
And the river running down;

And the smoke of the burning scrub,
And my two uncles tall,
And the smell of earth new-ploughed,
And the antlers in the hall,
Sings Harry.

Then Uncle Jim was off to the wars
With a carbine at his saddle
And was killed in the Transvaal
—I forget in just what battle.

263

And Uncle Simon left the farm
After some wild quarrel,
Rolled his blanket and rode off
Whistling on his sorrel.

My father held to the land
Running good cattle there,
And I grew up like a shaggy steer
And as swift as a hare
While the river ran down.

But that was long ago
When the hawk hovered over the hill
And the deer lifted their heads
And a boy lay still
By the river running down.

Sings Harry.

From *Sings Harry And Other Poems* by permission of DENIS GLOVER.

Denis Glover, "I Remember", with illustrations by Russell Clark, *School Journal*, Part 4, November 1952

Twentieth-century classics of New Zealand verse, such as R. A. K. Mason's "On the Swag" and Glover's "The Magpies", Allen Curnow's "Wild Iron" and Mary Ursula Bethell's "Pause", found their way into the *Journal* after first being published elsewhere in book form. Yet, as late as 1954, there was an almost apologetic tone when New Zealand poetry was being introduced in the *Journal*. Often local poems would be linked to some part of the social studies curriculum. A case in point, a New Zealand poetry feature in the *School Journal*, Part 4, Autumn 1954, presented a miners' song, "Off to the Diggings"; an evocation of moonlit landscape by David McKee Wright; one of Jessie Mackay's translations of a traditional Māori battle song; and from the ubiquitous William Pember Reeves, an account of the early Dutch explorers, which began with both a head of steam and a regrettable rhyme:

> Southward and eastward had our seamen steered
> And borne back tales of lands wide, arid, weird.

A tendency to employ poets as School Publications editors for at least a decade after the mid-1950s ensured that not only would poetry remain on the agenda but also the verse selected would get a lot better. Looking at the contents of a Part 4 *Journal*, Spring 1961, it is tempting to read the literary preferences reflected therein as being those of Baxter, Johnson, and Campbell. The issue contained a translation of Federico Garcia Lorca, some poems from the Greek Anthology, "The Bedpost" by Robert Graves and, to lighten things, "Some Natural History" by Don Marquis.

When I am very earnestly digging
I lift my head sometimes, and look at the mountains
And muse upon them, muscles relaxing.
I think how freely the wild grasses flower there,
How grandly the storm-shaped trees are massed in their gorges
And the rain-worn rocks strewn in magnificent heaps.

"Pause" by Mary Ursula Bethell, illustrated by Juliet Peter, *School Journal*, Part 4, June 1948

When Tom and Elizabeth took the farm
The bracken made their bed,
And Quardle oodle ardle wardle doodle
The magpies said.

"The Magpies" by Denis Glover, illustrated by Juliet Peter, *School Journal*, Part 4, June 1948

The poet-editors did, however, meet some resistance during the 1960s. For a time, Louis Johnson (Parts 1 and 2) and Alistair Campbell (Parts 3 and 4) "were compelled", writes Brent Southgate:

> *to support the new social studies syllabus with "theme" issues; they can't have been happy about that, because it obviously put the* Journal *in a straitjacket. But by the end of the 60s the* Journal *became a miscellany again, and it really took off*.[6]

Poetry was certainly back in force in 1969: the Part 1 *Journal* contained a suite of eight poems by James K. Baxter, and the Part 2 *Journal* not only ran eleven of Baxter's poems – among them the classics "The Seagull" and "The Firemen" – but also an article by Louis Johnson, "Making Your Own Poems". Having used Baxter's "The Rooster" as a model to explain rhythm, Johnson stated:

> Many children, and older people too, like to write poems when they feel strongly about something or get excited by things. Even quite young children have written poems which are so good that people have printed them in books.

He went on to feature a group of poems by schoolchildren, among them "Telephone Wires", by a twelve-year-old called Mary from Northland, which first appeared in Elwyn Richardson's *In the Early World* (1964) and was later anthologised by Bill Manhire in his *100 New Zealand Poems* (1994).

Telephone Wires

In the far away distance
I can hear the telephone wires
Singing in churches
Like pakehas.

Louis Johnson did not adopt one set of principles for *Journal* poetry and another when pursuing his own literary endeavours. His *Journal* essay ends with a manifesto-like statement that could just as easily have appeared in *Landfall*, extolling emotional content as the crux of poetry:

> You will see that in each of them, the person writing the poem has either had very strong feelings about what he has seen – or has seen it often in an unusual way. Very often, trying to find the right words to describe something makes you look at it more closely. You start to think of things in ways you might not have thought of before. When this happens, you should try writing it down.
>
> Although all sorts of word and sound tricks can be used to help write poems, the important thing is how well you feel what you are writing about.

Mist

A hill full, a hold full,
You cannot catch a bowlful.

Anonymous poem, illustrated by Evelyn Clouston, *School Journal*, Part 2 Number 4, 1970

Among the poems Sam Hunt published in the *Journal* during the 1970s were his much-reprinted "Four Bow-Wow Poems". Interestingly, with a few notable exceptions such as Hunt, poets of the generation after Baxter and Johnson tended to write a kind of poetry that was less accessible to younger readers. Poetry printed in the *Journal* in recent decades has tended to be by poets who write specifically for children – notably among them, Margaret Mahy, Elizabeth Pulford, Alan Bagnall, Pauline Cartwright, and Philippa Werry. Occasionally poems by contemporary "adult" writers have appeared – verse by Lauris Edmond, Elizabeth Smither, Brian Turner, Rachel Bush, Bernadette Hall, Jenny Bornholdt, James Brown, and Glenn Colquhoun.

Four Bow-Wow Poems

The First Bow-Wow Poem

BOW WOW

You woke my mother up this morning
At six o'clock with your barking

So she took away your barks
And put them in the bow-wow box

She tied you up and took your barks away
Now all you do is smile at strangers all day

You aren't a guard dog any more
You aren't even a dog any more!

2

Sam Hunt's "The First Bow-Wow Poem", illustrated by Robin White, *School Journal*, Part 1 Number 4, 1972

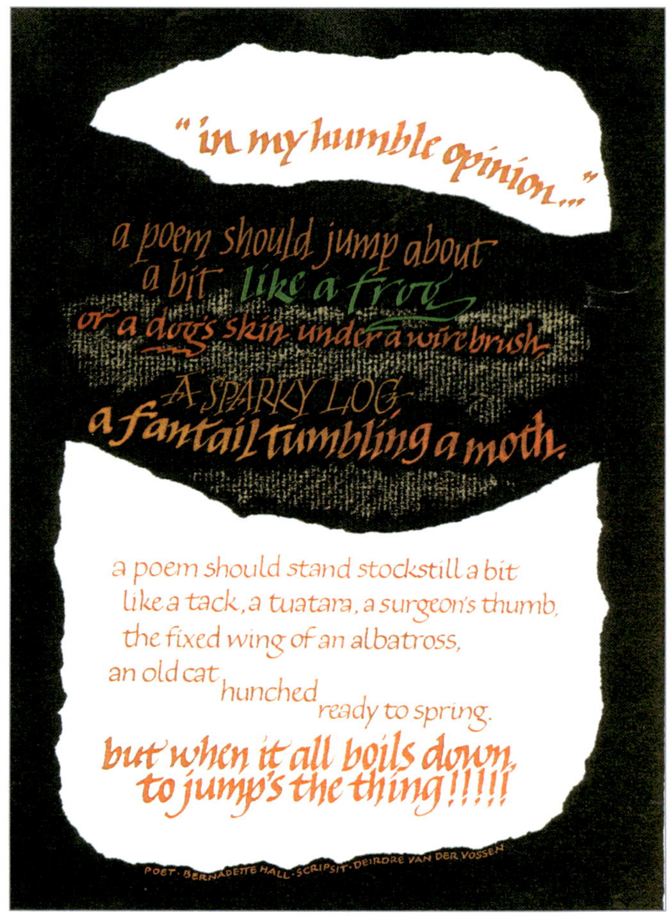

Poem by Bernadette Hall, handwritten by Deirdre van der Vossen, *School Journal*, Part 4 Number 1, 1991

Alan Bagnall, photographed by Meredith Biberstein, for "Stories in My Head: What Inspires the *School Journal's* Most Prolific Writer?", *School Journal*, Part 4 Number 2, 1997

The things I write about are usually based on true events: incidents I've witnessed or heard about ... I store most of my ideas in my head, sometimes for months or even years. Sometimes two or more ideas join together to make one story – that's magic!

There's an old car
Over the fence,
V 8 motor and
Just a few dents.
We kids often
Go for a drive
And pretend the big
Motor comes alive.
I know it really doesn't go,
The fuel it saves
Is real though.

Alan Bagnall

Poem by Alan Bagnall, illustrated by Margaret Nieuwland, *School Journal*, Part 3 Number 2, 1982

Dinosaurs

Tyrannosaurus
Lived before us.
Ultrasaur
Is no more.
Pteranodon
Has been and gone.
Triceratops
Were awful flops.
And as for archaeopteryx,
They ended up in quite a fix.

Poem by Judy Ling, illustrated by Bruce Mahalski, *School Journal*, Part 2 Number 4, 1997

The Drawing Board:

Visual artists and the School Journal

Fraser Williamson, illustration for *School Journal*, Part 1, Number 4, 1999

The Journal has provided generations of illustrators with the opportunity to learn their craft. Until recently you couldn't go anywhere to learn illustrating. It was the Journal and its editors that taught us how to do it, by providing paying work.

Bob Kerr, 2006 [1]

S. B. Maclennan, illustration for "How Books Are Illustrated", *School Journal*, Part 3, August 1945

S. B. Maclennan, illustration for *School Journal*, Part 1, June 1945

Having studied at the Royal College of Art, London, S. B. Maclennan believed in the tradition of finely wrought art, marrying elements of the local scene with fastidious craftsmanship. His work as a painter as well as an illustrator was featured in the *Year Book of the Arts in New Zealand* in 1948 – the same year he was appointed Director of the National Art Gallery, Wellington, a position he would hold for two decades.

Up until the 1940s, the vast majority of illustrations in the *Journal* were sourced from overseas publications. In the course of the Second World War, however, a confident and accomplished local visual element emerged. At the foot of these illustrations were the signatures of Yvonne Bendall, Nancy Parker (nee Bolton), George Woods, Russell Clark, S. B. Maclennan, and E. Mervyn Taylor. Initially, their art accompanied texts reprinted from overseas publications: extracts from *Gulliver's Travels*, *Don Quixote,* and miscellaneous Persian tales. It was as if New Zealand visual art had arrived at the *School Journal* a good few years in advance of New Zealand literature. It would not be until the end of that decade that locally produced fiction began to figure prominently in the *Journal's* contents.

Accompanying this 1940s surge in local content was a concerted effort to educate the readership in the visual language of the illustrator, graphic artist, and typographer. An essay in the Part 1 *Journal,* 1945 by Stuart Maclennan (1903–73) explained how images in the *Journal* were reproduced from metal and wood blocks.

Maclennan concluded his essay – or manifesto, to be more exact – by spelling out his design objectives:

> A worthy book deserves to be beautifully made. The printing must be clear and easily read, and the margins nicely planned. The paper should be strong, pleasant to touch, and neither too white nor too deep in tone ... The illustrations must be in harmony with the author's thoughts and with the type of printing used.

Maclennan's aspirations are worth noting as they encapsulate commonly held objectives for the visual art, typography, and design of the *School Journal* from the mid-1940s at least until the 1960s, at which point design – along with much else in the culture – began to loosen up considerably.

George Woods, illustration for *School Journal*, Part 1, June 1945

George Woods, illustration for "Jacko and the Crocodile: A Story from India", *School Journal*, Part 1, August 1943

Russell Clark, illustration for *School Journal*, Part 4, April 1948

Nancy Bolton, illustration for "The Water Boy", *School Journal*, Part 1, May 1941

"Next Day at Dawn I was awakened by a Comely Old Man."

Yvonne Bendall, illustration for "The Princess and the Serpent – from the Persian Tales", *School Journal*, Part 2, February 1941

Rather than appearing particularly child-friendly, the post-war *Journals* feel more intent on reflecting the ideals of elegance, eloquence, and harmony that their artists and designers held dear. Shades of John Ruskin and William Morris hover over the *Journals* of this period, just as they did the studios of Russell Clark and E. Mervyn Taylor. The thinking was that the values inherent in the publication – equal parts classicism and romanticism, with a dash of New Zealandism – would nourish the aesthetic sensibilities as well as the reading skills and general knowledge of the youthful nation. In that respect, the *School Journal* of this time could be seen as a visionary as well as a pragmatic enterprise. While Maclennan's views on art and culture were essentially conservative, a more radical, modernist cast of mind would enter the *Journal* in the person of Roy Cowan, who was an art editor at School Publications between 1949 and 1959.

As indicated earlier, a desire to explore New Zealand identity became more and more evident in the *Journals* throughout the 1940s. While a few covers immediately after the war bore Tourism Board-style images of idyllic New Zealand landscapes (see page 19), it was the graphic arts that would give the *Journal* its particular look in the decade to come – as it incrementally made the transition from black and white booklet to bound book with coloured covers. Subjects from Māori mythology, history, and contemporary life were increasingly prominent, as were images of local bird life. E. Mervyn Taylor's avian woodcuts came to define not only a period in the history of the *School Journal* but also an important moment in the story of New Zealand art generally – prefiguring the 1960s paintings of Don Binney and Robin White and influencing the work of contemporary photographer Peter Peryer. [2]

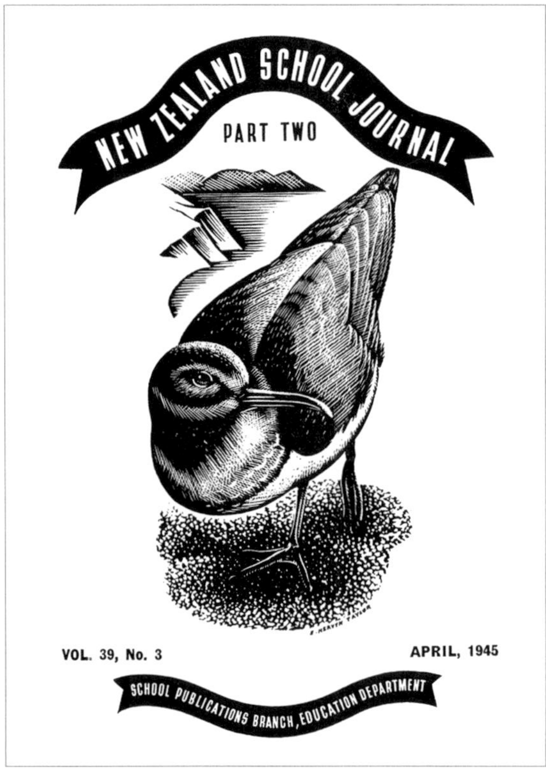

E. Mervyn Taylor, cover illustration, *School Journal*, Part 2, April 1945
Courtesy of the E. Mervyn Taylor Estate

Juliet Peter, cover illustration, *School Journal*, Part 1, May 1946

E. Mervyn Taylor, cover illustration, *School Journal*, Part 4, July 1946

Struggling to find enough drawings for the forthcoming *Journals*, the editorial staff post-1945 busied themselves enlisting new artists. Roy Cowan wrote:

> *The ability to form characters out of their minds, and do a human figure, and so on, turned out to be the rarest qualities, and we were constantly on the lookout. One of the most effective people, and most used, was Russell Clark. Another was Mervyn Taylor. George Woods was a very powerful and dramatic artist. He had a sculptural style of drawing, and an unabashed relish for the human figure.* [3]

During this period, the *School Journal* had some of the country's greatest painters and printmakers on its regular payroll. Other artists employed casually included the French-born painter Louise Henderson (1902–94), who was living in Wellington during the 1940s. As well as contributing a memorable, modernist-inspired view of New York from the air (see page 9), Henderson drew on her French background to illustrate a feature on Paris in 1947.

Louise Henderson, cover illustration for *School Journal*, Part 3, November 1947

This cover illustrated Celia Manson's fictionalised account of growing up in a village near Paris, "Jean, a French Boy". Manson (1908–87) was a New Zealander who lived in France for some years and, with her husband Cecil, was instrumental in establishing the Katherine Mansfield Memorial Scholarship, an annual award enabling a New Zealand writer to spend six months working in Menton on the French Riviera.

During the 1950s, drawings by May Smith (1906–88) appeared intermittently in the *Journal*. Born in India, Smith had arrived in New Zealand in 1920 and studied at Elam School of Art before attending the Royal College of Art in London. She met Frances Hodgkins in Ibiza in 1933, and a friendship developed. Best known for her 1941 portrait *Characterisation in Colour* (in the Auckland Art Gallery Toi o Tamaki collection), Smith was adept at drawing, printmaking, and oil painting. (She also took up textile design with considerable flair and success during the Depression, when she was unable to find sufficient illustrating work.) Her line drawings in the *School Journal* for Roderick Finlayson's "In Auckland Fifty Years Ago" display her acute sense of pattern and design.

May Smith, illustration for "In Auckland Fifty Years Ago" by Roderick Finlayson, *School Journal*, Part 4, Autumn 1957

When interviewed by Peter Shaw in the mid-1980s, Smith was very eager to talk of her *School Journal* work. Shaw recalls:

> *She was a socialist and a stalwart of the WEA so* School Journal *work was a logical extension of her firm belief in the availability of education for all, regardless of social class or gender.* [4]

In 1951, Invercargill-born sculptor Molly Macalister (1920–79) illustrated a series of stories by Ruth Park about a Māori boy called Rupene. Best known for her sculpture *Māori Warrior*, sited at the foot of Queen Street, Auckland (and the subject of Hone Tuwhare's much anthologised poem "To a Maori Figure Cast in Bronze outside the Chief Post Office, Auckland"), Macalister was an insightful and sympathetic interpreter of Māori subjects – as her *Journal* illustrations attest.

Molly Macalister, illustrations for Ruth Park's "Rupene" stories, *School Journal*, Part 1, March–May 1951

Two years after completing her most famous painting, *The Pumping Station* (Auckland Art Gallery Toi o Tamaki collection), Christchurch-based Doris Lusk (1916–90) produced two covers for the Part 1 *Journal* (1960): the first, a playful screen-printed arrangement of dogs and cats, followed by a deftly screened two-colour image of a boy fishing in Lyttelton Harbour, the background hills echoing the landscape subjects for which Lusk is best known.

For Lusk, Macalister, Smith, and Henderson, illustrating was a sideline to their usual artistic practice. Their illustrative work was, however, inadvertently a lesson for them in economy of means, clarity of line, and how to develop the storytelling and scene-setting capabilities of a single image. Among the other prominent painters who contributed drawings during the post-war period were A. Lois White, John Holmwood, W. A. Sutton and, some years later, Eileen Mayo.

Doris Lusk, cover artwork for *School Journal*, Part 1 Number 4, 1960

Doris Lusk, cover artwork for *School Journal*, Part 2 Number 4, 1960

Russell Clark, "the first unofficial art editor"

Russell Clark photographed in 1944 while official war artist in the Pacific. Courtesy of the Alexander Turnbull Library

After working as a graphic designer and then as a teacher – who counted among his students Colin McCahon and Doris Lusk – Russell Clark (1905–66) began publishing in the *Journal* in the early 1940s. His career as an illustrator was interrupted when, during the final phase of World War Two, he was commissioned as an official war artist and stationed in the Solomon Islands. It was upon his return to Wellington after the war that Russell Clark's influence was felt in the *School Journal*. Michael Dunn, in his 1976 study of Clark's drawings, quotes one of the artist's contemporaries at School Publications, J. L. Ewing, who observed that it was Clark who "decided which stories, articles, poems, etc. would be illustrated by which artists. He was in fact the first, though unofficial art editor for School Publications." [5]

His sound academic training and acute powers of observation (particularly when dealing with Māori subjects) raised the artistic standards of the *School Journal* in the immediate post-war period. While his work echoed that of English neo-romantic artists such as Paul Nash and Eric Ravilious, he also introduced a strongly New Zealand flavour.

In a 1948 review, James Shelley praised the artist's responsiveness to his immediate surroundings: "One gets an impression that Mr Clark is part of a real, living community, and that he is very much alive to what is going on around him." [6] Described in the 1948 *Year Book of the Arts in New Zealand* as "a protean performer [whose] extraordinary versatility, wit and invention is rooted in sound drawing, a practical grasp of his materials and a delightful sense of design", [7] Clark went on to become highly regarded as a sculptor and muralist.

Russell Clark illustrations from Rosaline Redwood's "Mutton Birds", *School Journal*, Part 4, June 1947

Russell Clark, cover illustrations, *School Journals*, 1945–49

As with Taylor's images of birds, Clark's refined, energetic drawings of outdoor adventures – on sea as well as land – were immensely popular and have come to define the period in which they were created. He produced over one hundred of his finest drawings for the *School Journal Life in the Pa* series (see pages 22–23), and his drawings continued to appear well into the 1950s, by which time he was working for the *Listener*. In August 1949, the Part 4 *School Journal* included a feature about the artist, "Russell Clark's Illustrations". Following on from Maclennan's essay about book illustration a few years earlier, this profile reflected an eagerness, on the part of the *Journal*, to raise reader awareness of its aesthetic objectives.

In common with many who worked on the *Journal*, Russell Clark was deeply concerned with the public and social applications of art. Illustrating for School Publications – and also for the *Listener* – were tasks he took seriously, not only because they paid the bills and gave him practice as a draughtsman but also because they reached a wide audience.

While visiting the Ureweras in the late 1940s and working on a School Bulletin assignment, *Ruatahuna*, Clark began painting a series of Māori subjects that were to become his best known canvases. *Hokianga Crossroads* (c. 1950) is imbued with both the naturalism and the strong design sense he had developed during the previous decade and a half as an illustrator. The Hokianga painting is also a subtly voiced acknowledgment of the complexities of Māori family life during a century of major changes – as the "crossroads" in the title suggest. It was reproduced in the New Zealand *Arts Year Book*, Number 7 (1951), the same issue that featured J. C. Beaglehole's important essay about School Publications.

Russell Clark, *Hokianga Crossroads*, c. 1950, oil on canvas, 690 x 695 mm
Courtesy of the Fletcher Trust Collection

E. Mervyn Taylor, cover design, *School Journal*, Part 3, Winter 1960

Upon taking up a position as art editor at School Publications in 1944, E. Mervyn Taylor found illustrations for forthcoming publications were in such short supply that he had little choice but to produce them himself, often fishing around in his sketchbooks for images. Although he held the editorial position for under two years, Taylor contributed many drawings and woodcuts to the *Journal* between 1940 and 1964.

According to fellow artist and *Journal* contributor John Drawbridge, Taylor "established the beginnings of a tradition of high standards in illustration, typography and book design in all the School Publications' productions". [8] In a 1982 tribute, Drawbridge recalled, as a young schoolboy, seeing Taylor walking along the road with his artworks under his arm:

> *In those days, it was very unusual to see anyone with a portfolio, and I often wondered what sort of mysteries and magic were hidden inside it. That was in the mid-1940s, and I had no idea, then, that this man was E. Mervyn Taylor. But I knew that he was the first real artist I had ever seen – and there he was getting off the bus, walking home after work and perhaps taking more work home with him. I also had no idea then that many of the illustrations which I, together with thousands of children throughout New Zealand, were very privileged to know and to enjoy in the* School Journals *were made by him.* [9]

Cover images courtesy of the E. Mervyn Taylor Estate

The precise, perfectly poised birds for which E. Mervyn Taylor is best known hark back to his training in jewellery engraving during the 1920s. Taylor's graphic style is synonymous with the *School Journal* of the 1940s, reflecting both a fervour for local subjects and a virtuosic treatment of line and mass. His emblematic versions of kea, kākāpō, huia, and godwit announced the beginning of a new era.

After leaving the *Journal*, Mervyn Taylor established himself as one of the few professional artists working in New Zealand. In the decades since his death, aged 57, in 1964, Taylor's reputation has continued to rise, and prints produced for the *Journal* regularly fetch considerable sums at art auctions. An illustrated biography by Bryan James was published in 2006, further underlining his significance.

E. Mervyn Taylor, ink drawing for R. M. Wheeler's "Sam Albatross", *School Journal*, Part 2, September 1947

E. Mervyn Taylor, in his Karori studio. Courtesy of the E. Mervyn Taylor Estate

In moments of depression, one may feel that the craftsman is almost an extinct bird in New Zealand. It is good, then, to think of Mervyn Taylor chipping away at his block of Southland Beech.

Howard Wadman, *Year Book of the Arts in New Zealand*, Number 3, 1947

Roy Cowan, cover illustration, *School Journal*, Part 2 Number 6, 1960

Important as both a *School Journal* art editor (1949–59) and illustrator, Roy Cowan was a man divided between the art studio and the motor-racing track. "I was interested in motor sports and car-building and other mechanical exploits," he once wrote. "I joined the School Publications Branch in 1949, and contact there with the work of artist-illustrators revived my leaning towards the arts." [10]

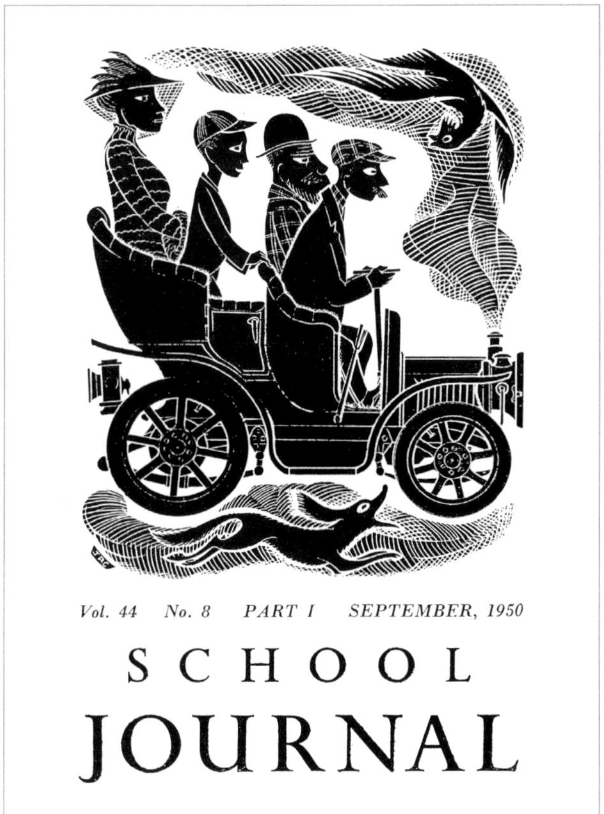

Roy Cowan, cover illustration for *School Journal*, Part 1, September 1950

Like two other prolific illustrators during this period, Joan Dukes and Joan Smith, Roy Cowan also contributed writing to the *Journal*. His fable "Away with Feet" was published in *School Journal*, Part 3, October 1950, and later reprinted. His fascination with automobiles is put to playful use in this Dadaist piece of verbal invention, which is also a madcap political satire. The story is set in the hilly island of Antippity, where a law has been passed forbidding feet – "instead, everyone must wear WHEELS!" All rolls along smoothly until one day a newborn baby, instead of crying, starts honking. The next morning, newspapers are announcing: "Infants can't speak, they toot!" and "Babies want Oil, not Milk!" The upshot of this is that wheels are banned and suddenly feet are reintroduced. And the tramcar coming down the street is much slower than usual – its wheels having been replaced with rows of bare feet.

Cowan met Juliet Peter at School Publications, where she held the position of staff artist from 1946 until 1951. They married in 1952 and, the following year, he was awarded a scholarship that enabled them both to study in England. There Cowan immersed himself in printmaking, drawing, book design, and art history, while Peter studied lithography and pottery. When they returned to work at the *School Journal* – Cowan as editor and Peter as freelance contributor – they brought fresh ideas and a knowledge of the latest techniques in colour printing.

Cowan's work, in particular, marries an awareness of English landscape art with an interest in earthy, porous surfaces more readily associated with pottery than with printmaking – the patterning on his cover for the Summer 1959 Part 3 *Journal* is a striking example (see overleaf).

Roy Cowan, illustrations for his story "Away with Feet", *School Journal*, Part 3, October 1950

Roy Cowan, cover illustration, *School Journal*, Part 3, Summer 1959

The waves looked like mountains. I don't know how to explain what it was like except to say that Mount Ranier, Mount Fuji, and the Rocky Mountains were chasing us. They rose high above the boat, but usually slid under us.

Every once in a while a wave came over and soaked the man at the tiller but the water always drained out quickly through the scuppers. The water was rather warm.

"Jessica's Diary", illustrated by Roy Cowan, *School Journal*, Part 2 Number 6, 1956

Roy Cowan and Juliet Peter with their pottery. Courtesy of Juliet Cowan

Roy Cowan, illustration for "Jessica's Diary", School Journal, Part 2 Number 6, 1956

At the same time as Cowan and Peter were prominent in the *School Journal*, they were becoming respected figures in the art world. Their lithographs had been exhibited at the Architectural Centre Gallery, and their prints, drawings, and ceramics regularly featured in the New Zealand *Arts Year Books*. Drawings by both featured in the December 1957 issue of Charles Brasch's *Landfall*. (Juliet Peter's work had appeared earlier in that publication, in March 1953, alongside that of two other *Journal* contributors, Rita Angus and John Drawbridge.) In 1959, Cowan left the *Journal* to become a freelance artist and potter. After his death in 2006, Cowan's obituary in the *Dominion Post* noted his pride in both his art and his cultural origins – he could reputedly recite his Ngā Puhi whakapapa back thirty-three generations.

Juliet Peter, cover illustration, *School Journal*, Part 3, Summer 1956

One of the most prolific designer-illustrators of the period 1945–60, Juliet Peter contributed hundreds of drawings and dozens of covers to the *Journal*. While she eventually found being a full-time staff artist too restrictive, her remarkable work of the late 1950s suggests that the limitations imposed upon her art in fact worked to her advantage. Her line drawings and two-colour covers are as intrinsic to the identity of the 1950s *School Journal* as E. Mervyn Taylor's and Russell Clark's drawings had been a few years earlier.

Juliet Peter, back cover illustration, *School Journal*, Part 4, Spring 1956

Peter was clearly valued by School Publications as she was profiled more than once on the *Journal's* pages. In *School Journal*, Part 2, October 1948, an episode of R. M. Wheeler's "Te Awa Awa" – which Peter had illustrated with great aplomb – was followed by a feature about both writer and illustrator. A far cry from the days when *Journal* authors did not even get their names acknowledged, Rae Wheeler was profiled enthusiastically while, on the facing page, a striking studio portrait of Juliet Peter by Spencer Digby was accompanied by an apposite, albeit quaint, note:

Juliet Peter, cover illustration for R. M. Wheeler's "Te Awa Awa", *School Journal*, Part 2, October 1948

Juliet Peter was a land girl during the war; and, working with dogs and sheep and horses, she came to know them well. That is why her animals seem as lively as the animals you know on your own farm or in your own street.

Miss Peter does not do all her drawings in the office. Last week she went out stalking a milkman and his horse to get sketches for a story in the Part 1 *Journal*, and another day she walked through half a mile of sticky mud to make drawings inside a wool-shed for the shearing chapter in "Te Awa Awa".

Photograph of Juliet Peter by Spencer Digby, reproduced in *School Journal*, Part 2, October 1948

Peter continued illustrating for the *Journal* into the 1960s although, by this time, much of her energy was directed into making pottery in the studio she shared with Roy Cowan at their Wellington home. Peter's work as a painter and printmaker was acknowledged in 1999, when a solo exhibition was held at City Gallery, Wellington. An extensive interview with art historian Damian Skinner appeared in *Art New Zealand* in 2005, further acknowledging her significance.

Juliet Peter, cover artwork for *School Journal*, Part 2, February 1950

One day Miss Peter looked out of the office window and saw five elephants walking along the street. The elephants had chains on their legs so that they would not move too fast, and the men who were leading them took them along very gently. These men knew there would be trouble if five elephants bolted down a city street.

Now, Miss Peter, who is the artist at the *Journal* office, wanted to see where the elephants were going. She took a notebook and a pencil with her, and she followed the elephants to the park where the circus people were going to pitch their tent.

A circus is a good place for an artist to find pictures, and Miss Peter stayed there most of the day. She watched everyone getting ready for the circus at night. She made a lot of quick drawings of the horses and the elephants and the clowns and the circus riders. When she came back to the office, she used the small pictures in her notebook to help her, and drew two circus covers for the Standard 1 and 2 *Journals*.

Juliet Peter, cover illustration,
School Journal, Part 4, Summer 1956

From the mid-1950s, Juliet Peter, Roy Cowan, Dennis Beytagh, Jill McDonald, and others took masterful advantage of new colour-printing technology, which allowed them to use two-colour screens (with a third colour where the two colours overlap) to create richly textured, atmospheric covers. Current art editor Penelope Newman notes that "the printing techniques that were available at this time influenced the way the illustrations turned out to a certain degree. The colours were mixed specially for each image – they weren't simply from a process colour chart."

Jean Angus, cover drawing for *School Journal*, Part 1, May 1952

A regular *School Journal* contributor during the 1950s, Jean Angus (1915–2005) produced numerous drawings, using heavy and light outlines to create flattened, modernist-inspired designs. Notable among them were her illustrations for the writer/art historian/musician Peter Cape's serialised story "The Caravanners". At times, Jean Angus's work also echoed the decorative traditions of medieval manuscripts – see her rhythmical rendition of two boys and a magpie for Barry Mitcalfe's story "Ricky and Boodle".

For Angus's sister, Rita, freelance work for the *School Journal* provided a useful supplement to her meagre income from painting. In the mid-1950s, Rita Angus (1908–70) produced over fifty drawings for the *Journal*. Importantly, Angus's friendship with Juliet Peter grew over the period they were both involved in the *Journal*, and their relationship became a sustaining one.

It all started one afternoon when my father came home and said that he wasn't going to work any more. I was so surprised that I nearly knocked the model aeroplane I was making on to the floor.

"Not ever any more?" I asked.

"No," said my father. "At least, not the sort of work I've been doing."

"But what are we going to do?" I asked. "Where are we going?"

My mother, who was getting things ready for tea, laughed and said, "Don't sound so worried, Peter; we're not going to starve." She smiled across at my father, and I knew that whatever the secret was, they were both in it.

"You tell him," Father said. He dropped his satchel on the floor and sat down.

Mother wiped her hands on a towel. "Well," she said, "we're going to leave Northcote, and we're going back on the road."

"Back on the road?" I said slowly, because it was very hard to believe. "You mean, in a caravan again?"

Peter Cape ,"The Caravanners", illustrated by Jean Angus [Jones], *School Journal*, Part 3, July 1951

Jean Angus [Jones], illustration for Barry Mitcalfe's "Ricky and Boodle", *School Journal*, Part 3, Winter 1954

In the 1960s, the two would go on sketching expeditions around Thorndon, Island Bay, and elsewhere. Juliet Peter and Roy Cowan, along with Russell Clark, supported Angus by purchasing works directly from her.

In a letter to composer Douglas Lilburn, dated 23 June 1954, Rita Angus apologised for taking so long completing an Otago landscape painting he had commissioned from her. The delay was on account, she wrote, of a drawing commission for School Publications:

> *31 drawings since I began these last November. In these drawings I've hoped to maintain an artistic standard, high as possible; drawing helps painting and vice versa.* [11]

Rita Angus, "Kie-Kie", illustration for A. W. Anderson's "The Maori as a Plant Hunter", *School Journal*, Part 4, Autumn 1954

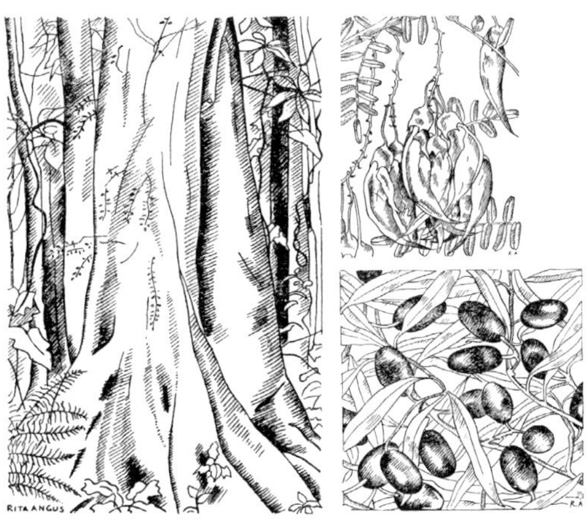

Rita Angus, illustrations for A. W. Anderson's "The Maori as a Plant Hunter", *School Journal*, Part 4, Autumn 1954

Rita Angus, cover illustration for *School Journal*, Part 1, August 1955

The *Journal* assignments demanded painstaking analysis of native plants and some very refined drawing. While Angus found working in black and white a challenge, it could also be a frustration. She wrote to her sister on 23 June 1954: "I'm getting through the last set of drawings only by painting as well. I cannot continue to draw without paint." [12]

Angus's drawings also appeared on the covers of the *School Journal* Parts 1 and 2 in August 1955; and a further suite of nature studies – these ones sketchier in quality – appeared in the Part 2 *Journal* in 1956. Technically, Angus's drawings share the refinement – almost Oriental in its distilled quality – and flattened spatial treatment of the botanical watercolours that she produced intermittently from the 1940s until the 1960s. No doubt considering the drawings serious pieces of work, Angus initialled or signed most of them. Less successful than the botanical studies were two portrait studies published in 1954 – of Dr D. C. Solander and Sir Joseph Banks – which appear strictly made to order.

Tellingly, she left these unsigned. Portraiture, for Angus, was always a serious, slow process, and cooking up portraits from historical source material was not in her nature.

Rita Angus, illustration for "Plants", *School Journal*, Part 2 Number 3, 1956

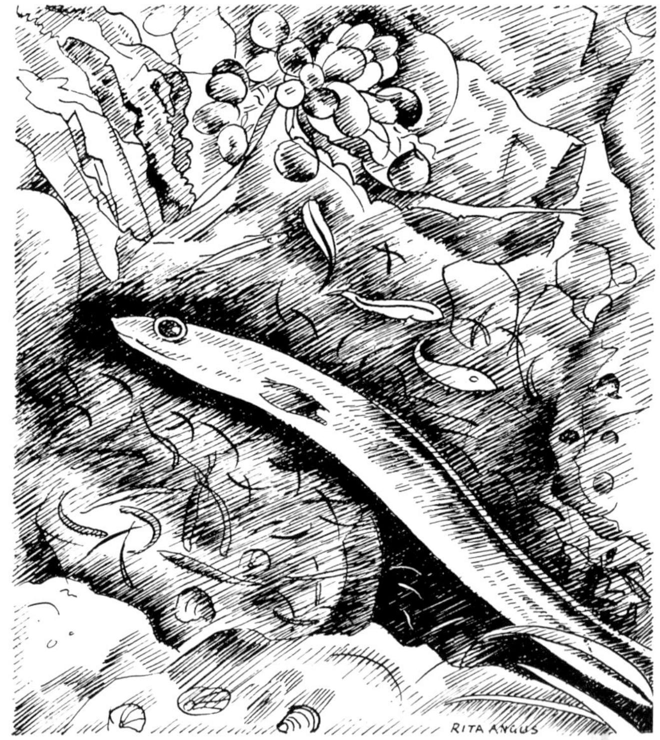

He found a hole in the rock, then rose again, searching for food. His dark thin body flicked towards an insect floating on the water. He knew he was a child no longer. Now he was tuna, he was a young eel.

He waved his long fins, felt the fresh cool water flowing in his mouth and over his gills, and gazed eagerly about him. He heard the sound of a young trout rising. The valley grew darker. A bright star came over the mountains and sent its pale, blue light sparkling into the pool.

John Caselberg, "The Story of Tuna", illustrated by Rita Angus, *School Journal*, Part 4, Autumn 1957

Rita Angus, "Mountain totara, *Podocarpus nivalis*", *School Journal*, Part 4, Spring 1954

On other occasions, Angus produced a drawing of a tuna and a memorable table-top still life (a single image that deftly incorporated a number of perspectival views). In 1956, she illustrated Ruth Ross's "The Family Tree", a story about a boy visiting a rural graveyard and coming to a realisation of his own Māori ancestry. Here, the clearly delineated architecture and foregrounded gravestone prefigure the last suite of paintings Angus produced: the oil paintings of Bolton Street Cemetery, Wellington, where she and Juliet Peter spent many hours sketching. The *Journal* illustration, with its fastidious rooflines and gravestone contour, is echoed dramatically in Angus's 1969 painting *Untitled (Demolished Cemetery)*.

Rita Angus, illustration
for A. W. Anderson's
"The Pioneer Plant Hunters",
School Journal, Part 4, Winter 1954

Rita Angus in her studio,
working on *Untitled (Demolished Cemetery)*,
photographed by Marti Friedlander.
Courtesy of the photographer

Ted walked from stone to stone. "Who's this?" he asked, stopping in front of one and reading out the inscription: "'Miriama Matthews, died June 1871.' Who was she?"

"Old John's wife. Maori of course. I suppose you knew your great-great-grandmother was a Maori?"

"I'd heard there'd been a Maori somewhere in the family, but I didn't know just where."

"Man, there's a whole tribe of them, not just one." But Ted wasn't listening, he was counting tombstones.

From Ruth Ross, "The Family Tree", illustrated by Rita Angus, *School Journal*, Part 4, Winter 1956

Contributions from down the Corridor

In 1954, Director of the Arts and Crafts Branch Gordon Tovey wrote a series of instructive features for the *School Journal*, the first about making models using cardboard and paint (see page 11) and the second instructing children in the art of wire sculpture. To accompany the latter, John Drawbridge produced Alexander Calder-inspired line drawings of a horse, a cow, and a very kinetic skier (see page 146) to suggest the kinds of things children could make.

John Drawbridge, cover illustration and drawings for Esther Archdall's article "Puppets", *School Journal*, Part 3, Spring 1954

(left) John Drawbridge, cover illustration, *School Journal*, Part 3, Spring 1955

In a similarly pedagogical vein, Drawbridge contributed a homely modernist cube as the cover motif for a subsequent *Journal*. The latter cover – which feels like a good-natured joke about modernist house design – accompanied a feature about making "pictures in a box" or dioramas. Drawbridge also illustrated an enthusiastic Part 3 article by Esther Archdall on puppet shows, in which the author laid out reasons why puppet shows were superior to ordinary plays: "you can make better costumes, and once you have prepared the play you can show it with a very little fuss almost at a moment's notice."

As well as producing *Journal* covers, John Drawbridge designed a series of covers for School Publications' Sāmoan language journal, *Tusitala mo Vasege Tetele Samoa*. Fifteen years later, an abstract cover design by Drawbridge was included in a series of covers by contemporary artists (*School Journal*, Part 4 Number 1, 1970).

John Drawbridge, cover illustration and drawings to accompany "Pictures in a Box", *School Journal*, Part 4, Spring 1954

Anne McCahon and Colin McCahon

In the early 1950s, painter Colin McCahon, his artist wife, Anne, and their children were living in uncertain circumstances in Christchurch. McCahon had yet to establish himself as an artist, and family life was precarious, emotionally as well as financially. In 1953, they moved north to a damp house in Titirangi, Auckland. Encouraged by editor Roy Cowan, Anne McCahon, who had trained as an artist before family life took over, began producing drawings for the *School Journal*. Art historian Linda Tyler records that Cowan became a mentor figure for Anne McCahon at a time when all eyes were on her husband's career:

> *For Anne, who was just emerging from an intensive few years of raising four children – her youngest was now a year old – this was a significant opportunity ... It meant regular payments to supplement the meagre family income.* [13]

Anne McCahon contributed to the *Journal* regularly over the next eight years, producing over fifty illustrations in 1955 alone. With their heavy outlines, the drawings have an affinity with Colin McCahon's early figurative paintings, hinting at a common interest in folk and religious art. Anne McCahon's drawings are impressive for their economy of means and also – something in short supply amongst New Zealand illustrators at this time – their sense of humour.

Anne McCahon, illustration for "Lazy Jack", *School Journal*, Part 1, October 1954

When Cowan left the *Journal* in 1959, Anne McCahon ceased regularly contributing illustrations, although her drawings appeared in the *School Journal* as late as 1975, when a suite of ink and wash drawings accompanied "The Wise Man – A folk tale from Korea". While Anne McCahon's career as an exhibiting artist effectively ended in 1945, her drawings are a highlight of the 1950s *School Journal* and a significant achievement on their own terms. In an era characterised by the fastidious, detailed art of Maclennan, Clark, and Taylor, she introduced not only an element of the spontaneous and playful but also a robust earthiness.

Anne McCahon, illustration for "Lazy Jack", *School Journal*, Part 1, October 1954

Anne McCahon, illustration for "The Wise Man – A folk tale from Korea", *School Journal*, Part 3 Number 4, 1975

Anne McCahon, cover illustrations, *School Journals*, 1953–55

Colin McCahon, cover artwork for *School Journal*, Part 4 Number 2, 1971

Like many artists of his generation, Colin McCahon believed in the artist's responsibility to communicate ideas about art to audiences of all ages. To this end, he regularly taught at summer schools around the country. In 1981, he contributed a memoir to the School Publications journal for teachers, *Education* (Volume 30 Number 3), looking back on the experiences of primary school that galvanised his decision a decade later to become an artist:

> Tennyson, Wordsworth, struggling with the moderns, and wonderful exercises in formal English spelling. You never knew what was happening to you. Poetry – words – words and pictures – and music – and grabbing it all ...
>
> "Tales out of School: Well-known New Zealanders Look back at their Education", pages 32–33

Reminiscent of the paintings of Barnett Newman, this minimalist design was, on a scale of School Publications designs, very abstract. Art editors Terence Taylor and Gordon Walters plucked it from their file of commissioned images and installed it on the *Journal* cover in 1971.

Peter Campbell, cover illustration, *School Journal* Part 3, Winter 1959

Among the other painters of the 1950s who found themselves lugging a folio along the corridor to the *Journal* office was Dennis Knight Turner (born 1923), whose most considerable assignment for School Publications was a 1962 Bulletin entitled *East Coast Village*, which was followed by a larger-scale collection of drawings for A. H. and A. W. Reed, *Tangi*.

Known internationally for his illustrations for *Pippi Longstocking*, the English artist Richard Kennedy was a frequent contributor during the late 1950s, sending by long-distance mail numerous drawings in his characteristically flowing, rhythmical style. Notable among them were illustrations for stories by Alistair Campbell.

Around the same time, Robert Ellis (born 1929) illustrated numerous stories, including Ruth Dallas's "The Elephant" and "At the Show". Born in England, Ellis had served as an aerial photographer shortly after World War Two before emigrating to New Zealand. At the time he started producing freelance illustrations for the *Journal*, he was a lecturer in design at Elam School of Art, Auckland University. Among his other assignments were "Two Maori Stories" (retold by Margaret Orbell) in *School Journal*, Part 3, Winter 1960, one of which was the now-famous legend of Paikea, the whale rider.

Richard Kennedy, illustration for Alistair Campbell's "The River", *School Journal*, Part 3, Spring 1958

There was no mistaking Uncle Mick's walk, hands in pockets, head down, peering this way and that, as he walked along. Nora jumped beside him, in bare legs and sandals, wearing the same old dress that she wore to school; but her hair was combed and tidy, and she smiled so widely her white teeth glistened. Nora didn't care about not having a new dress; she never knew what she had on; she would have been happy in any dress.

From Ruth Dallas' "At the Show", illustrated by Robert Ellis, *School Journal*, Part 4, Summer 1959

Then Ruatapu recited a magic spell, and sent five great waves across the ocean after Paikea. But Paikea was too far away, and he came to land just before the waves reached him. The waves hit the shore and bounced off again, and went back across the ocean. They rushed over Ruatapu, who was still in the sea, and Ruatapu was drowned through his own magic.

"Two Maori Stories – Ruatapu and Paikea", retold by Margaret Orbell, illustrated by Robert Ellis, *School Journal*, Part 3, Winter 1960

John Pascoe, Ans Westra, and Photography in the School Journal

John Pascoe. Photograph courtesy of the Alexander Turnbull Library

> New Zealand in the past has suckled men who have photographed barrels of lush pastureland dominated by posterish Egmont, trainloads of pseudo-Maori dancers, while Mount Cook from the bathroom window of the Hermitage has sadly slunk through lots of lenses. Where are the documentary stories of the gold prospectors, the deer killers, the growth of a dairy factory, the monotony of wharf labour, the discomfort of a miner's calling, the adaptation of the Maori worker to city life and environment?
>
> John Pascoe, *Landfall*, December 1947

A contributor to the *School Journal* and *Post-Primary School Bulletins* between 1947 and 1970, John Pascoe (1908–72) has been described as New Zealand's greatest unrecognised photographer. An outdoorsman, editor, and writer as well as a photo-artist, Pascoe divided his considerable energy between his wide-ranging pursuits, often marrying his numerous enthusiasms by writing about mountaineering or by incorporating his photographs into his writing. In *School Journal*, Part 4, August 1953, he proffered some practical instruction on how to make a snow cave and build a "snow house", having himself built one "at 7000 feet on Ruapehu" and slept in it for one night. The article ended on an upbeat note, with Pascoe announcing that "New Zealand snowfields have the raw material, and we like living there as a change from a home in the city" – a hearty highland sentiment shared by poets such as James K. Baxter around that time. In a lighter vein, John Pascoe's other contributions included a serial, "Was Wicky Lazy?" (1950), which was illustrated by Juliet Peter and prefigured the madcap rural escapades of Jack Lasenby's Uncle Trev three decades later.

Wicky had two dogs, whose names were Sou-wester and Nor-wester because they could both run after the sheep as fast as the wind. Wicky called them Sou and Nor for short. One day Wicky was told by the farmer Scrumshaw to climb a range of hills and bring the sheep back for their bath. Sheep do really have a bath, but it is usually called a dip.

Wicky climbed fast up the hill which was something he liked doing. Sou and Nor trotted alongside him and swept the grass with their tails. Soon they climbed above the grassy part of the hill and met some steep rock. Wicky climbed that too, and he could see that Sou and Nor would not fall off the rock, because they were swishing their tails like men on a tight rope at a circus who keep their balance by waving umbrellas.

Above the rock, Sou and Nor sat down to scratch their fleas. A baby flea had jumped on to Wicky, and Wicky scratched away too.

From John Pascoe's "Was Wicky Lazy?", illustrated by Juliet Peter, *School Journal*, Part 2, February 1950

John Pascoe, cover photograph for *School Journal*, Part 1 Number 5, 1961

John Pascoe, Rene children and Jane, D'Urville Island, January 1961
Courtesy of Dorothy Pascoe and the Alexander Turnbull Library

John Pascoe, Te Momo and son fishing, D'Urville Island, January 1961
Courtesy of Dorothy Pascoe and the Alexander Turnbull Library

Pascoe's photographs appeared in two significant features in 1961 and 1970 respectively. In 2005, images from these were included in a major touring exhibition of his work, *Songs of Innocence – Photographs of a New Zealand Childhood*. Pascoe's "family" images, considered primarily of interest to children aged six to eight in 1970, were belatedly given their due recognition as significant works of "serious" photography. The two images from the 1970 photo-essay reproduced above were both included in *Songs of Innocence*.

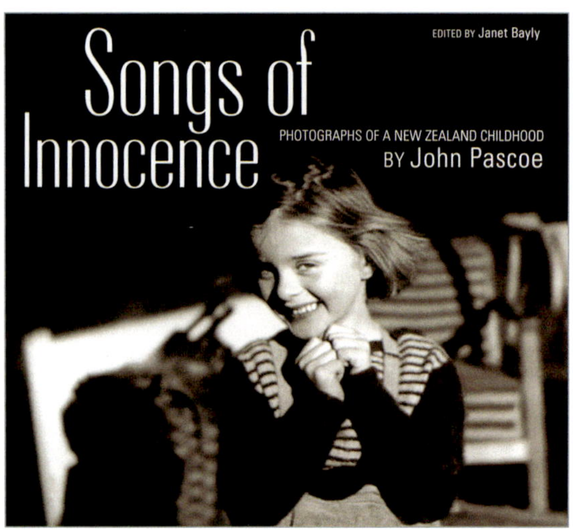

Songs of Innocence: Photographs of a New Zealand Childhood,
John Pascoe, edited by Janet Bayly,
Waikanae: Mahara Gallery, 2005
Courtesy of Mahara Gallery and Pacific Press

Although photography has been less integral to the *School Journal's* visual identity than drawings and screen-printed images, the work of John Pascoe and others has played an important part in the *Journal's* history. As far back as the First World War, photographs were reproduced in the *Journal* – initially using a primitive dot-screen process, which offered a very grey version of reality (and one that reflected the writing accurately, a less than charitable commentator might add). With the rise of high-quality graphic art during the 1940s and 50s, photographs became much less prominent, although they bounced back in the 1960s with the advent of increasing social-studies-based content and improved printing technology.

Most notable among the *School Journal* photographers from the late 1950s onwards is Ans Westra (born in Leiden, Holland, 1936), who, while working for School Publications, established herself as one of New Zealand's leading documentary photographers. An all-photography issue, *School Journal*, Part 1 Number 2, 1966, opened with the photo-essay "What's Tommy Doing?" by Ans Westra with text by Louis Johnson. This was followed by "Mountain Holiday" with text by Joyce Royle and photographs by Grieg Royle – and, to close, "Suzie's Family", scenes from the life of a domestic cat, written and photographed by Ans Westra.

Ans Westra, cover photograph for *School Journal*, Part 1 Number 2, 1966. Courtesy of the photographer

Ans Westra, photograph from "The Circus Comes to Town", *School Journal*, Part 2 Number 2, 1965
Courtesy of the photographer

Tommy was whistling a merry tune very softly. He was leaning against the wall of a wharf-shed.

"What's Tommy doing?" we all asked at once.

"Stand back, stand back," called Tommy. "There's something there!" The string was bobbing up and down in his hand. Quickly Tommy hauled the string up.

We all gathered around. With a final flick, Tommy hauled it through the hole in the wharf. And on the end, wriggling and squirming, was a fat little herring.

From Louis Johnson's "What's Tommy Doing?", with photographs by Ans Westra, *School Journal*, Part 1 Number 2, 1966. Courtesy of the photographer

Ans Westra, cover photograph for *Washday at the Pa*, School Publications, 1961
Courtesy of the photographer

Westra took photographs for the 1961 School Bulletin *Washday at the Pa*, which was famously withdrawn from circulation soon after its appearance, following protests from both Māori and Pākehā groups. She also produced book-length photo-essays for the *Journal*, including *Children at Play* and *Holiday in the Capital* (both 1964) and *The Circus Comes to Town* (1965). The latter publication was an extended piece of accessible photo-journalism although, as was the case with much of Westra's commissioned work, there were some remarkable pictures amidst the workaday ones. Westra's touching photograph of a child peering through a gap in the side of the circus tent reflects her fascination and empathy with children – the same qualities so evident in her iconic photograph *Students Performing, Whatatutu Primary School, near Wairoa*, 1963.

Ans Westra, *Students Performing, Whatatutu Primary School, near Wairoa*, 1963.
Courtesy of the photographer

Among other photographers contributing to the *Journal* was Helen Buttfield, whose nature photographs were a staple of the *School Journal* during the 1970s. Other established photo-artists whose work appeared in the *Journal* were Les Cleveland, who contributed a photo-essay about film-making in 1961; Robin Morrison, whose contributions included a photo-essay about water purity levels at an Auckland beach; and Marti Friedlander, whose photograph *Fakaofo, Tokelau* graced the inside cover of a 1979 Part 4 *Journal* and was included in the Auckland Art Gallery exhibition and catalogue *Marti Friedlander: Photographs* (2000). Tom Shanahan, whose day job was playing trombone with the New Zealand Symphony Orchestra, also contributed work during the 1980s, notably a suite of Hong Kong photographs to accompany "The Camp of the Boat People" by Norman Bilbrough in *School Journal*, Part 4 Number 3, 1989. A doyen of contemporary documentary photographers, Auckland-based Gil Hanly continues to produce work for the *School Journal* (see page 140).

Jill McDonald, illustration for "AEIOU", *School Journal*, Part 2 Number 2, 1966

Jill McDonald, Graham Percy, Clare Bowes, and the 1960s

By the mid-1960s, specialist illustrators were emerging on the New Zealand scene – among them Graham Percy, Clare Bowes, and Olga Volger. Inspired by the rise in children's picture-book art internationally, these artists began producing work that was more attuned to young readers, presented more overt narrative content and more humour, and increasingly used colour. Gone were the refined strategies of E. Mervyn Taylor, although the best of the new wave of artists certainly maintained Taylor's degree of commitment and technical prowess.

Illustrator and art editor Clare Bowes recalls:

> *During the summer of 1964–65, an Elam friend and I scored a holiday job at School Publications in Upper Willis Street. This was the result of a suggestion from Graham Percy that we visit School Publications in Wellington and show them work we had been doing. We learned a large amount at that job, and it was there that I met Jill McDonald who, I believe, single-handedly changed the look of the* Journals *in the mid-1960s. I admired her work hugely – her originality, humour, draughtsmanship, intelligence. Graham Percy's work, too, was superb.* [14]

Jill McDonald at Penguin Books in the 1960s
Courtesy of the McDonald family.

Born in Auckland in 1927, Jill McDonald was educated at Marsden School, Wellington before studying architecture at Auckland University. During the 1950s, she was a member of the Architectural Centre and established herself as an illustrator before taking up the position of art editor on the *School Journal*. After emigrating to England in 1965, she was employed by Penguin Books to reinvigorate the Puffin Books imprint – a task she achieved with consummate skill and vision.

After her untimely death from melanoma in London in 1982, an obituary in *The Times* by Puffin Books editor Kaye Webb acknowledged her "brilliant use of colour and unique style. Everything she drew or wrote contained the same joyfulness and delight in life which was the essence of her personality". When asked by schoolchildren what thrilled her most in life, she replied, "Dribbling cerulean blue into a puddle of rose carthamine, and bashing a bully."

Jill McDonald, cover illustration for Margaret Mahy's *The Wind between the Stars*, *School Journal*, Part 3 Number 3, 1965

Jill McDonald, cover illustrations for *School Journals* 1955 56

Jill McDonald is a towering figure in the history of the *School Journal* – as an editor and as a practising artist. Under her art editorship between 1959 and 1965, the *Journal* adopted a far more relaxed, playful, and irreverent character. "The only overall credo I've ever had regarding books for children," wrote McDonald, "is that if they look entertaining or exciting or amusing enough to be worth the effort of reading them, children will make that effort." [15]

As early as 1955, McDonald's immensely detailed drawings had become a feature both inside and on the covers of the *School Journal*. These intricate images manifested a drawing technique that was the envy of other *Journal* artists. Fellow illustrator Peter Campbell recalls the extraordinary evolution of her work:

> *Jill McDonald had trained as an architect and produced artwork of a perfection beyond the ability of most of us. Once, as a kind of game, she fitted all the detailed drawings for a book onto a single sheet of watercolour paper, as neat as a jigsaw puzzle. By the mid-1960s, McDonald's drawing style had changed dramatically. Gone were the cross-hatching and academic rendering of figures and nature. By the time she illustrated stories by Margaret Mahy, the line was softer and warmer, the works full of youthfulness and a kind of folk-art-derived optimism.* [16]

Having found, by the mid-1960s, the perfect creative partner in Margaret Mahy, McDonald illustrated two of the classic *School Journals* devoted entirely to the writer: *A Lion in the Meadow* (see pages 64–65) and *The Wind between the Stars* (1966). In the 1970s, McDonald was quick to soak up some of the pop-inclined energy of the times and she began producing hard-edged, angular images(see page 68).

Graham Percy illustration for Patricia Mason's "Coal and Mrs Cat" in *Ten Tales*, *School Journal*, Part 1 Number 5, 1965

Jill McDonald, cover illustration, *School Journal*, Part 1 Number 5, 1965

Another prolific contributor to the *School Journal* during the 1960s, Graham Percy was born in Stratford in 1938. He studied at Elam School of Fine Arts, University of Auckland and the Royal College of Art, London. Based in England for the past three decades, he has illustrated many books, including *The Fantastic Flying Journey* by Gerald Durrell (1987) and a remarkable picture book for adults, *Arthouse* (1994).

The tradition of commissioning painters to design covers or illustrate stories continued in the 1960s and 70s, with work appearing from Gretchen Albrecht, Michael Smither, Don Binney, and Julia Morison. Brent Wong – who later became well known for his super-real depictions of New Zealand landscape with vast geometric, concrete clouds floating above it – was enlisted in 1965 to illustrate stories by Louis Johnson and Marilyn Duckworth. He also produced a delightful cover for a Part 1 *Journal* – his birds located resolutely at the far end of the aviary from Mervyn Taylor's. Maybe Ronald Barber's owls from a 1966 *Journal* would be perched somewhere in the middle?

THE OLD MAN AND THE BEAR

by Jack Lasenby

an old story from Lapland

DRAWING BY JULIA MORISON

An old man, a wolf, a reindeer and a bear stood by a river. Winter was coming.

"We must cross the river," said the old man, "or we'll die of the cold. You have warm coats, but the cold water will kill me."

"Wolf," said the old man, "will you help me across the river?"

"No," said the wolf, "help yourself!" and he swam across the river.

"Reindeer," said the old man, "will you help me?"

"No," said the reindeer, "help yourself," and he swam across the river.

"I will help you," roared the bear. "Climb on my back." The old man was carried across the river. He was dry, and the bear's thick coat kept him warm.

The wolf and the reindeer laughed at the bear.

"Wolf and Reindeer," said the old man, who was really a god, "you would not help me, so I will not help you. All winter, you will be cold and you will have to search for food."

"Bear," he said, "you were kind to me, so I will be kind to you. All winter you will sleep in your warm coat until spring comes again."

That is why the bear sleeps all winter. ★

Julia Morison, illustration for Jack Lasenby's retelling of "The Old Man and the Bear", *School Journal*, Part 1 Number 2, 1976.
The spikiness of the forms and the taut outlines in Morison's 1976 illustrations subtly prefigure her later art. It was nearly three decades later that Morison wrote and illustrated a children's book of her own: a Gothic shopping odyssey for grown-up children, *The Butler's New Clothes* (2002). In the meantime, Morison established herself as one of New Zealand's most accomplished, if often perplexing, artists.

Ronald Barber, illustration for Irene Pearl's "The Eagle's Dinner", *School Journal*, Part 2 Number 3, 1966

Like many other art students at Wellington Polytechnic during the 1960s, Ron Barber was encouraged by his teacher, John Drawbridge, to take up freelance work for School Publications.

Brent Wong, cover illustration for *School Journal*, Part 1 Number 2, 1965

Michael Cox, cover illustration for *School Journal*, Part 1 Number 2, 1969

While New Zealand's bicentenary in 1969 was met with the predictable series of informative historical articles in the *Journals*, all dutifully presented, the art department commissioned a series of mischievously fluorescent cover designs for the Parts 1 and 2 *Journals* from Michael Cox and Trevor Plaisted. Here we had, in stereo, a "Captain Cook for our times".

By the early 1970s, the pollen-laden winds of the flower power movement were blowing through School Publications. Cover designs by Graham Percy figured well into that decade, his energetic circus-inspired scenes being used for successive *Journals*. What little remained of the *Journal's* conservative former self was well and truly vanquished by a new generation of designers. "Psychedelia held sway amongst commercial designers and illustrators during the late '60s", observed Athol McCredie in *Fabulous and Familiar: Children's Reading in New Zealand, Past and Present* (1991):

Trevor Plaisted, cover illustration for *School Journal*, Part 2 Number 3, 1969

Nan Reid, cover illustration for *School Journal*, Part 2 Number 4, 1970

> *Flattened perspective, fussy decoration (often composed of parallel wavy lines) and broad colour were hallmarks, as were young women of the knock-kneed, wide-eyed, innocent looking, nature's child variety. Graham Percy and Vanya Lowry were two exponents of the style at this point in their careers.* [17]

Using repetitive patterns usually associated with textile design, Nan Reid's cover art for a 1970 *Journal* (see above) was inspired by Susi R. Collins' story "Ted and his Canada Geese". While, during the 1940s, the graphic style of the *School Journal* owed much to E. Mervyn Taylor's iconic depictions of native birds, over the next three decades artists like Anne McCahon, Juliet Peter, Jill McDonald, and Nan Reid added geese, roosters, pigeons, and sparrows to the ornithological rostrum.

Ralph Hotere c. 1979
photographed by Marti Friedlander
Courtesy of the photographer and
Ralph Hotere

Ralph Hotere, painting reproduced on the cover of *Maori Children and the Teacher*, School Publications, 1972

Reminiscent of his work published in *Te Ao Hou* earlier in the 1960s, two organic designs by Ralph Hotere accompanied "Drift", a short story by his friend O. E. Middleton. The two would later collaborate, at *Landfall* editor Charles Brasch's behest, on a book of stories and drawings, *The Loners*, published by Square and Circle in 1972. The same year, Hotere's oil study of the giant Northland kauri, Tāne Mahuta, appeared on the cover of the Department of Education publication *Maori Children and the Teacher*.

Ralph Hotere, illustrations for O. E. Middleton's "Drift", *School Journal*, Part 4 Number 2, 1969

These drawings are from a folder of illustrations by Ralph Hotere, many of them relating to Māori myths, which are held in the School Publications files at Archives New Zealand.

Robin White, cover illustration, *School Journal*, Part 3 Number 1, 1972

Robin White's stylised images of New Zealand people, birds, and landscape are icons of the 1970s. As well as designing this *Journal* cover, White also produced a cover image of hill country and water, which illustrated an article on "The Soil Conservation and Rivers Control Council" in *School Journal*, Part 1 Number 3, 1971. In a much less characteristic vein, she illustrated Sam Hunt's poems in a 1972 *Journal* (see page 92).

Gordon Walters, cover illustration for *School Journal*, Part 4 Number 1, 1972

Painter Gordon Walters worked as an art editor at School Publications for two years in the early 1970s. Terence Taylor, who shared an office with him, recalled that the artist considered the job primarily a meal ticket. However, during his stint as an art editor, he did produce a *Journal* cover – a hybrid of one of his famous koru paintings and an aerial view of a hotplate cooker. (Terence Taylor remembers it fondly as the "paper-clip" cover.)

Mass Appeal and Mass Disapproval: Comics in the School Journal

In the 1950s, the education system was, for the most part, at odds with the phenomenon of the comic book. So was the general public. A panel of experts – including poet A. R. D. Fairburn – on a National Radio programme devoted to the "problem" famously reached the conclusion that "allowing children to read comics at school was rather like giving them free methylated spirits to drink in schools instead of free milk". Certainly comics were considered anathema to the *School Journal* of the time. This was, after all, the heyday of the cover art of E. Mervyn Taylor and Russell Clark.

By the mid-1960s, however, *Journal* artists were drawing upon comic-book techniques and approaches – witness Graham Percy's carnivalesque assemblages and the pop-inspired images of Clare Bowes and Michael Cox. Things would become even more comics-friendly in the 1970s with the arrival of Vanya Lowry. By then, School Publications was seeking out the best cartoonists and comic artists in the country – among them Rosemary McLeod, who was well known in the mid-1970s for her weekly column in the *Listener*.

Trace Hodgson, illustration for Maryan Moss's "Carlos Comes to Stay", *School Journal*, Part 2 Number 1, 1988

Other cartoonists in the *School Journal* included Murray Ball, David Bromhead, and Tom Scott – who illustrated a 1976 account of aviatrix Jean Batten completing her England–New Zealand flight, "Flying Alone across the Tasman Sea". Inspired in equal parts by two gurus of comic art, Robert Crumb and Ralph Steadman, Trace Hodgson produced suitably shrill drawings to illustrate Maryan Moss's "Carlos Comes to Stay", a tale of a problematic canine house guest.

During the 1970s, comic-book formats were used to introduce readers to foreign languages and, by the 1980s, to introduce Māori language. By the 1990s, a few "orthodox" comic strips were being included in the *Journal* – among them Michael Wilson's "The Phantom Door Knocker" (Part 4 Number 1, 1997) and the four-part series "Suzie and the Space Nuts" (2000), written and drawn by Lorenzo Van Der Lingen. Such cartoon features have, however, tended to be sporadic rather than long-running. Most recently, comic artists including Hicksville author Dylan Horrocks (born 1966) and Tim Bollinger (born 1962) have been enlisted to illustrate stories in the *School Journal*.

Far more noticeable than comics themselves in the *School Journal* is the influence comic strips have had on virtually all the illustrators who have contributed in recent decades, an influence immediately apparent in the work of Phillip Webb, Eleanor Meecham, Ali Teo, Trevor Pye, Steve Templer, and Jennifer Lautusi, among others.

Tim Bollinger, illustration for David Hill's "Once Bitten", *School Journal*, Part 4 Number 3, 1994

Rosemary McLeod, illustration for "The Thirteen Flies", *School Journal*, Part 3 Number 4, 1975

Cover of *School Journal*, Part 4 Number 2, 2006

Whereas the *School Journal* in earlier decades featured cover artwork alongside standardised typography and formatting, by the 1970s and 80s graphic designers were reinventing the *Journal's* appearance issue by issue, introducing new typefaces and sometimes using the art of more than one artist to create composite covers – as is the case with the *School Journal*, Part 4 Number 2, 2006, which was designed by Penelope Newman, incorporating cartoon drawings by Dylan Horrocks and a well-rendered crocodile from Pepin van Roojen.

From Bare Feet to Sneakers – Dick Frizzell

Dick Frizzell in his Ponsonby studio, 1994, photographed by Robert Cross
Courtesy of the photographer

Dick Frizzell, illustration for Jane Buxton's "The Fleas at the Pet Show", *School Journal*, Part 1 Number 3, 1990

Widely known for his pop-art-inspired images of New Zealand life, Dick Frizzell (born in Auckland, 1943) is one of the country's leading contemporary artists. From the time he ceased working as a commercial artist in 1973 and launched himself as a freelance painter, designer, and illustrator, Frizzell has contributed hundreds of illustrations to the *School Journal*.

A major retrospective exhibition of his paintings that toured New Zealand in 1995–96 was titled, tongue firmly in cheek, *Portrait of the Serious Artiste*. Frizzell's paintings have always blurred the boundary between "fine art" and popular culture. He resists differentiating between his work as a "serious artiste" and the work he has produced for publishers, agencies and, importantly, for the *School Journal*. In a 1994 interview, he said that producing illustrations for the *School Journal* was "where I get off my civic responsibility rocks; I struggle away drawing hairs for the flea family to crawl through".[18] In his own unabashed, high-spirited way, Frizzell is following very much in the footprints of Russell Clark, who similarly believed that the artist had a role to play in the community. In April 2006, Dick Frizzell answered a few questions by email from his Hawke's Bay home.

How did you stumble upon the School Journal *– or how did they stumble upon you?*

Vanya Lowry, who was an editor during the early 1970s, bullied me into illustrating a story about pirates. She was convinced I'd be able to do it. I wasn't so sure, having failed Russell Clark's paper in Book Illustration [at Canterbury School of Fine Arts]. But I did do it, after a rather titanic struggle for something so little. She was impressed and sent me another … and another … (Years later I received the Russell Clark Memorial Medal for book illustration for *The Magpies*!)

I assume the School Journal *work led towards your other work for children – such acclaimed books as* The Magpies *and* Pyjamas Don't Matter*?*

It certainly did. All those sweatshop hours led to some pretty well-developed skills – and theories.

Did the School Publications work affect your development as a "serious artiste"?

There was no cross-over at all for years! It was like having two totally separate identities! I know it did lead to an amazing confidence with vast scale shifts. We had to do all those pictures for the *Journal* actual size because School

Dick Frizzell, illustration for Jane Buxton's story "The Fleas at the Pet Show", *School Journal*, Part 1 Number 3, 1990

Publications were too skint to do reductions and so on – you found yourself illustrating casts of thousands in spaces like 10 centimetres by 15 centimetres! I've been a sharp-pencil addict ever since.

What other skills did this kind of work give you?

Drawing, drawing, drawing – getting it tight. I learned a lot about compression.

What do you think a good "illustration" should do?

It should illustrate the story – and not illustrate how clever the illustrator is. I did so many that I quickly ran out of "favourite tricks" and had to fall back on the actual demands of the story, where the composition is entirely at the mercy of the moment's legibility – the clearest presentation of the "facts". So you swiftly move on from all your fine-art "classical training" – that was handy!

Did you have anything to do with the writers/editors, or was everything conducted at a distance?

All long distance – until they flew me down once to lecture me about all the aggression and "subliminal" sex in my Māui comic-book stories (written by Sydney Melbourne). All the old heads of department – all old "chalkies" – couldn't stand comics, couldn't resist the old "confiscation principle". Ha, ha … they wanted me to "smooth" Māui's muscles out! Leave out the gouts of blood. And when we got to the episode when Māui had to re-enter his mum's womb, they pulled the plug on the whole thing.

What would you like to think your illustrations offered children?

I think one of the most significant things I did when I was in there was to catapult the style of the illustrated kiwi kid from *Washday at the Pa* to *Sesame St* … you know – from bare feet to sneakers …

Dick Frizzell, illustration for Jack lazenby's "Uncle Trev and the Pukeko Dog", *School Journal*, Part 3 Number 2, 1990

From East Cape to Wellington, Past to the Present

On a sketching trip to the East Cape in 1955, E. Mervyn Taylor spent time at Te Kaha School, where he met, and encouraged, two young Māori artists, Para Matchitt and Cliff Whiting. The following year, embarking upon teacher training, Whiting was a boarder in Mervyn Taylor's Wellington household. The contact with Taylor was no doubt formative in Whiting's creative growth. Two decades later, he would illustrate one of the most considerable pieces about Māori history published in the *School Journal*: Michael Keith's 1978 two-part account of Māori–Pākehā conflict in nineteenth-century Taranaki, "Bitter Payment". A tour-de-force, Whiting's illustrations ran like a frieze or tāhuhu along the top of the text, linking together historical and mythical figures.

Just as impressive were Whiting's illustrations the following year for "Captain Cook Visits Mercury Bay", a retelling of a tale John White attributed to Hore-ta-te-taniwha. In Whiting's drawings, the interweaving shapes anticipate the sculptural work he would produce in subsequent decades.

The drawings of the interwoven carvings in the illustrations represent the close presence of the tipuna, the ancestors, in all things Maori, particularly in matters concerning land.

The peaked heads of the tipuna reflect the shape of the mountain, Taranaki, sacred to the Atiawa, as is the head of a person. In some of the drawings, Taranaki itself is represented as a carved head.

The tipuna are there to be called upon by the living people, to argue for them, to protect them, to guide them, to fight for them.

In the drawing [on left], the carved figures represent the land both Wiremu and Ihaia live on, every gully, stream and cultivation that they know … In the drawing [on right], the coming of the Pakeha's taua (war party) brings together those who are prepared to fight. The tipuna here represent the people as a whole, facing downward to defend themselves and their way of living against an ignorant stranger.

A note by Cliff Whiting on the drawings for "Bitter Payment: The Taranaki Troubles"

Cliff Whiting, illustrations to accompany Michael Keith's "Bitter Payment: The Taranaki Troubles", *School Journal*, Part 4 Number 1, 1978

Cliff Whiting, illustrations for "Captain Cook Visits Mercury Bay", a story told by Hore-ta-te-taniwha last century to John White, *School Journal*, Part 4 Number 2, 1977

Painter-sculptor Para Matchitt provided drawings for a special issue of the *Journal* celebrating the International Year of the Child in 1979. Entitled *Stones from the Spring – Events in the Lives of Young New Zealanders*, the issue also featured sculptor Robert Jahnke's illustrations for Roger de Vere's story "Freight Train North".

Para Matchitt, illustration for *School Journal*, Part 4 Number 2, 1979

Cliff Whiting photographed by Helen Mitchell, 1986

Although Matchitt and other Māori artists of his generation illustrated primarily for *Te Ao Hou* and Māori-language publications, painters of Māori descent who contributed to the *Journal* in the 1970s and 80s included Robin White (see page 132) and Robyn Kahukiwa. Kahukiwa, after contributing drawings to the *Journal* in the early 1980s, devoted her subsequent energies as an illustrator to producing picture books with Patricia Grace and, later, Roma Potiki; while continuing to develop as one of New Zealand's most important painters. Among recent Māori artists, Te Maari Gardiner was profiled, alongside Russell Clark, in a feature about changing illustrative styles in 2000.

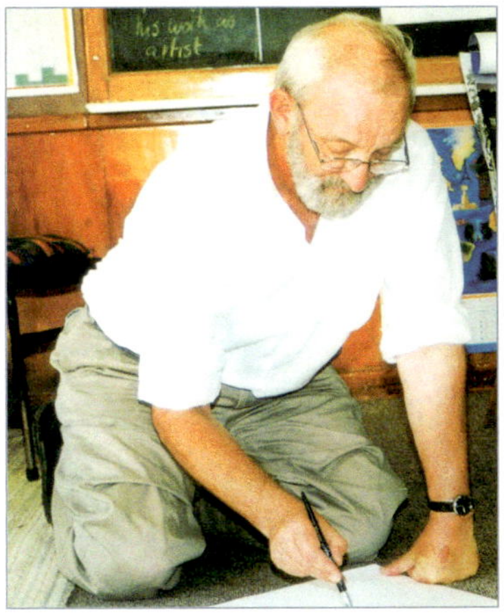

Murray Grimsdale painting in a classroom at Halfmoon Bay School, Stewart Island, photographed by Lee Wadds, *School Journal*, Part 2 Number 1, 2000

Murray Grimsdale, illustration for Kelly Haitana's story "Eeling", *School Journal*, Part 2 Number 3, 1990

Philip Paea, illustration for Sheridan Waitai-Cherrington's "Te Pūpū Harakeke", *School Journal*, Part 2 Number 3, 2003

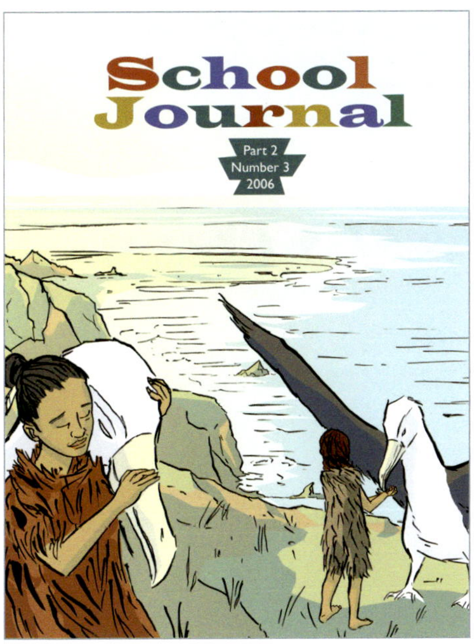

Mathew Hunkin, cover illustration for "Tears of the Albatross" by Tawai Te Rangi (retold in English by Radha Sahar), *School Journal*, Part 2 Number 3, 2006

An artist with a particular empathy for Māori and Pasifika subjects, Murray Grimsdale has, since the early 1970s, produced strongly delineated images, at times reminiscent of work by other New Zealand artists, such as Russell Clark, Eric Lee Johnson, and Nigel Brown. Perhaps more than the work of any other regular *Journal* artist, his images hark back to the publication's artistic past. In his frieze-like illustration for Kelly Haitana's story "Eeling", the stylised trees echo those in Russell Clark's paintings (see above and page 77). In 1999, Grimsdale visited Stewart Island, where he met the students of Room 1, Halfmoon Bay School. The following extract is from a child's account of the visit, which subsequently appeared in the *Journal*:

> Murray Grimsdale visited our class recently. He brought some of his paintings of Stewart Island and also showed us some of the artwork he has done for the *School Journal*.
>
> Then he showed us an easy way to draw a face. "Just imagine it's a hot cross bun," he said.
>
> First he drew a big circle on a piece of paper and painted a cross on it. "That's where the eyes, nose, and mouth will go," he said.
>
> We all had a go at drawing one another's faces.
>
> Then Murray Grimsdale showed us how to draw action figures. He told us to draw each part of the arms and legs as a cylinder. "Start off with pale colours," he suggested. "Then you can easily change it later if you're not happy with it."

Grimsdale's emphasis on clear outlines and strong narrative is shared by Vaitoa Baker and Philip Paea, both of whom illustrate for the *Journal* while also working for Learning Media as art editors. Much of Paea's work is set in contemporary New Zealand, although stories such as Sheridan Waitai-Cherrington's "Te Pūpū Harakeke" have provided an opportunity to revisit Māori mythology and history.

Fraser Williamson, cover artwork for *School Journal*, Part 2 Number 3, 2003

Increasingly, as the twentieth century progressed, the *School Journal* engaged with New Zealand's place in the Pacific, acknowledging Polynesian traditions and the contribution Pacific peoples were making to this country's cultural life. Here Fraser Williamson's frangipani-blooming, tapa-cloth masthead floats above an imaginary South Seas island. A net resembling a speech balloon is tossed into the fish-laden ocean, and an outrigger heads towards the horizon, where a dark headland looms, capped appropriately by a long white cloud.

Fraser Williamson photographed by Gil Hanly, *School Journal*, Part 1 Number 1, 2003

Artist as Illustrator as Writer, Bob Kerr

Born in 1951, Bob Kerr was a frequent contributor to the *School Journal* during the 1990s. Following in the tradition of Roy Cowan and the two Joans (Dukes and Smith), he has developed into a writer as well as an illustrator, producing the much acclaimed *Mechanical Harry* (1996), with its sequel, *Harry and the Flying Bicycle* (1999), and *After the War* (2000). While the clear outlines of his drawings hark back to earlier artists in the *Journal's* history, his colour sense is entirely contemporary.

In recent years, Kerr has exhibited narrative paintings, producing notable sequences about Rua Kenana – *The Rua Expedition*, which toured North Island galleries in 2003–04, and *Number One Field Punishment*, a retelling of Archibald Baxter's story. Both sequences represent a further elaboration on his concerns as a *Journal* illustrator.

From his Wellington studio, Kerr answered a few questions about his work as an illustrator and artist.

Over what period have you been producing work for School Publications/Learning Media?

John Bonallack gave me my first illustrating job for the *Journal* – a story called "The Rich Girl's Party" in Part 1 Number 2, 1981 – and then gently rejected my first efforts because my eight-year-olds looked like eleven-year-olds. I remember doing the drawings again and taking them in, and John said, "That looks OK." I am not doing much work for the *Journals* at all now. That is mostly to do with my career shift into painting but also because I really got to know a generation of editors who were my age: John Bonallack, Brent Southgate, Jim Gorman, and Clare Bowes. On one of my first visits to School Publications, when it was in the old wooden building, one of the editors had just had a play put on at Downstage called *Middle Age Spread*. So that really dates me, I guess. The last work I did for the *Journals* was probably about eighteen months ago. The new, younger editors at the *School Journal* are employing people from their own generation, and that is as it should be.

Is there any work you did for them that, in hindsight, you're particularly pleased with (and why)? Any writer you worked with …

"Fixing the Playground" – Hazel [Armstrong] and I worked on this story together. I started photographing the run-down playground at the beginning of the year, hoping that a story would develop and, as things turned out, it did. It was great seeing those kids go and address the council meeting. The other story I'm fond of is "The Bishop, the Boeing, and Billy the Pigeon" from 2003.

Bob Kerr, in his Wellington studio, 2006
Courtesy of the artist

Bob Kerr, photograph to accompany his article "Fixing the Playground", *School Journal*, Part 2 Number 2, 1995

Bob Kerr, story and illustrations, "The Bishop, the Boeing, and Billy the Pigeon", *School Journal*, Part 3 Number 1, 2003

Were you aware of the visual arts history of the School Journal*? What illustrators inspired you?*

I can still remember my delight when I was at school at seeing illustrations by Juliet Peter and Mervyn Taylor in the *School Journal*, of the country I lived in. Most of the illustrations I saw in my childhood were British or North American. I was rather pleased to be awarded the Library Association's Russell Clark Medal for my book *After the War*. I think he is the great New Zealand illustrator. He could effortlessly and convincingly draw the human figure in action and, as *Journal* editors will tell you, that is a rare skill.

Did the School Journal *give you much creative freedom? Or was the content/mood of the drawings pretty rigorously laid down for you?*

Usually the editors would give you an A4 page with the type already in place and spaces for your drawings. Sometimes there would be suggestions about what the drawing in that space should be, but usually there was a fair amount of freedom, particularly if they knew your work. If you timed your visit right, particularly to the old wooden building, you could usually score a cup of morning or afternoon tea and the editors would (in those days) have a leisurely chat with you about what was required.

You usually sent along a pencil rough before you coloured up the final illustrations, and at that stage, the editors would make any helpful suggestions.

What qualities do you think infuse your work?

I certainly took my lead from those illustrators you mentioned – Clark, Peter, Taylor – and wanted to follow in their tradition. I wanted my landscapes and townscapes and people to be from here. My trees were pōhutukawa, my houses were wooden with corrugated iron roofs, and the hills were borrowed from McCahon.

What do you think a great illustration does?

I think illustrations are the hook. An illustration will get to you before the story; the information you can get from an illustration can be instant and complex. It is the illustration that will seduce the reader into the story or make the person in the bookshop pick the book up off the shelf, but after that, it's story that is important.

The other thing illustration can do is bring in subplots and jokes that aren't even mentioned in the text.

Illustration Today

At various points in the *Journal's* history, the primary purpose of the illustrations has been questioned: are they to enhance, to alleviate comprehension difficulties, to add new meanings, or to simply be beautiful? The role of the art editor is crucial in balancing the visual–verbal equation. Art editor Clare Bowes says she always looked for an illustrator who:

> *would be empathetic to the story and would enhance it with, say, humour, maybe a subplot, competent draughtsmanship, someone who would get details correct. The following illustrators come to mind as providing outstanding work: Trevor Pye, Dick Frizzell, Christine Ross, Murray Grimsdale, Scott Kennedy, Caroline Campbell, Jennifer Cooper, Philip Webb, and Deirdre (Te Maari) Gardiner.* [19]

The overall look and feel of the *Journal* has to be kept in mind as well, as Terence Taylor has pointed out:

> *To avoid monotony, illustrations are commissioned from artists with different styles and in a variety of forms and sizes. Drawn illustrations are mixed with photographs and diagrams, and ideas can be represented through the varied techniques of fine line, pen, water colour, flat colour, coloured inks, wash and line, crayon, spatter, lino cut, pastel, colour pencil, and collage.* [20]

For Taylor, the primary point of illustration has to be to "assist the reader through the text". With that concern in mind, artist Bob Kerr recalls, during a school visit, observing a pupil reading the *School Journal* in class:

> *his eyes kept moving from the words to the pictures. He was scanning the illustrations for clues about the words he didn't understand. This was a revelation to me. I realised that it wasn't my job just to decorate. It was my job to teach kids to read.* [21]

Shortly after that encounter, Kerr set to work illustrating "Filling the Bins" by Marion Rego (Part 1 Number 3, 1987). He decided to list all the nouns in the story and to include all of them in the illustration (see p. 143):

> *So if you take a look at pages 4 and 5, everything named in the text on the left-hand side appears in the picture on the right-hand side. I was particularly pleased to be able to get in not only every noun but every action as well.* [22]

Certainly illustrators, graphic artists, and designers remain a dynamic and integral presence in "the nest of singing birds" that is the *School Journal*. Whether they are visually unpacking the contents of a text, as is the case with "Filling the Bins", or launching forth into adjacent imaginative territory, as in Fraser Williamson's visualisation of "Watching Wildlife" (see page 81), their work is a fundamental and hugely valued component in the publication.

"Someone else has put rubbish in our bin," we said.
"If I find out who did it," said Dad, "I'll dump it on their lawn." But he didn't know who it was, so we left it in the bin.
We spent a lot of time on Saturday hauling rubbish from our house and dumping it in the bin. By night time it was nearly full.
"We'll fill it up tomorrow," said Dad.

3

Bob Kerr, illustration for Marion Rego's "Filling the Bins", *School Journal*, Part 1 Number 3, 1987

I can't emphasise enough how the advent of the computer in the nineties revolutionised the design of the Journals and, I believe, the illustrations. For the first time, you could actually see everything laid out in front of you. This gave the designers a much greater freedom when commissioning artists. The illustrations were more integrated with the text, and the artists responded so that the Journals really began to sizzle with energy. The current illustrative styles are certainly attuned to today's children with their ready access to all forms of visual presentation.

Clare Bowes, Art Editor[22]

Andrew Burdan, illustration for Jacqui Brown's "Aunty", *School Journal*, Part 3 Number 2, 2004

Donovan Bixley, illustration for Sue Gibbison's "Great-grandpa", *School Journal*, Part 2 Number 1, 2006

Along for the Ride:

The School Journal and changing ideas about childhood

A red-wetsuited figure, arms flailing, cuts back off the top of a green wave breaking from left to right across the cover of a recent *School Journal*. When you look a little harder, you realise the sparkling wave is actually contained within an even bigger wave – this one drawn with a computer mouse – which continues around onto the back of the publication. It is an appropriate cover for a *School Journal* at the beginning of the twenty-first century: alive to the energies and excitement of youth and the rhythms of the natural world while engaging the latest technologies. Only a few decades back, surfing would have been deemed unsuitable territory for the *Journal*, being associated, as it was, with dissolute and selfish lifestyles, the misspent youth of many a Kiwi male. When you flip to the back cover of the 2006 *Journal*, however, the first thing you realise is that the surfer up front is, in fact, a young woman – Jessica Santorik. Her story, "Red Surfer Riding" (a modern-day rephrasing of "Little Red Riding Hood", no doubt) is told inside the *Journal*.

Cover, *School Journal*, Part 4 Number 3, 2006

(left) Cover illustrations *(clockwise from top left)* are by Stephen Templer, Mat Tait, Scott Kennedy, Andrew Burdan, Freya Blackwood, Nic Marshall, Philip Webb, Daron Parton

The *School Journal*, like the surfer on the cover, has had to move fast to keep up with the times. By way of some fancy footwork, it has had to put a contemporary spin on Allen Curnow's lesson concerning "the trick of standing upright here".[1] One of the most notable developments in the *School Journal* over recent decades is the way it now places young people – like the surfer on her wave – at the very centre of the action. Whether riding a left-hander or crossing a city street, girls and boys are presented as self-assured and empowered – at the opposite end of the spectrum to the refectory girls drawn so gracefully, if somewhat mournfully, by Russell Clark in a 1947 *Journal*.

Russell Clark, illustration for "Jane Eyre", *School Journal*, Part 4, July 1947

Joan Dukes, illustration for Frank Sargeson's "The Beginning of the Century – Games", *School Journal*, Part 4, June 1953

Comparing the "Red Surfer Riding" cover of 2006 with earlier depictions of outdoor pursuits suggests how notions of recreation and, indeed, childhood have changed. Accompanying Frank Sargeson's 1953 article, "The Beginning of the Century – Games", Joan Dukes' illustration is almost comical in its flighty decorum; the world of childhood is presented as an orderly English park in which girls skip and boys play with hoops and kites. It is very much the kind of view an adult might project onto the young. By comparison, Jessica Santorik is finding her own feet, making her own way, ruffling a few feathers quite probably, but taking responsibility for herself.

when the fisherman in John Pascoe's photo-essay in a 1970 *Journal* (see page124) starts gutting a fish while puffing on a cigarette, you just have to shrug your shoulders and admit that times have changed. The characters in recent *School Journals* eat fewer treats, an indication that fish and chips and ice creams get little approval in a society where childhood obesity has become an issue.

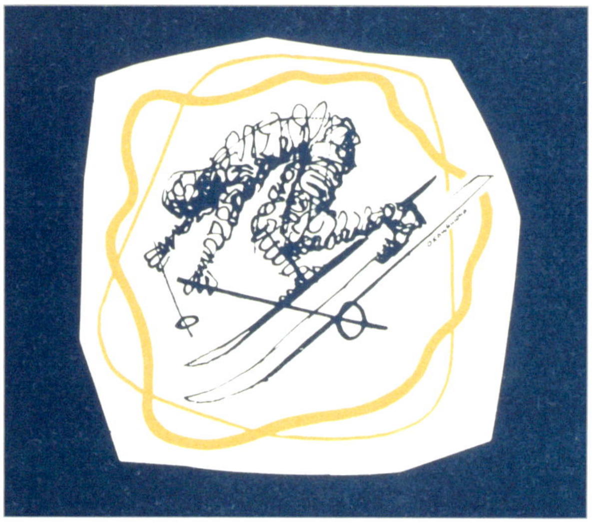

John Drawbridge, cover illustration for *School Journal*, Part 4, Winter 1954

Cover, *School Journal*, Part 3 Number 2, 1999

In contrast to *School Journal*, Part 4, Winter 1954, which featured a stylised drawing of a skier by John Drawbridge, the 1999 *Journal* features a high-speed photograph of a somersaulting snowboarder. Adrenalin would seem to have replaced decorum in the art studio as it has on the slopes. The figure in Drawbridge's 1954 cover drawing looks like an adult, whereas our contemporary snow hound is, importantly, a teenager or possibly even younger. Again, we find young people at the centre of the action.

It is certainly true that the *Journal* has, in recent decades, adapted to accommodate more of the young person's world and world-view – but it has done this in a cautious and qualified way. Skateboarding might be a permissible topic for a contemporary *School Journal*, but the skaters have to wear helmets and regulation safety gear. On one hand, the *Journal* has become far more liberal but, on the other, it has also grown more sensitive and, in a way, troubled. If the children who inhabit the branches in Clare Bowes' illustration for Merlene Young's 1966 story "The Fig Tree" were to appear in a 2007 *Journal*, safety issues and implications would need to be worked through. All children riding bicycles in present-day *Journals* must have helmets on their heads – and tales abound of illustrators having to redo their artwork to introduce appropriate headgear or footwear. Occupational safety and health issues would be raised by the girl curled inside the tyre in Murray Grimsdale's illustration for "Tyred Tumblers" in *School Journal*, Part 3 Number 1, 1990; and

Clare Bowes, illustration for Merlene Young's "The Fig Tree", *School Journal*, Part 2, Number 3, 1966

Murray Grimsdale, illustration for Authur Curtis's "Tyred Tumblers", *School Journal*, Part 3, Number 1, 1990

Graham Percy, illustration for K. M. Bradley's "Little Girl Lost" in *Ten Tales*, *School Journal*, Part 1 Number 1, 1965

Conrad Frieboe, illustration for "The Traffic Officer", *School Journal*, Part 2, September 1947

Conrad Frieboe, illustration for Captain Marryat's "The Black Tom Cat", *School Journal*, Part 3, October 1944

Then Aunt Billie goes downstairs and leaves me with the dreaded Bess. Bess plugs in the lamp, and her eyes glint in an evil kind of way in its glare.

My heart bangs in my chest, in my throat, and between my ears. Why? Because my most secret secret is that I'm scared of the dark. Really, really scared of the dark. And I know Bess knows.

I see Bess's smile slide around her face. "Let's play shadow puppets," she says.

From Janice Marriott's "Heartbeats in the Dark", illustrated by Jared Lane, *School Journal*, Part 2 Number 4, 2005

"I'D SOONER BE BY MYSELF."

George Woods, illustration for "The Three Prize Essays", *School Journal*, Part 3, September 1941

Yvonne Bendall, cover illustration for *School Journal*, Part 2, October 1952

Markedly, the *Journal* in recent years has become less willing to portray children at risk or in trouble. It is hard to imagine in the contemporary context an illustration with the predatory undertones of Conrad Frieboe's 1947 depiction of a policeman in an unmarked car confronting a young girl on the roadside. Graham Percy's brooding evocation of a lost girl in the 1965 *Journal*, with a silhouetted figure approaching from behind, might prove just as problematic. The abiding tone in recent *Journals* is positive and inherently responsible. Might this quite possibly be the legacy of the "Our Street" and *Washday at the Pa* controversies? Or does this simply reflect a desire to present society, and the world at large, as manageable and inviting – as long as you obey the rules?

Would an art editor at the *School Journal* in the era of political correctness find the group in George Woods' 1941 illustration (right) too languid, the girls displaying far too readily what Roy Cowan once called the artist's "unabashed relish for the human figure"? Most editors would, I am sure, feel more comfortable with Yvonne Bendall's sensible skipping girl from a few years later.

If New Zealand, until the late twentieth century, was characterised as a practical, commonsensical, pragmatic nation, the *Journal* of the early century may well have played a part in establishing that limiting self-definition, advocating, as it did, the sturdy colonial virtues of honest toil and uncomplicated thinking. Certainly the *School Journal* until the 1950s did little to resist that stereotype.

In recent decades, New Zealand has been reconstructed as an independent and imaginative nation, with a good many of its citizens engaged in "creative industries". It is interesting to ponder if this might in some way be the delayed effect of the more dynamic, imaginative *Journals* that began to appear from the late 1950s onwards. And, if you follow this line of thought, what does the present day *Journal* bode for the future?

David Elliot, illustration for Marion Rego's "Ice Cream", *School Journal*, Part 1 Number 4, 1994

Penelope Newman, illustration for Alice Robertson's "The Captive", *School Journal*, Part 2 Number 3, 2004

I was tired of trying to interest children in stories which were set in a cosy world where things didn't really go wrong… I wanted stories where children could hear echoes of things they'd seen and felt and heard of themselves – their own dramas, conflicts and adventures.

Brian Birchall, School Journal editor, 1972–78

Rebecca ter Borg, illustration for Anna Kenna's "Bike Day", *School Journal*, Part 3 Number 3, 2005

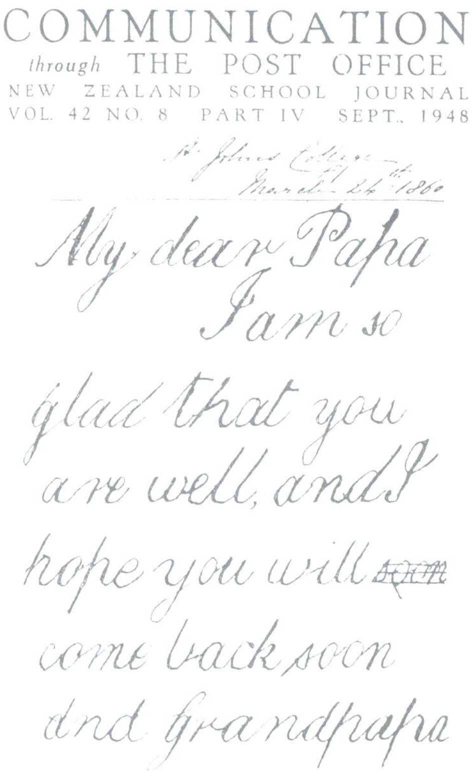
COMMUNICATION
through THE POST OFFICE
NEW ZEALAND SCHOOL JOURNAL
VOL. 42 NO. 8 PART IV SEPT., 1948

My dear Papa I am so glad that you are well, and I hope you will ~~soon~~ come back soon and grandpapa

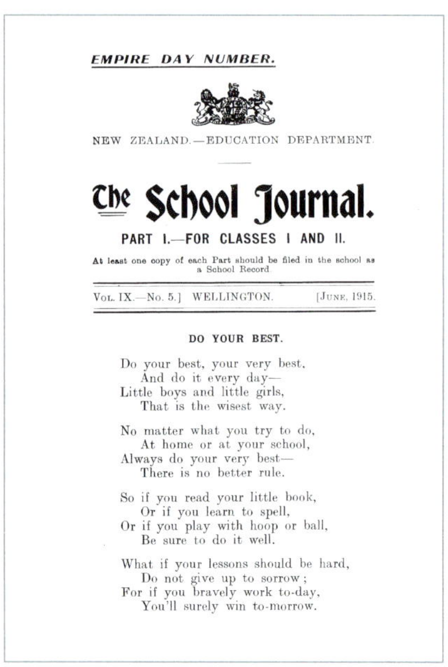
EMPIRE DAY NUMBER.

NEW ZEALAND.—EDUCATION DEPARTMENT.

The School Journal.

PART I.—FOR CLASSES I AND II.

At least one copy of each Part should be filed in the school as a School Record.

VOL. IX.—No. 5.] WELLINGTON. [JUNE, 1915.

DO YOUR BEST.

Do your best, your very best,
And do it every day—
Little boys and little girls,
That is the wisest way.

No matter what you try to do,
At home or at your school,
Always do your very best—
There is no better rule.

So if you read your little book,
Or if you learn to spell,
Or if you play with hoop or ball,
Be sure to do it well.

What if your lessons should be hard,
Do not give up to sorrow;
For if you bravely work to-day,
You'll surely win to-morrow.

CELLPHONE

Norman liked to be alone;
his best friend was his mobile phone.
He preferred the glowing case
to any boring human face.

Even wearing swimming gear,
he kept the phone pressed to his ear.
Speed-dial, redial, email too,
he even used it on the loo.

Each new model was a blast,
and each was smaller than the last.
His latest was the Buzz-4-Free –
half the size of a bumblebee.

He took the phone to bed one night,
snoozing by its tiny light.
But while he was in deepest slumber,
someone tried to call his number.

In error, sleepy from his doze,
he held the phone up to his nose.
Then, sniffing, Norman felt a pain –
the phone had lodged inside his brain.

Now this is what young Norman does –
his eyes light up, his nostrils buzz.
When people call, he's always home,
a walking, talking, mobile phone!

Raymond Huber, illustration by Kirsty Lillico,
School Journal, Part 3 Number 2, 2003

Over the years, there have been sparks and, occasionally, smoke surrounding the *School Journal*. The publication is constantly juggling the fact that it has to serve and reflect a diverse, multicultural society while providing a common ground for all its readers.

Early in the *Journal's* history, the British Empire was the moral and social template from which it took its shape. A 1908 issue of the *School Journal* proposed the following virtues to the young citizens of New Zealand: faith, courage, duty, self-discipline, fair dealing, even justice, good citizenship, loyalty, patriotism, and sympathy – all of which should be put to the good end of "elevating the British character, strengthening the British Empire, and consolidating the British Race". The list was reiterated in a 1917 *Journal* (see page 16). As recently as 2005, the Education Ministry was mulling over what values should be taught in New Zealand schools – and, it follows, promoted or at least acknowledged in the *Journal*. They came up with a list markedly different from that of 1908: diversity, community, respect and care, equity, integrity, environmental sustainability, enquiry and curiosity, and excellence.

Alongside the persistent question of what values and ideals the *School Journal* should reflect, numerous other debates will continue as long as the *Journal* exists: how children are depicted, how ethnic groups are represented, and what roles women and girls are shown in, for a start. There is also the recurrent question of what young people should be exposed to, and inversely, what they should be sheltered from.

Should children be told things or taught to discuss them and formulate their own responses? These issues, so central to the "Our Street" flare-up of 1949, remain central to the *Journal* as it finds its way in the twenty-first century. What exactly is childhood, and where do children stand in relation to the rest of society and the wider world around them? Such is the territory in which the *School Journal* must continue to function.

In 2007, the *School Journal* remains centred on the need for children not only to be able to read but also to imaginatively engage with the world. Elspeth Williamson's illustration for Bill Manhire's poem "Girl Reading" (on right) sums up this ongoing concern: reading is a tree for all of us to climb, and – hopefully – when we get to the top, we acquire knowledge, nourishment, and a new perspective.

Girl Reading

She overhears the sound of things in hiding.
She bites an apple and imagines orchard starlight.
Each time she licks her thumb, its tip,
she tastes the icy branches,
she hears a sigh migrate from page to page.

Bill Manhire

As well as imparting "the trick of standing upright here", the *Journal* is concerned with the trick of tree-climbing, of being curious and adventurous, of being lifted above the everyday by words. The *Journal* is predicated on the equation – call it a miracle, if you like – that learning to read a page of a book is, in fact, learning to read the world.

The *School Journal* continues to be attentive to its readership and responsive to the writers, artists, and editors who have given the publication its dynamic, unpredictable, irrepressible character. Prominent in the 1993 National Library exhibition *Working Titles: Books That Shaped New Zealand* just as it was in the 1951 *Arts Year Book*, the *Journal* has not only taught generations of New Zealanders how to read, it has been influential in subtle and less predictable ways. As we have seen, it has funded the literary and artistic activities of generations of talented New Zealanders while also offering them a forum where remarkable work could be presented. Looking back to the early *Journals* of 1907, there is a sense that, while the publication began life as the most rational and pragmatic of ventures, it always had it in its nature to become something of an adventure. And that is what it certainly became, and what – after one hundred years – it remains.

Juliet Peter, illustration for R.M. Wheeler's "Te Awa Awa", *School Journal*, Part 1, February 1948

Notes

Foreword

1. James K. Baxter, "Time and the Bell", *Education*, vol. 5 no. 3, October 1956, p. 47.
2. C. E. Beeby, Introduction, *The New Zealand School Publications Branch*, Educational Studies and Documents, no. 25 (Paris: UNESCO, 1957; hereafter referred to as UNESCO report), p. 7.

Revisiting the School Journal

1. Athol McCredie, "Growing up with the *School Journal:* The Illustrations since 1940", in *Fabulous and Familiar: Children's Reading in New Zealand, Past and Present* (Wellington: National Library of New Zealand, 1991), p. 42.
2. Peter Campbell to Greg O'Brien, 2006.
3. James K. Baxter, *Collected Plays*, ed. Howard McNaughton (Auckland: Oxford University Press, 1992), p. 167.

Both Ends of the Telescope

1. P. R. Earle, "The Official Connection", *Education*, vol. 31 no. 1, 1982, p. 12.
2. J. C. Beaglehole, "A Small Bouquet for the Education Department", *Arts Year Book*, no. 7, 1951 (Wellington: The Wingfield Press, 1948), p. 123.
3. Tricia Glensor, unpublished lecture notes.
4. Brent Southgate, entry on School Publications in *The Oxford Companion to New Zealand Literature* (Auckland: Oxford, 1998), pp. 480–481.
5. P. R. Earle, cited above, p. 5.
6. Michael King, *The Penguin History of New Zealand* (Auckland: Penguin, 2003), p. 40.
7. ibid., p. 46.
8. Diana Beaglehole, "The Maori in the *School Journal:* 1907–1981", *Education*, vol. 31 no. 1, 1982, p. 39.
9. P. R. Earle, quoted in *The Beeby Fascicles*, vol. 2, (Wellington: Te Aro Press, 1992), p. 4.
10. UNESCO report, p. 5.
11. Roger Hardie, "*... the buds of flowering": An Archive List of the Department of Education Art and Crafts Specialist Staff 1938–1989* (Auckland: R. Hardie, 2005), inside front cover.
12. P. R. Earle, quoted in *The Beeby Fascicles*, vol. 2, p. 12.
13. P. R. Earle, "The Official Connection", pp. 6–7.
14. *Revised Syllabuses* (Wellington: Department of Education, 1948), p. 78.
15. Brian Sutton-Smith, "Our Street", *Education*, vol. 2 no. 2, 1949, p. 50.
16. Memo from Education Department to the Minister of Education, 20 August 1949, copy in Archives New Zealand.
17. Letter from Acting Director of Education to the President, Headmasters' Association, 12 September 1949, copy in Archives New Zealand.
18. Brian Sutton-Smith to Greg O'Brien, 2006.
19. Alistair Campbell, quoted in *Education*, vol. 31 no.1, 1982, p. 16.
20. Gordon Tovey, quoted in Hardie, cited above, p. 79.
21. John Drawbridge, quoted in *A Blaze of Colour: Gordon Tovey, Artist Educator* by Carol Henderson (Christchurch: Hazard Press, 1998), p. 97.
22. UNESCO report, p. 2.
23. Alistair Campbell, quoted in *The Beeby Fascicles*, vol. 2, p. 5.
24. UNESCO report, p. 5.
25. ibid., p.5.
26. ibid., p.5.
27. ibid., p.6.
28. Interview with Terence Taylor, 2006.
29. *A Guide to the School Journal* (Wellington: Learning Media, 1994), p. 7.
30. Margaret Mahy, "Countries of the Mind", in *Education*, vol. 31 no. 1, 1982, p. 3.
31. Penelope Newman to Greg O'Brien, 2006.

The World as We Know It

1. Alistair Campbell, quoted in *Education*, vol. 31 no.1, 1982, p. 14.
2. William Pember Reeves, "The Passing of the Forest", *An Anthology of New Zealand Poetry (in English)* (Auckland: Oxford University Press, 1996), p. 498.

A Literary Perch

1. Alistair Campbell, quoted in *The Beeby Fascicles*, vol. 2, p. 19.
2. ibid., p. 23.
3. Southgate, cited above, pp. 480–481.
4. Letter from James. K. Baxter to Ruth Dallas, 14 March 1957, copy in Archives New Zealand.
5. Letter from Maurice Duggan to Alistair Campbell, 18 December 1956, copy in Archives New Zealand.
6. Roderick Finlayson, *Beginnings*, ed. Robin Dudding (Wellington: Oxford University Press, 1980), p. 64.
7. Bill Pearson, Introduction to *Brown Man's Burden and Later Stories* by Roderick Finlayson (Auckland University Press/Oxford University Press, 1973), p. vii.
8. Ian Richards, *To Bed at Noon: The Life and Art of Maurice Duggan* (Auckland: Auckland University Press, 1997), p. 210.
9. ibid., p. 210.
10. Peter Campbell to Greg O'Brien, 2006.
11. ibid.
12. Ruth Dallas, *Curved Horizon: An Autobiography* (Dunedin: University of Otago Press, 1991), p. 129.
13. ibid., p. 45.
14. Betty Gilderdale, "Children's Literature" in *The Oxford History of New Zealand Literature (in English)* (Auckland: Oxford University Press, 1998), p. 548.
15. Janet Frame, *An Autobiography* (New York: George Braziller, 1991), p. 34
16. Michael King, *Wrestling with the Angel: A Life of Janet Frame* (Auckland: Viking, 2000), p. 143.
17. James K. Baxter, *Collected Plays*, pp. 166–167.
18. ibid., p. 167.
19. ibid., p. 169.
20. Frank McKay, *The Life of James K. Baxter* (Auckland: Oxford University Press, 1990), p. 189.
21. ibid., p.189.
22. Peter Campbell to Greg O'Brien, 2006.
23. Charles Doyle, *James K. Baxter* (Boston: Twayne Publishers, 1976), p. 32.
24. Letter from James K. Baxter to Pat Wilson, 27 September 1960, copy in Archives New Zealand.
25. Letter from Alistair Campbell to Barry Mitcalfe, 21 June 1960, copy in Archives New Zealand.
26. Brian Sutton-Smith to Greg O'Brien, 2006.
27. ibid.
28. John Kelly, quoted in *Education*, vol. 31 no.1, 1982, p. 16.
29. Tricia Glensor, unpublished lecture notes.
30. Margaret Mahy to Greg O'Brien, 2006.
31. Paul Millar, entry on Jack Lasenby in *The Oxford Companion to New Zealand Literature*, (Auckland: Oxford, 1998), p. 300.
32. Jack Lasenby, quoted in *Education*, vol. 31 no.1, 1982, p. 17.

33. Beaglehole, cited above, p. 39.
34. McCredie, cited above, p. 43.
35. *A Guide to the School Journal*, p. 8.
36. Albert Wendt, quoted in the entry on him by Briar Wood, *The Oxford Companion to New Zealand Literature,* p. 582.
37. *A Guide to the School Journal*, p. 28.
38. Diana Noonan to Greg O'Brien, 2006.

For a Song

1. *A Guide to the School Journal*, p. 9.
2. Frame, cited above, p. 34.
3. Michael King, *Wrestling with the Angel*, pp. 28–29.
4. Mahy, cited above, p. 4.
5. Memo from the Department of Education to the Minister of Education, 30 August 1949, copy in Archives New Zealand.
6. Brent Southgate to Greg O'Brien, 2006.

The Drawing Board

1. Bob Kerr to Greg O'Brien, 2006.
2. Peter Peryer noted in his December 2006 online blog: "While at Primary School, one of the biggest influences on me were the *School Journals*, which arrived perhaps two or three times a year. They were remarkable publications, filled with writing and illustrations by our very best. One contributor whose work made a big impression on me was E. Mervyn Taylor. The woodcuts had a lot of presence I felt ..."
3. Roy Cowan, quoted in *Education*, vol. 31 no.1, 1982, p. 19.
4. Peter Shaw to Greg O'Brien, 2007.
5. J. L. Ewing, quoted in Michael Dunn, *The Drawings of Russell Clark* (Auckland: Collins, 1976), p. 10.
6. James Shelley, "Canterbury Society of Arts Annual Exhibition", review in *Art in New Zealand*, no. 24, June 1934, p. 178.
7. Comment in *Year Book of the Arts in New Zealand*, no. 4, 1948, (Wellington: The Wingfield Press, 1948), p. 40.
8. John Drawbridge, "New Zealand Printmakers: Number One: E. Mervyn Taylor, 1906–1964", *Education*, vol. 31 no. 1, 1982, p. 49.
9. ibid., p. 49.
10. Roy Cowan, "The Pottery of Roy Cowan and Juliet Peter", *Ascent*, vol. 1 no. 2, July 1968, pp. 37–38.
11. Letter from Rita Angus to Douglas Lilburn, 23 June 1954, Alexander Turnbull Library manuscript collection.
12. Letter from Rita Angus to Jean Angus, 23 June 1954, Alexander Turnbull Library manuscript collection.
13. Linda Tyler, "I do not want to be Mrs Colin: Anne and Colin McCahon", in *Between the Lives: Partners in Art*, ed. Deborah Shepard (Auckland: Auckland University Press, 2005), p. 48.
14. Clare Bowes to Greg O'Brien, 2006.
15. Jill McDonald, quoted in *Education*, vol. 31 no.1, 1982, p. 20.
16. Peter Campbell to Greg O'Brien, 2006.
17. McCredie, cited above, p. 45.
18. Dick Frizzell, quoted in *Lands and Deeds: Profiles of New Zealand Painters* by Gregory O'Brien (Auckland: Godwit, 1996), pp. 36–37.
19. Clare Bowes to Greg O'Brien, 2006.
20. Terence Taylor, " 'What is the use of a book without pictures?' thought Alice", *Education*, vol. 31 no.1, 1982, p. 22.
21. Bob Kerr to Greg O'Brien, 2006.
22. ibid.
23. Clare Bowes to Greg O'Brien, 2006.

Along for the Ride

1. Allen Curnow, "The Skeleton of the Great Moa in the Canterbury Museum, Christchurch", *An Anthology of New Zealand Poetry (in English)*, p. 400.

Christine Ross, cover illustration, *School Journal*, Part 2 Number 1, 1990

Trevor Pye, illustration for David Hill's "Stranger Dog", *School Journal*, Part 1 Number 1, 1997

Index

Bold page numbers indicate main passages and italics illustrations. "Passim" indicates the subject is not discussed continuously in a page range.

Dennis Beytagh, cover illustration, *School Journal*, Part 4, Summer 1957

Gretchen Albrecht, cover illustration, *School Journal*, Part 3 Number 3, 1968

Michael Smither, cover illustration, *School Journal*, Part 4 Number 1, 1973

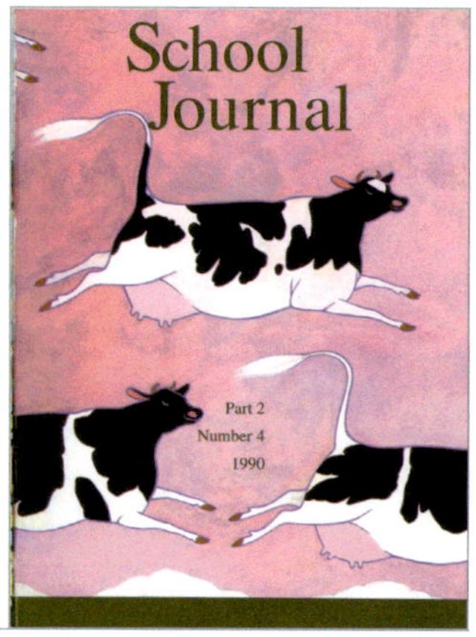

Caroline Campbell, cover illustration, *School Journal*, Part 2 Number 4, 1990

Wol Jobson, cover illustration, *School Journal*, Part 2 Number 3, 1994

Victoria Purdie, photograph; Jodi Wicksteed, design, *School Journal*, Part 1 Number 2, 2005

Scott Kennedy, cover illustration, *School Journal*, Part 1 Number 3, 2002

Further Reading

Barr, Jim and Mary. *Working Titles: Books That Shaped New Zealand*. Wellington: National Library Gallery, 1993.

Baxter, James K. *Collected Plays*, ed. by Howard McNaughton. Auckland: Oxford University Press, 1980.

Baxter, James K. *Collected Poems*. Auckland: Oxford University Press, 1982.

Bayly, Janet (ed.). *Songs of Innocence: Photographs by John Pascoe*. Waikanae: Mahara Gallery, 2005.

Bayly, Janet and Athol McCredie. *Witness to Change: Life in New Zealand: John Pascoe, Les Cleveland, Ans Westra: Photographs, 1940–1965*. Wellington: PhotoForum, 1985.

Beaglehole, Diana. "The Maori in the School Journal: 1907–1981". *Education* (special issue), vol. 31 no. 1, 1982: pp. 38–41. Wellington: School Publications Branch.

Beaglehole, J. C. "A Small Bouquet for the Education Department" in *Arts Year Book*, no. 7, 1951: pp. 123–129. Wellington: The Wingfield Press, 1951.

Bornholdt, Jenny et al. (ed.). *An Anthology of New Zealand Poetry (in English)*. Auckland: Oxford University Press, 1996.

Chapman-Taylor, Ray. *Life in the Pa* (illustrated by Russell Clark and E. Mervyn Taylor). Auckland: Paul's Book Arcade, 1963.

Dallas, Ruth. *Curved Horizon: An Autobiography*. Dunedin: University of Otago Press, 1991.

Dictionary of New Zealand Biography, vols 1–5. Wellington and Auckland: Allen and Unwin/ Bridget Williams /University of Auckland and Department of Internal Affairs/Ministry for Culture and Heritage, 1990–2000.

Duder, Tessa. *Margaret Mahy: A Writer's Life*. Auckland: Harper Collins, 2005.

Duffy, Mary-Jane (ed.). *Outdoor People: A Tribute to Juliet Peter*. Wellington: City Gallery Wellington, 2001.

Dunn, Michael. *The Drawings of Russell Clark*. Auckland: Collins, 1976.

Earle, P. R. "The Official Connection". *Education* (special issue), vol. 31 no. 1, 1982: pp. 5–12.

Fabulous and Familiar: Children's Reading in New Zealand, Past and Present. Catalogue for exhibition curated by Mary Atwool, Mary Hutton, Peter Ireland, and Athol McCredie. Wellington: National Library of New Zealand, 1991.

Frame, Janet. *To the Is-land*. Auckland: Century Hutchinson, 1982.

A Guide to the School Journal. Wellington: Learning Media, 1994.

Hardie, Roger. *"… the buds of flowering"; An Archive List of Department of Education Art and Crafts Specialist Staff 1938–1989*. Auckland: R. Hardie, 2005.

Henderson, Carol. *A Blaze of Colour: Gordon Tovey, Artist Educator*. Christchurch: Hazard Press, 1998.

James, Bryan. *E. Mervyn Taylor: Artist: Craftsman*. Wellington: Steele Roberts, 2006.

King, Michael. *The Penguin History of New Zealand*. Auckland: Penguin, 2003.

King, Michael. *Wrestling with the Angel: A Life of Janet Frame*. Auckland: Viking 2001.

Mahy, Margaret. "Countries of the Mind". *Education* (special issue), vol. 31 no. 1, 1982: pp. 2–4.

McDonald, Geraldine and Richard Benton (eds). *The Beeby Fascicles*. Wellington: Te Aro Press, 1992.

McDonald, Lawrence (ed.). *Handbook: Ans Westra Photographs*. Wellington: BWX, 2004.

McKay, Frank. *The Life of James K. Baxter*. Auckland: Oxford University Press, 1990.

Maclean, Chris. *John Pascoe*. Nelson: Craig Potton, 2003.

Main, William and John B. Turner. *New Zealand Photography from the 1840s to the Present*. Wellington: PhotoForum, 1993.

Ministry for Culture and Heritage. *Dictionary of New Zealand Biography* (online resource). Wellington: Ministry for Culture and Heritage, 2001. Available at www.dnzb.govt.nz

O'Brien, Gregory et al. *John Drawbridge: Wide Open Interior*. Wellington: Mallinson Rendell/City Gallery Wellington, 2002.

O'Brien, Gregory. *Lands and Deeds: Profiles of Contemporary New Zealand Painters*. Auckland: Godwit, 1996.

O'Brien, Gregory and Robert Cross. *Moments of Invention: Profiles of New Zealand Writers*. Auckland: Heinemann Reed, 1988.

Paul, Janet (ed.). *Rita Angus*. Wellington: National Art Gallery, 1982.

Richards, Ian. *To Bed at Noon: The Life and Art of Maurice Duggan*. Auckland: Auckland University Press, 1997.

Robinson, Roger and Nelson Wattie (eds). *The Oxford Companion to New Zealand Literature*. Auckland: Oxford University Press, 1998.

Shallcrass, Jack. "The School Journal: Fifty Years On". *Education* (special issue), vol. 31 no. 1, 1982: pp. 44–45.

Shephard, Deborah. *Between the Lives: Partners in Art*. Auckland: Auckland University Press, 2005.

Skinner, Damien. "A Modest Modernism: A Conversation with Juliet Peter". *Art New Zealand*, no. 119, Winter 2006: pp. 66–71, 88–91.

Smith, Allan. *Dick Frizzell: Portrait of a Serious Artiste*. Wellington: City Gallery Wellington, 1996. (NB: author and curator Allan Smith was himself an illustrator – see *School Journal*, Part 3 Number 3, 1985.)

Southgate, Brent. Entry on School Publications in *The Oxford Companion to New Zealand Literature*, ed. Roger Robinson and Nelson Wattie, pp. 480–481. Auckland: Oxford University Press, 1998.

Sturm, Terry. *The Oxford History of New Zealand Literature* (in English), rev. ed. Auckland: Oxford University Press, 1998.

Sutton-Smith, Brian. *Our Street*. Wellington: Reed, 1950 and Wellington: Price Milburn, 1975.

Sutton-Smith, Brian. *Smitty Does a Bunk*. Wellington: Price Milburn, 1975.

Taylor, Terence, "'What is the use of a book without pictures?' thought Alice". *Education* (special issue), vol. 31 no. 1, 1982: pp. 22–25.

Thomson, Jane. "Shaping the *Journal*". *Education* (special issue), vol. 31 no. 1, 1982: pp. 14–21.

Trevelyan, Jill and Vita Cochran. *Rita Angus: Live to Paint, Paint to Live*. Auckland: Godwit/City Gallery Wellington/Hocken Library, 2001.

Trevor, Ruth. "This Singular Publication". *Education* (special issue), vol. 31 no. 1, 1982: pp. 26–30.

UNESCO. *The New Zealand School Publications Branch*. Educational Studies and Documents, no. 25. Paris: UNESCO, 1957.

Wadman, Howard (ed.). *Arts Year Book*, no. 7, 1951. Wellington: The Wingfield Press, 1951.

Lesley Moyes, cover 3-D illustration, *School Journal*, Part 1 Number 3, 1990

"Some might say this is the happy ending," said Jack, "but I say, brisk and seamanlike as is my nature, it is just the happy beginning."

Then the parrot shouted, "Hoist aloft the sails!" The monkeys began to climb the palm tree, and the island moved merrily out of the harbour into the sunset. The Board of Governors waved goodbye.

"Perhaps they will be back," they said.

But the floating island, Jack, Emily, and the boys never ever came back again, for they were bound for places of enchantment about which no ordinary tale dares to tell.

From "Sailor Jack" by Margaret Mahy, illustrated by Jill McDonald, included in *A Lion in the Meadow and other stories and poems*, *School Journal*, Part 1 Number 3, 1965

Acknowledgments

The task facing any anthologist, historian, or critic is to find their way to "the true orchards of fruit". Working on this book made it abundantly clear to me that the *School Journal* is one such "true orchard". Whether you approach it as a literary critic, an art historian, an educationalist, or an interested child (of any age), the *Journal* over the past century is an immensely rich and rewarding territory. I am grateful to Gillian Candler, Tricia Glensor, and Margaret Styles for inviting me, an outsider, to set forth into the universe that is Learning Media (née School Publications). This timely celebration of the *School Journal* will, I hope, encourage other writers and researchers to produce further studies and, in due course, a comprehensive history.

Much of the reading and scouring of archives was done by my collaborators and co-authors in this project, Susanna Andrew and Jenny Bornholdt. Their archival industry, opinions, and energy were integral not only to this publication but also to the National Library exhibition that accompanies it. I am grateful also to the designer, Penelope Newman, editor, Margaret Cahill, and style editor, June Hannah, and to Charlotte Ellis and Kelly Dix who kept track of the many images included in this book. Thanks too to Robin Briggs who compiled the index.

Many thanks to all those who helped us source material for this book. In particular, I would like to thank the following individuals for information, opinions, and encouragement: Luit Bieringa, Clare Bowes, Peter Campbell, Robert Cross, Pat Earle, Marti Friedlander, Dick Frizzell, Bob Kerr, Jack Lasenby, Glen McDonald, Margaret Mahy, Paul Millar, Diana Noonan, Graham Percy, Peter Shaw, Brent Southgate, Brian Sutton-Smith, Michele Taylor, Terence Taylor, Hamish Thompson and Jill Trevelyan (who provided invaluable assistance researching Rita Angus's involvement in the *School Journal*), and Ans Westra. At the National Library, Penny Carnaby, Peter Ireland, Chris Cane, Aaron Lister, Damian Skinner, Courtney Johnston, and Brendan O'Brien were all generous with their time and expertise. Thanks also to the staff at National Archives, Wellington, and of course to the artists, writers and editors, designers, and typographers of the *Journal*, many of whose work is reproduced in this publication.

Gregory O'Brien

How Journals Are Notated within the Text

The way of referring to individual issues of the *School Journal* has varied during its hundred years of publication. In this book, the relevant "Part" for each *Journal* mentioned is denoted by the numerals 1 to 4, for example, *School Journal*, Part 2. Until 1950, however, the Parts were denoted by Roman numerals. References to quoted material from the *Journals* identify the relevant Part, then the month, season, or number is given according to the system at the time of publication, followed by the year of publication.

Until the 1980s, some *School Journal* stories were reused – either with their original illustrations or with new artwork (sometimes, as technology improved, the original artwork would have colour added, for better or worse). Publication dates indicate the first publication, with a very few exceptions (such as Roderick Finlayson's "The Cave", which is reproduced here in its abridged 1975 version, which incorporated Dick Frizzell's art).

Part 1 *Journals* are published for seven- and eight-year-olds; Part 2 for eight- to nine-year-olds; Part 3 for nine- to eleven-year-olds; and Part 4 for eleven- to thirteen-year-olds.